CRIME
IS
CALLED
VIRTUE

I'm not against the police,
I'm just afraid of them.

I'm not against the police;
I'm just afraid of them.

you're wasting my motherfucking time

not crimes and scandals

POLICE 13th TALES FROM THE PRECINCT

BY ALAN ALEXANDER AND CLAYTON OLIVER

INTERDEPARTMENTAL RE

The Midway Police Department: Trying to pull itself from beneath

By BRAD LASSITER and MACE CALHOUN

Excerpts from a May 2005 interview of Midway Tribune crime reporter Mace Calhoun as conducted by Brad Lassiter, a junior journalism major attending Midway University. Mr. Calhoun has recently retired after 37 years in the journalism profession, during which he received numerous awards for his crime reporting, including a Pulitzer nomination for investigative reporting for his series on the 1987 Citadel Heights police brutality scandal in Midway.

Brad Lassiter: There we go. Sorry about that. I hope I don't run out of tapes before we're done. [laughter] Now, before the break, we were just getting into the discussion of the political side of police work. How all these different agencies work together, or don't work together, as in the Belinda Miller murder case.

Mace Calhoun: Well, see, the first thing you have to remember is that individual police officers, except for the really crooked ones, see themselves as law enforcement agents first and foremost, as opposed to "public officials." But as you advance up the food chain from beat officer to lieutenant to captain to police chief, your decisions tend to be based less on solving specific cases and more on doing what is politically advantageous. That's not to say that the chief of police doesn't care about crime. Even the most venal police chief knows a high crime rate is certainly bad

ATIONS

shadow of corruption.

good news coverage. Meanwhile, violent crime in the projects continues to escalate, even as more resources are diverted to protecting upper-class, white neighborhoods. The problem is made worse by the competing interests of other law enforcement agencies, which often try to undermine each other's authority out of a desire for a public relations boost or simply out of petty animosity.

We have four basic entities to keep track of when we're talking about law enforcement in Midway: the city police, the various county sheriff's departments (most prominently, Washington County), the state police and the feds. We'll start with the Midway PD. The head of the MPD is currently Police Chief Elliot Tyler, who has been on the job for about two years, so I'm still making up my mind about him. The police chief is a political appointee who serves at the pleasure of the mayor, and, consequently, the job requires a politician much more than a brilliant criminologist. The appointment of a new police chief is also a statement by the mayor indicating his views on

for his job prospects. It's just that, at a certain career level, you tend to prioritize cases based on how they'll affect your coverage on the nightly news. As the saying goes, "if it bleeds, it leads," so the crimes that get the highest priority are the crimes that most frighten middle- and upper-class whites: rape, robbery and murder, especially in white neighborhoods. Drug crimes are also a big deal, especially in and around the public school systems. Narcotics and prostitution sweeps always give

POLITICAL PUPPET OR PUBLIC SERVANT? : Many speculate that the appointment of Police Chief Elliot Tyler was a "cave in" to the mayor's affluent (and mostly white) political campaign contributors. After two years on the job, crime in the predominantly poor parts of town have increased while police presence in these areas has decreased.

law enforcement within the city. After the Citadel Heights scandal, the mayor appointed an African American as police chief to blunt accusations of racism in the MPD. Nine years later, we had a new mayor elected on a "clean up Midway's gang problem" ticket, and suddenly the new police chief is a no-nonsense white guy with a military background who rose up from the Gang Crimes Division.

The police chief has three direct subordinates. One deputy chief runs the Operations Division, which means that all the uniformed cops in the city, from beat cops up to precinct captains, answer to him. He's in charge of all major investigative divisions — Homicide, Personal and Property Crimes, Narcotics, Vice, etc. Detectives assigned to any of those divisions answer to him, even if they're technically assigned to a precinct and formally answer to a local precinct commander. Another deputy chief runs the Administrative Division, and, although she has 20 years on the force and is a decorated officer, at the moment, she's a glorified office manager. A third deputy chief runs the Support Division. Analysis, surveillance, things like that fall under his leadership.

Naturally, this can lead to a certain amount of tension among investigators and local beat cops, particularly when the beat cop stops to arrest a hooker and finds out that she's an undercover vice squad member. Investigative Services is notorious for failing to inform Field Ops about the activities of undercover officers, mainly out of a not-unjustified fear of beat cops on the take passing on the information to the targets of sting operations. Unfortunately, I suspect that, one day, it's going to get an officer killed, but even that won't stop the turf wars.

Cut from article... the pig has his snoot in a lot of troughs..

It's even worse with some of the other agencies. The Washington County Sheriff's Department has been mired in scandals since the 1920s when Sheriff George O'Dell's election campaign was bankrolled by rum-runners. Even today, the current sheriff is distantly related to George O'Dell, two of the three deputy sheriffs are cousins of his and the third is the sheriff's best friend going back 20 years. The whole department's just a shoddy old boy's network. They've been sued five times in the last eight years, three times by African Americans for employment discrimination and twice for firing departmental personnel who refused to campaign for the sheriff in the last election. Of course, it's still a lot better than it used to be. Back in '63, a couple of civil rights workers who were investigating claims that the sheriff at the time was in the Klan were found in the woods basically ripped to pieces. They must have used chainsaws or something on the poor guys. Needless to say, no one ever connected the Sheriff's Department to it.

The Sheriff's Department is charged with patrolling all the unincorporated land in Washington County. The duties of the sheriff are roughly the same as those of the chief of police, except that the sheriff is actually an elected official in his own right. So, while the police chief can be fired by the mayor for almost any reason, the sheriff can lose his job only by being voted out of office. If memory serves, at least two sheriffs have remained in office while under indictment, and one served a one-month jail sentence for public drunkenness back in the 1950s and then went back to work as if nothing had happened.

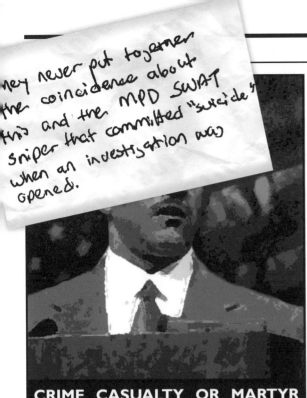

[handwritten note] they never put together the coincidence about this and the MPD SWAT sniper that committed "suicide" when an investigation was opened.

CRIME CASUALTY OR MARTYR FOR THE CAUSE? Reginald Dubois attempted to become the first African-American Sheriff in Midway history. He was gunned down in his front yard the night before the election. The crime was blamed on street violence, however the three shots that the coroner had determined to be the kill shots were pefectly grouped centermass and came from an MP5. Most gangs in Midway tend to favor the standard Glock or the now discontiued MAC10.

BL: Wow! So the county sheriff doesn't have to answer to anyone?

MC: Well, technically no, but the entire operational budget for the Sheriff's Department has to be approved by the Board of Supervisors and so the sheriff generally has to maintain at least the pretense of following their advice on setting departmental policy. Also, since the sheriff is elected, even the appearance of corruption can end his career at the ballot box. Both the sheriffs I mentioned who had been under indictment lost their re-election campaigns, even though they were never successfully prosecuted.

There's also a long history of petty rivalry between the Sheriff's Department and the Midway Police Department. For instance, both agencies will happily work with the feds on a drug case or something similar, but they hate working with each other, at least at the administrative levels. I suppose it's because career politicians run both departments, and they all have vested interests in appearing more competent than the guy on the other side of the city limits. MPD doesn't want to waste hundreds of man-hours setting up a drug operation only to have the Sheriff's Department sweep in and hog the cameras, and the Sheriff's Department feels the same way. There are also class and race issues, I suppose. Washington County is a fairly parochial, white-flight area, and Midway residents tend to view county residents almost as hillbillies. Meanwhile, Washington County politicians have been railing for years about Midway and its "gang problems," which is, of course, a euphemism for "too many black people."

The state police play a fairly limited role in Midway law enforcement. The jurisdiction of statewide police agencies varies from state to state, and ours has a fairly limited mandate. State troopers mainly have jurisdiction over enforcement of traffic laws on state and interstate highways. They are also authorized to detain someone found on a state or interstate highway who is the subject of a BOLO — "be on the look out." Being a state trooper pays about the same as being a city police officer, and it's about as dangerous, since troopers rarely have backup when they pull someone over on the highway. When you pull someone over for speeding, you really don't know who you're dealing with until you get his license in your hand. Troopers also get about five weeks' more certification training than city police, so troopers tend to think that makes them vastly more qualified to be law officers, which, of course, tends to grate on the average street cop's nerves.

The state police also run the State Crime Lab, which can provide more sophisticated technical and scientific support than the local crime labs can handle. Stuff like DNA tests, for example. Lastly, if the State Attorney General sets up a multi-jurisdictional task force of some kind, the state police coordinate the involved jurisdictions, so they can basically make the MPD and the Sheriff's Department work together whether they want to or not. The last time that happened was about two years ago when the state went after organized crime figures involved in the Leon Figueroa killings.

BL: Interesting. So what about the feds?

The "Thrilla from Manilla" Killer

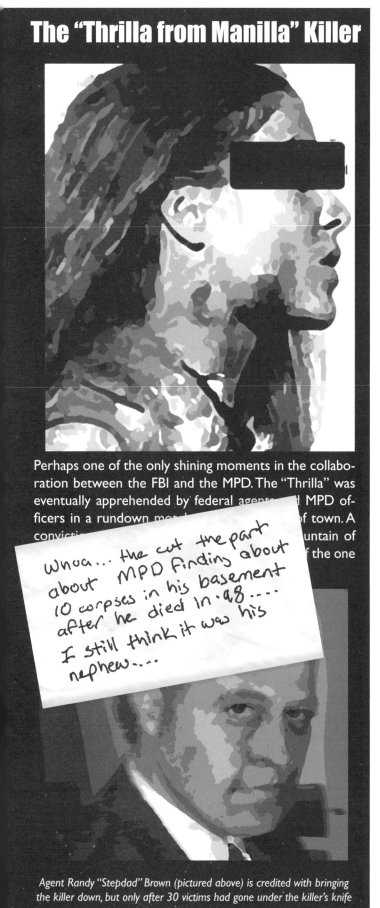

Perhaps one of the only shining moments in the collaboration between the FBI and the MPD. The "Thrilla" was eventually apprehended by federal agents and MPD officers in a rundown motel ~~~~~~~~ of town. A convicti~~~~~~~~~~~~~~~~~~~~~~~~~~~~ untain of ~~~~~~~~~~~~~~~~~~~~~~~~~~~~ f the one

Whoa... the cut the part about MPD finding about 10 corpses in his basement after he died in '98.... I still think it was his nephew....

Agent Randy "Stepdad" Brown (pictured above) is credited with bringing the killer down, but only after 30 victims had gone under the killer's knife

MC: Depends on which kind of fed and what local crimes he's sticking his nose into. The FBI is basically the federal police force. It has the authority to investigate any crime "against the United States." Technically, FBI agents lack jurisdiction to investigate state crimes or even the authority to arrest someone they see breaking a state law, though they can still investigate what they suspect are federal crimes. Congress has been busy, however, and there are a lot of federal crimes. Robbery of federally insured banks, kidnapping across state lines, serial killing — the list is plenty long. I seem to recall a lot of conflicts between the MPD and the FBI about 12 years ago, when the feds were investigating a serial killer active in Midway's Asian community. Some psycho prostitute who liked to tear out the throats of her johns. I seem to recall that a young Filipino woman was arrested, but I don't recall if she ever went to trial.

The big problem with the FBI is that they seem almost genetically predisposed to be arrogant when dealing with local police. The locals in turn tend to be a bit insecure and touchy about cocky FBI agents with their overcoats and shiny badges walking into a local crime scene like they own the place. It's generally not conducive to healthy relations. The only exception is if there is any suspicion of "terrorist activities." The average police officer is just as caught up in post-9/11 hysteria as any other citizen, and if a new mosque opens up in town, the MPD won't hesitate to call in the FBI for some contrived reason. Similarly, any sufficiently violent activity that might be attributable to terrorism — random explosions, mass killings, other weird events — can also lead to the FBI being called in to coordinate with the MPD. The locals are always ready to palm off things they can't explain or deal with to somebody else. Besides, there's always an outside chance of hitting the mother lode and getting some big, fat Homeland Security grants if there's actually any legitimate evidence of terrorist activity.

Local cops get along much better with Drug Enforcement Administration agents. They often coordinate together on drug sweeps. [pause] Are you familiar with the concept of drug sweeps?

BL: Generally, but I'd like your take on them.

MC: Well, basically, a federal agent, usually DEA, will ride along with patrol officers in a squad car as the officers make a circuit through various high-crime neighborhoods. The local cops stop anyone they see who might arguably be violating some local law or city ordinance. Busted taillights, running stop signs, littering, what have you. Until it finally got struck down as unconstitutional just last year, there was even a law on the books that made it a misdemeanor for more than two people to be caught standing together on a sidewalk for any length of time. Anyway, the local cops arrest whoever they reasonably can for whatever convenient reason presents itself, and once the invariably poor, minority perp is properly arrested, he can be fully searched. Then, any drugs, guns or other contraband found on him are simply handed over on the spot to the DEA agent, who

MIDWAY'S FINEST: Officers Walter Brown (l) and Oscar Garza (r) load evidence obtained in a joint DEA sweep on Lombardo Street.

then Mirandizes the perp and arrests him again, this time on federal charges.

BL: And that's constitutional?

MC: Oh, definitely. Hey, it's constitutional to arrest, handcuff and strip search you if the wrong cop gets you for driving without a seatbelt.

BL: It sounds like the whole exercise is set up to arrest people just for the purpose of getting their help in arresting other people. Do these sweeps over minor drug offenses actually

why'd they cut this.... every suy I knew in college knows they dothis.. is it like the ticket quota thing... unspoken truth or something?

BL: I'll remember that on the way home. Now, I understand why the DEA is interested in drug crime, but why guns and other paraphernalia?

MC: Because things like crack pipes and empty needles are enough evidence to at least threaten a perp with jail time. Just paraphernalia is illegal in most jurisdictions, and even if a conviction is unlikely, you might be able to get a junkie to flip on his dealer. As for the guns, it's illegal for anyone with a felony conviction to possess a gun. The penalty for that is real time, often measured in decades for repeat offenders. Most people caught up in sweeps will eventually cooperate with the feds and plead out to avoid jail time. Some of them might even be willing to become full-time informants. The MPD likes sweeps because the mayor's office can point to all those convictions obtained with MPD help but the city doesn't actually have to pay to prosecute anyone. The feds like it because they can use local police as proxies to search people that the feds would never have probable cause to search themselves.

TACTICS OR TORTURE: The tactics and practices of the MPD and ATF have come under fire more than once in the last few years. This photo taken from a dashcam reel, shows an ATF agent extracting a little payback from an uncooperative perp. Spokespeople for the ATF still contend the suspect was not in cuffs at the time and the agent was simply trying to restrain him...although clearly in the photo you can see his hands bound behind him.

lower the crime rate or do they just make politicians look good?

MC: That's a very cynical outlook. It'll serve you well as a journalist. To answer your question, I've never seen any reliable studies suggesting that sweeps actually reduce crime at the street level. Whether they make politicians look good is debatable, but the prison guards union is one of the largest and most politically active unions in the state, and they just love politicians who put lots of people in jail.

Anyway, the FBI and the DEA are the two biggest federal law enforcement agencies that regularly interact with the MPD. The ATF very rarely involves itself in local criminal activity. Occasionally, there'll be something involving illegal firearms shipments or bootleg whiskey, but that's about it. That's probably best for all concerned, since the ATF has a reputation for coming in with all the subtlety of the Normandy invasion. Actually, that's unfair. There have been some unfortunate situations over the past 20 years involving the ATF attempting to storm fortified compounds guarded by crazy militia groups or wacko religious cults and things going very badly. For instance, there was a big shootout 12 years ago when the feds went after a local gun club called the Diamondhead Arrow Hunting Club that had been stockpiling automatic weapons. Generally, though, the ATF does its fair share of undercover work, mainly enforcing gun control legislation and making sure idiots in pawn shops don't sell

SOCIETY

Desert Eagles to every guy who walks in off the street.

Investigators for the Secret Service show up when there's evidence of counterfeiting activity, since the Treasury Department has jurisdiction over any crimes relating to currency. Also, they oversee all security operations whenever the president or any other figure entitled to Secret Service protection comes to town.

Lastly, the U.S. Marshals Service will coordinate with local cops to apprehend escaped federal fugitives or to safely transport federal prisoners. They also compete with the local cops for a valuable resource, though: confiscated property. The Marshals Service is the federal agency is tasked with managing assets seized and forfeited as the proceeds of drug trafficking and organized crime. Since both the MPD and the Sheriff's Department also love to get their paws on seized and forfeited assets, there's some tension there.

BL: You don't sound like a fan of drug forfeiture laws. If someone's convicted of being a drug dealer, why shouldn't he have all his assets seized?

MC: Well, you see, in the real world it works like this: Johnny's a drug dealer. His father, Jimmy, buys a new tractor for the family farm with some money that Johnny gave him that Jimmy doesn't know came from secretly running a meth lab somewhere on Jimmy's property. The feds arrest Johnny and also get Jimmy

Midway Citizens' Groups Demand Justice !

After the acquital in the Leon Figueroa shooting case of Sheriff's Deputy Ron Kardrotti, the newly formed Midway Citizens' group staged a protest outside the courthouse. The protest drew more national attention to a case most federal invesigators had wanted to deal with quietly.

Local government watchdog Jamie Biron stated for the record, "If the government won't stop the widespread corruption of law enforcement in our city, it is up to the citizens of Midway to do so. If we cannot get justice in a court of law, then we will take our case to the court of public opinion."

as an accomplice. But they can't prove beyond a reasonable doubt that Jimmy was involved so he gets off. So then, they turn around and sue Jimmy on civil drug charges. The standard now becomes "Is it more likely than not that Jimmy was somehow involved in the drug trade?" If the jury says yes, then the government can take the tractor, and the farm and possibly the shirt off Jimmy's back.

BL: I thought the double jeopardy clause prevented that.

MC: Not in civil cases. Jimmy just can't be tried as a criminal again. The MPD just bought two shiny new helicopters for its "Aerial Division" or whatever they're calling it with money acquired after selling a lot of cars seized from drug dealers. You can even go to the MPD website and bid electronically on seized and forfeited property. It's a little sordid, but politically, it's a lot more palatable than raising taxes. ∎

Credits

Written by: Alan Alexander and Clayton Oliver
Additional Material: Andy C. Davis
13th Precinct Original Concept: Richard Thomas with Adam Geibel
World of Darkness created by Mark Rein•Hagen.
The Storytelling System is based on the Storyteller System designed by Mark Rein•Hagen.
Consultation, Assistance and Special Thanks: Bishop Lewis, Andy C. Davis, Alex Flagg, the Lexington Division of Police and its Citizen Police Academy program
Developer: Justin Achilli
Editor: Scribendi.com
Art Director: Mike Chaney
Layout & Typesetting: Pauline Benney and Mike Chaney
Interior Art: Sam Araya, Travis Ingram, Brad Williams, Phil Hilliker, nik Stakal, James Cole and Matt Milberger
Front Cover Art: Katie McCaskill
Front & Back Cover Design: Pauline Benney and Matt Milberger

For Use with
the World of Darkness® Rulebook

1554 LITTON DR.
STONE MOUNTIAN,
GA 30083
USA

Introduction

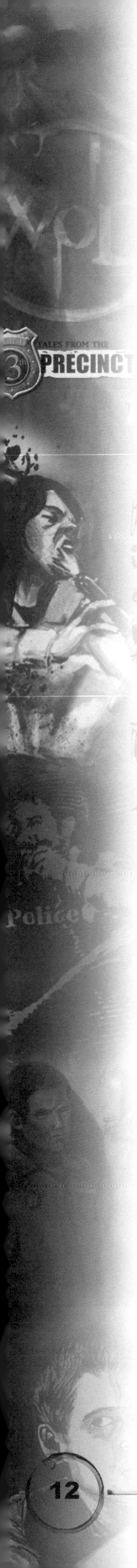

Follow your
inclinations with due
regard to the policeman
round the corner.

—W. Somerset
Maugham,
Of Human Bondage

The beleaguered, divorced detective studying a trail of evidence growing more grisly by the night. The forensics expert who's given a ritual athame of unknown material to analyze. The nervous beat cop who finds a junkie in the alley who's killed a bum and is lapping at his blood. The traffic officer who just pulled over a rusted pickup with out-of-state plates and an unsettlingly hairy driver.

Cops see some weird shit. In addition to an officer's usual array of circumstances and evidence — which can be horrific on their own — the subtle (or gross) supernatural hallmarks of the World of Darkness occasionally intrude in the police jurisdiction.

This book presents an entire working legal system, ready for plug-and-play use in any World of Darkness chronicle. This legal system is a three-tiered split, including the following elements:
- Sidebars introducing real-world verisimilitude
- Object lessons in how the American legal system functions
- Ready-to-use characters for interaction with players' characters

Plug-and-play means just that. This book contains a ready-for-my-chronicle legal system that you can drop into the story and not miss a beat. You'll see specific, named characters in there with whom your players' characters can interact. You'll see through their activities how the legal system works. If you choose not to use the plug-and-play characters, you can still use the procedural walkthrough as the basis for your own city's unique characters and system.

To approach it from another angle, you're holding a playable chronicle here. As a Storyteller, you can use this as a foundation for your own chronicle, having the players assume characters presented herein. Secondarily, you can also use it as background for a chronicle in which the players portray vampires, werewolves, etc.: these characters will be their antagonists.

Think of this like a city setting book. Instead of a full city, however, you're witnessing the stuff that the precinct experiences. This is a more focused approach, but it's also one that comes ready-to-order with supernatural and horrific implications.

A Few Central Concepts

You'll do well to keep these cornerstone ideas in mind while reading Tales From the 13th Precinct and using it to design characters or chronicles.

Midway: In the interests of keeping the immediately playable aspect of the setting functional, we're placing our police department in the possibly fictional city of Midway, in the possibly fictional Washington County. "Midway" is one of the most frequently occurring population center names in the United States. If you happen to be planning a chronicle for a city not named Midway, simply do a mental find-and-replace function when you read this book. You won't have to scratch off any other informational serial numbers unless you want to introduce specific local customs or police procedures into your stories.

We're going to hit the ground running with the city of Midway. In the interests of keeping the precinct suitable for as many chronicles as possible, we're not going to detail a lot of city history. You'll find several references to places and neighborhoods, but none that come with backstory demands to make of your chronicle. We make similar assumptions with significant personalities, such as high-ranking public officials. Your chronicle surely already has a mayor for its home city, so we're not going to assume that the one we created for this book should trump that. The same goes for high-ranking police, such as the commissioner, the chief of police, deputy chiefs and the like. Again, you can just drop the precinct into your story and start right away.

Use of the word "precinct": We often use "precinct" here in this book to define anything that involves the legal system. Precinct is a convenient term for the reader that encapsulates the whole idea of things happening to police, at the police station, in an investigation or at an actual, physical precinct house. The word "precinct" signifies that we're talking about the whole phenomenon of police activity, as opposed to just a literal police precinct.

Locality: We've kept most of the attention on local systems and authorities. We're dealing with local cops and city-level affairs. The World of Darkness eschews global plots and worldwide conspiracies, instead focusing on the concerns of individual cities or regions. This book continues that trend. One of the central tenets of horror is the visceral impact of monstrous events on the individual — national and global is too large a scale for our looks at law enforcement. You'll see individual officers driving their shift-assigned cruisers rather than secret FBI departments devoted to exterminating vampires. The government and massive conspiracies are your last concern — you're worried about the satanic sorcerer next door. The local authorities' concern is the growing tide of strangeness that they're unable to stem, and the average local citizen's concern is the mysterious horror from which conventional authorities are unable to protect the citizens. You'll see a little bit in here on federal agencies (notably at the end of this Introduction), but not much, and it's predominantly in the context of how they react with local agencies.

A Focus on Law Enforcement: As opposed to bureaucracy and the courtroom. We don't spend too much time on the DA, the stenographer, a priori, voir dire or other details of the courtroom.

Super Troopers

The police officer and SWAT officer on pp. 205–207 of the **World of Darkness Rulebook** are veteran characters. They're designed to be challenges to characters who have supernatural edges. A "stock" cop will have a much humbler spread of capabilities, as you'll see herein.

They Don't Know

The precinct, by and large, doesn't know about the existence of the supernatural. Sure, the precinct is often up to its ears in weirdness, but the precinct lacks the insight, cohesion and story role of knowing that the supernatural exists.

Bear in mind that this is a horror game, and horror often lies in the unknown. Various agents of the precinct will certainly face horror in the form of the players' characters. *This is the point* — use the events encountered by the precinct to "peel back" the layers of the World of Darkness and expose its malignance. The characters themselves will face personal horror in the form of what they encounter while on the beat, their reactions to precinct agents or what the precinct is able to do to them.

Among the ranks of the precinct, a comparative minority of its agents know about the supernatural. Their knowledge, naturally, is flawed, and those individuals don't exactly trumpet what they've discovered to their fellows officers. What these individuals know is bits and pieces about the supernatural world, and they probably keep it to themselves, quietly following hunches rather than trying to convince the other cops that a ghost committed the murder. (How would you like to be at a crime scene with a partner who looks you in the eye and says, "It's probably a vampire, Roberts. Or maybe a werewolf"?)

Indulge this a bit in your own chronicles and stories. What would it mean if the commissioner believed in monsters? What about the racist, redneck beat cop two months away from retirement? What about the assistant DA who's seen inexplicable behavior come from her boss and slowly puts two and two together? This should be a fun part of Storytelling, climbing into the fraying personality of the guy who knows just enough to scare himself to the point of madness.

Theme and Mood

The theme is a refinement of the larger World of Darkness' theme. Weird, scary, incomprehensible things lurk in the shadowed corners of the world, and they're waiting to prey upon us. Specifically for this book, the theme is responsibility. How do we, as members of the precinct, protect those who depend on us from these mysterious and horrific entities, especially when we don't necessarily even know they're out there or what they can do?

The mood works something like a dial in this book. At one end of the dial is dread — the inherent, endemic dread of a malignant world that's unconcerned with its individual denizens and allows its malefic presences to victimize them. At

the other end of the dial is hope — the whole point of society and authority is to protect individuals from the depredations of those who would harm them. Over the course of a chronicle, the Storyteller will toggle that dial back and forth with the participation of the players' characters. Tonight's crime-scene atrocity turns to tomorrow's victory for humankind as the supernatural horror responsible comes to justice.

How to Use This Book

Chapter One introduces the precinct house itself and describes its look and function.

Chapter Two, the bulk of this book, describes police procedure, equipment, law enforcement and a variety of topics an officer might encounter while on the job.

Chapter Three details a variety of law enforcement officials and professionals who might be encountered in the 13th Precinct.

Chapter Four covers the blotter, numerous entries regarding calls made to police and story suggestions for handling them.

The **Appendix** includes a ready-to-play story, in which officers must confront a supernatural threat exposed by an unwitting offender.

Radio Communication

Official radio communication, similar to an official report, requires both brevity and clarity. Background noise and RF interference can render a speaker almost unintelligible. The academy course on radio communication teaches officers to speak slowly and distinctly, even when their adrenaline is up. The first part of this is a phonetic alphabet that officers use to indicate individual letters with greater verbal clarity. Most officers use the MPD standard, but those with prior military or civil aviation experience often revert under stress to the standard they knew first:

Letter	MPD	Military/Aviation
A	Adam	Alpha
B	Boy	Bravo
C	Charles	Charlie
D	David	Delta
E	Edward	Echo
F	Frank	Foxtrot
G	George	Golf
H	Henry	Hotel
I	Ida	India
J	John	Juliet
K	King	Kilo
L	Lincoln	Lima
M	Mary	Mike
N	Nora	November
O	Ocean	Oscar
P	Paul	Papa
Q	Queen	Quebec
R	Robert	Romeo
S	Sam	Sierra
T	Tom	Tango
U	Union	Uniform
V	Victor	Victor
W	William	Whiskey
X	X-ray	X-ray
Y	Young	Yankee
Z	Zebra	Zulu

Occasional creative supplements to the official list are also heard, particularly late at night when supervisors aren't likely to be listening.

In addition to the phonetic alphabet, the MPD has a unique vocabulary of numeric codes. Through the late 1990s, the department used a much larger set of codes, known as "10 codes" because each one began with a 10. First developed in 1940, these codes provided additional brevity for radio communication, as well as obfuscating the meaning of a conversation from non-department listeners. Over the years, every police department supplemented the initial set of 10 codes with its own additional signals until no two agencies used the same codes. This created communication problems that led the U.S. Department of Justice to recommend the termination of 10 code use in favor of plain English speech. The MPD officially phased out 10 codes in 2003. However, veteran officers still use a handful of the most common ones out of habit, most commonly "10-4" for "message received" and "10-20" for "location." The following list summarizes MPD's much shorter current list of radio codes, which serve much the same purpose as 10 codes: brevity and security. Following the current codes, we include the outdated 10 codes for Storytellers who want to suggest veteran cops stuck in their ways or who might be running games set in a period other than the present.

Code Zero	Possible safety hazard, caution is advised
Code One	Respond at normal safe speed
Code Two	Respond quickly, but no lights or sirens needed
Code Three	Respond immediately, with lights and sirens
Code Four	All is well; situation is secure; no additional help needed (used as interrogative or statement)
Code Five	Suspect has an outstanding arrest warrant or is otherwise a potential threat
Code Five Mary	Warrant is for a misdemeanor
Code Five Frank	Warrant is for a felony
Code Five Adam	Subject believed to be armed
Code Six	Busy; unavailable for other service calls
Code Seven	Out of service for meal or coffee break
Code Eight	Officer needs immediate help
Code Eight Frank	Firefighters or paramedics need immediate help
Code Nine	Back in service; available for calls
Code Ten	Clear this channel of all non-essential transmissions
Code Eleven	On scene
Code Twelve	Headquarters
Code Thirteen	Precinct house

Code Fourteen	City jail
Code Fifteen	Hospital
Code Sixteen	Area is under temporary surveillance; all units should avoid it except in response to an emergency or call for service
Code Twenty	Speaker needs assistance but requesting it in clear speech would provoke an undesirable reaction from the person with whom he's in contact
Break	Pausing transmission in case someone else needs to speak
Clear	Done transmitting for now
Copy	Understood last transmission
Go Ahead	Ready to listen
Stand By	Wait for further transmissions
10-1	Unable to understand
10-2	Signal is good
10-4	Message received
10-6	Busy, stand by
10-7	Out of service
10-8	In service
10-9	Repeat information
10-10	On specific assignment unless otherwise needed
10-15	Subject under arrest
10-16	Pick up ___
10-18	Anything for us?
10-19	Nothing for you
10-20	Location
10-21	Call ___ by phone
10-22	Report in person
10-23	Arrived at scene
10-24	Assignment finished, report filed
10-25	Assignment finished, no report filed
10-26	Detaining subject
10-27	Driver's license or identification
10-28	Vehicle registration
10-29	Check records for warrants
10-30	Domestic disturbance
10-31	Unspecified disturbance
10-32	Burglary
10-33	Robbery at business
10-34	Burglar alarm
10-35	Prowler
10-36	Fight
10-37	Subject with deadly weapon
10-38	Shots fired
10-39	Subject shot
10-39A	Subject cut or stabbed
10-40	Hospital run
10-41	Get a report
10-42	Subject in view
10-43	Robbery other than business
10-44	Carjacking
10-45	Abandoned vehicle

10-46	Disorderly person
10-47	Drunk
10-48	Hit-and-run accident
10-49	Accident without injury
10-50	Accident with injury
10-51	Tow truck needed
10-52	Traffic problem
10-53	Wires down
10-54	Investigation
10-55	Drunk driver
10-56	Indecent exposure
10-57	Child molestation
10-58	Child left unattended
10-59	Meet another officer
10-60	Person tampering with vehicle
10-62	Noise complaint or party
10-63	Drug transaction
10-64	Prostitution
10-70	Disorderly person in vehicle
10-71	Reckless driving
10-72	Street racing
10-73	Fire in the open (field, trash pile)
10-74	Structure or vehicle fire
10-75	Bomb threat
10-76	Explosion
10-77	HAZMAT incident
10-79	Aircraft crash
10-80	Corpse
10-81	Heart attack
10-82	Injured person
10-83	Sick person
10-84	Critical illness or injury
10-85	Ambulance needed
10-86	Homeless person
10-87	Emotionally disturbed person
10-88	Lost or missing person
10-89	Barking dog or other animal complaint
10-90	Need phone number for ___
10-91	Talk closer to microphone
10-92	Talk further from microphone
10-94	Give radio test with voice
10-95	Officer being held hostage
10-96	Non-officer being held hostage
10-97	Rape

A wide variety of police slang and shorthand has originated from both past and current codes. For example, "what's your twenty?" is cop-speak for "where are you?" When one officer drives past another who's handling an incident, he'll hold up four fingers to ask if everything is okay ("Code Four"). A response of four fingers indicates that the situation is well in hand.

Like most police departments, the MPD uses the 24-hour military clock: 9 A.M. is "0900 hours," 9 P.M. is "2100 hours."

Call Signs

Every partner pair or lone officer is assigned a unique call sign for radio use. The MPD uses a standardized system: precinct (if applicable) plus assignment plus individual unit. The precinct and individual unit are numbers, while the assignment is a letter:

A	Aviation Squadron
C	Analysis Bureau
D	Detective Bureau
E	Patrol Bureau (first shift)
F	Patrol Bureau (second shift)
G	Patrol Bureau (third shift)
K	K-9 Unit
M	Administration Division (any bureau)
S	Surveillance Bureau
T	Traffic Bureau (first shift)
U	Traffic Bureau (second shift)
V	Traffic Bureau (third shift)
X	ERU
Z	Dispatch

Thus, "Thirteen George Fifteen" (or "13G15" in a written report) is the 15th numbered patrol unit working the 13th Precinct's third shift, while "Five Zebra" is the dispatcher for the 5th Precinct. The Aviation Squadron is notorious for using "Air" to identify its units instead of official "Adam" or "Alpha" call signs, but no one else gets away with this. On precinct channels, units usually drop the precinct identifier, as all the regular speakers on the channel should be assigned to the precinct in question. It's not uncommon for certain squads to use even less formal protocol when talking among themselves, going simply by individual unit numbers: "Hey, Twelve, we've got a domestic for you."

Other Specialized Terminology

ADW: Assault with a Deadly Weapon

AKA: Also Known As

AMBER: America's Missing: Broadcast Emergency Response. An AMBER alert makes information available to the public regarding the abduction of a child whose life may be in danger. Instigated by the National Center for Missing and Exploited Children (NCMEC).

Anonymous Report: The report issued by a victim of or witness to a crime who does not want to pursue any further action by police, but wants the incident investigated nonetheless.

B&A: Bomb and Arson

B&E: Breaking and Entering

BAT Van: Breath Alcohol Testing unit

BDU: Battle Dress Uniform

Beat: The area assigned to an officer for patrol, in which the officer answers calls for service.

BOLO: Be On the Look Out

CCW: Carrying Concealed Weapon

CST: Crime Scene Technician

CSU: Crime Scene Unit

DCS: Distribution of a Controlled Substance

Detail: A broad term for a station-assigned special assignment, such as a stakeout, pursuit of suspects, perimeter control, special event crowd control, etc. Also known as a station assignment.

DOA: Dead on Arrival

DOB: Date of Birth

DOJ: Department of Justice

Domestic: A domestic dispute

DOP: Destruction of Property

DUI: Driving Under the Influence

DWI: Driving While Intoxicated (or Impaired)

EDP: Emotionally Disturbed Person

ERU: Emergency Response Unit

Expedite: Emergency response, in which the officer will employ a vehicle's lights and siren.

GM: Identified street gang member

GOA: Gone on Arrival

HAZMAT: Hazardous Materials

History: Previous criminal records or outstanding tickets

Hit: A computer record that indicates a detained suspect is wanted or a vehicle is reported stolen. "We got a hit on the silver Lexus."

Job, The: An insider's term for salaried police work

Juvenile: A person under 17 years of age

Larceny: The act of stealing, usually in reference to shoplifting

LSA: Leaving the Scene of an Accident

MDT: Mobile Data Terminal. A portable computer used by police in the field.

Minor: A person under 21 years of age

MIP: Minor In Possession (of a controlled substance)

MPD: Midway Police Department

MVA: Motor Vehicle Accident

NCIC: National Crime Information Center. A computerized repository of criminal justice information such as criminal records, fugitives, missing persons, stolen property, etc.

NCMEC: National Center for Missing and Exploited Children

NDPIX: National Drug Pointer Index. A database managed by the DEA specializing in drug investigative targets/subjects. Searches and records are processed through the NCIC (see above).

NHTSA: National Highway Traffic Safety Administration

NRN: No Report Needed

OIS: Officer Involved Shooting

On-View: The officer discovered the incident in question. No call or report came though the dispatch center.

PBT: Portable Breathalyzer Test

PCR: Police Community Relations (Neighborhood Watch meetings, etc.)

PCS: Possession of a Controlled Substance

Peace Disturbance: A general complaint involving one party inhibiting the "right to peace" of another, such as with loud music, a barking dog, unsupervised children causing havoc, etc.

Person Down: An individual who is not moving for an unknown reason. Most persons down are discovered prone or supine.

POI: Person of Interest

POST: Police Officer Standards and Training

Primary: The officer responsible for writing the police report on a given incident.

Probe: A probationary police officer (PPO); a rookie

Proceed with Caution: A standard response offered by a police officer or dispatcher; a general acknowledgment of heightened awareness

Rolling Plate: A moving vehicle subjected to a records check to determine if the vehicle is stolen

Sally Port: A secure entrance into the police station where prisoners are transferred

Secondary: An off-duty police officer working a second job, such as security, crowd control, checking ID, etc.

Seeing Eye: A report given by a third party or uninvolved witness

SO: (Registered) Sex Offender

Standby to Keep the Peace: A station assignment that requests an officer to be present at a location (and potentially act as a witness). Most often assigned during the execution of an eviction or repossession job, but increasingly often in child custody situations.

Stealing Over: A theft in which the total loss is valued at over $500.

Stealing Under: A theft in which the total loss is valued at $500 or less.

Strong-Arm Robbery: A robbery in the commission of which an assailant steals private property without the use of a weapon, usually through threats or physical violence.

Trash Run: A station assignment to standby when a restaurant opens its service door to take the trash out. Usually assigned via MDT, and after dark.

UCR: Uniform Crime Report

Unfounded: No basis for a complaint at the time of the call; a "false alarm"

UUW: Unlawful Use of a Weapon

VIN: The standard 17-digit Vehicle Identification Number

VOP: Violation of Probation or Parole

Wrecker: A general term for a tow truck; may be further specified as a flatbed rollback, tilt-bed carrier or a heavy-duty tow truck

WT: Walkie-talkie

X-Patrol: Extra patrol to increase vigilance around a house whose owners are on vacation or in an area that has seen a recent increase in burglaries/crime

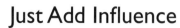

Just Add Influence

Interdepartmental relations can get even more complicated than Mace Calhoun (from the Prologue) might believe where the supernatural is involved. For example, while it is quite difficult for any single supernatural entity, or even a group of such entities working in concert, to "control the city's police force," such a scenario is much more feasible in a smaller and more insular organization, such as a small county sheriff's office. Thus, the Storyteller might decide that the antagonism between the city police and county officers is based on more than professional rivalry. The Sheriff's Department might be under the sway of a vampire, a mage or perhaps even the ghost of long-dead Sheriff George O'Dell, who can't let go of the office that meant so much to him in life. Of course, the Sheriff's Department need not be under the sway of a purely supernatural force. The Sheriff's Department might simply be in the thrall of organized crime, which can often infiltrate the small rural police forces at the periphery of an urban area.

To those police officers aware of the supernatural, the FBI presents both an opportunity for help in exposing the truth, or a dangerous adversary with no idea what it is up against. The FBI is charged with investigating kidnappings that cross state lines, and since most mages, vampires and werewolves must abandon their former lives upon gaining supernatural powers, such beings often end up on missing persons lists. Also, the FBI has jurisdiction over serial killers who cross state lines, and the many commonalities shared by victims of vampire attacks often show up in FBI serial killer profiles, despite the Kindred's best efforts to preserve the Masquerade. A character forced to work with an arrogant FBI agent may grow exasperated at the government agent's abject refusal to acknowledge clear evidence of supernatural events.

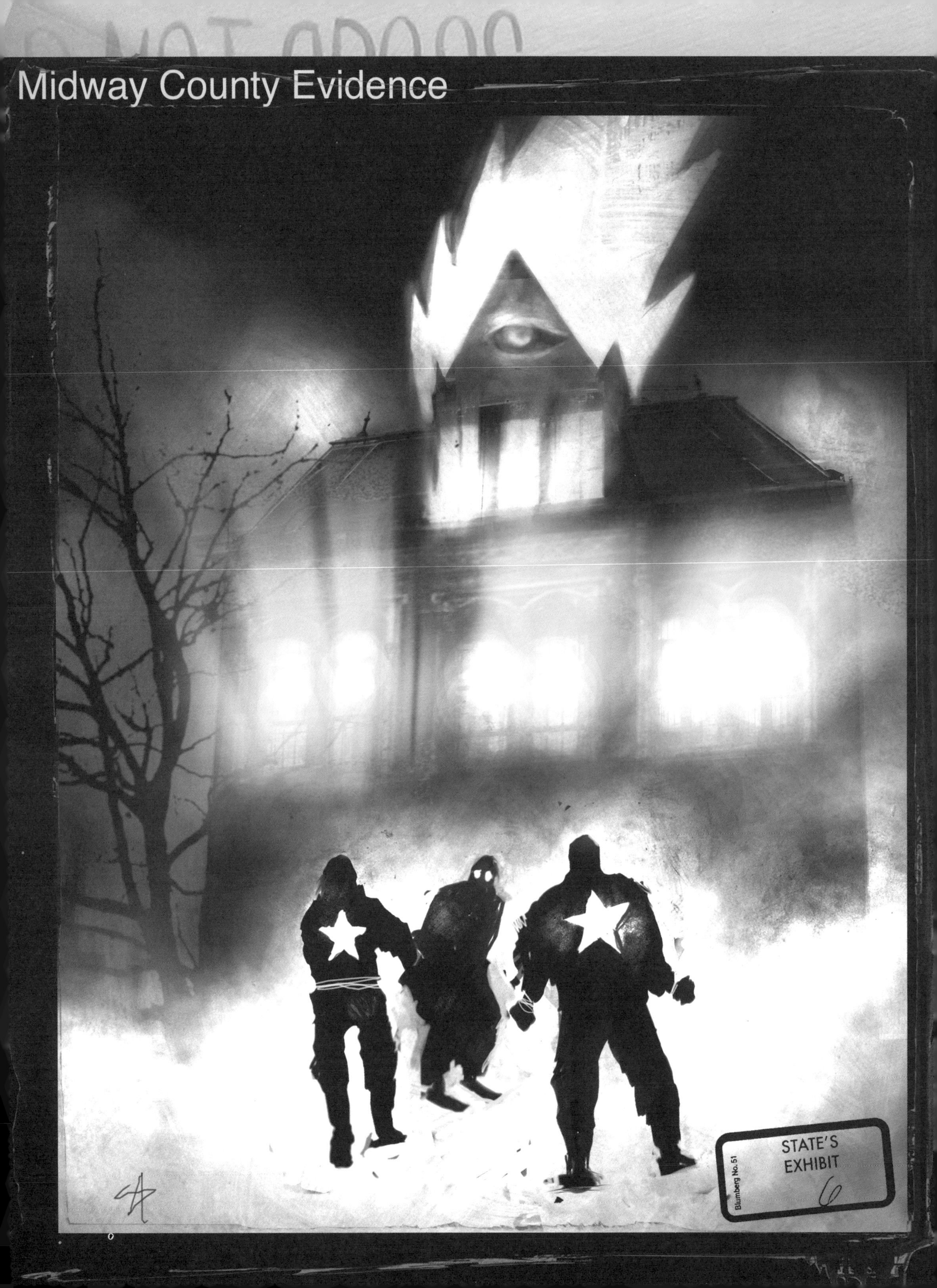
Midway County Evidence
STATE'S EXHIBIT
6
Blumberg No. 51

Chapter One: The Cop Shop

The city of Midway has organized and reorganized its police precinct layouts over a dozen times in the last century, often engendering great confusion in both the police and the citizenry in the process. At the peak, the city maintained 17 different precinct houses during the early 1980s as part of a program to foster better relations between police and the local communities they served. In the mid-1990s, however, budget cuts forced the city to close the majority of the police precincts and reconfigure the personnel and equipment into a six-zone structure.

While the mayor's office initially wanted to close the 13th Precinct and preferably raze it to the ground due to the building's age, those plans were stymied by protests from civil rights leaders (the 13th services a section of town with a high minority population) and the Midway Historic Preservation Society (the precinct house was originally built in 1904). Consequently, when the restructuring plan was enacted, the former 13th Precinct was officially renamed the Zone 4 Regional Precinct House and heavily renovated to restore its traditional features.

The precinct is still referred to conversationally as the 13th. The building, in addition to its historical name, is also located at the corner of 13th Street and Madison Avenue, with the station's parking lot taking up the rest of the block on 13th street all the way to Monroe Avenue. An additional reason for referring to the building as the 13th Precinct can be viewed as either police superstition or else just black humor: the precinct has a disproportionate number of officers killed or seriously injured in the line of duty. Some officers even claim that the 13th Precinct is cursed.

Like all precincts in Midway, the 13th Precinct maintains three shifts: First, Second and Third. Officially, First Shift lasts from 6 A.M. to 2 P.M., Second Shift from 2 P.M. to 10 P.M. and Third Shift from 10 P.M. to 6 A.M. However, Precinct 13 is divided into an A-shift and a B-shift. In practice, A-shift starts roll call 15 minutes before the hour and B-shift 15 minutes after the hour.

The precinct generally fields about 15 squad cars per shift. About a third of the squad cars are assigned to partnered officers, while the rest are assigned to solo officers, mainly on a seniority basis. There are also five bicycle officers on each shift except in case of inclement weather, in which case bicycle officers ride with solo patrol officers. Each shift generally has about 25 officers on patrol to respond to calls and to maintain a presence in the community. The precinct also has nine field investigators assigned to it, plus another 12 detectives assigned to the various task forces (including Homicide, Narcotics, Vice and Organized Crime).

The precinct captain generally stays in his office from 9 A.M. to 6 P.M. Each shift also has one shift lieutenant, two shift sergeants, one desk sergeant (stationed at the main reception desk), one evidence officer (stationed in the evidence lockup) and one booking officer (who floats between the booking room and the holding cell office). Typically, the precinct also hires at least one trainee per shift to assist as needed, usually in the holding cell office or with the desk sergeant. Such personnel are generally people who plan to enter the police academy and who want to gain contacts and practical police experience first.

The Exterior

The precinct house is a two-story (plus basement), steel-frame building in a Romanesque Revival style. The lower floor has a red sandstone facade, with two large, arched windows on the west and south sides. Identical windows used to exist on the east side, but they were bricked over in 1977.

Instead of red sandstone, the second floor of the precinct has a facade of red brick with gray brick accents. The windows are conventional rectangular windows without bars, and unlike the windows on the first floor, these actually open. Above the glass windows are tall, brick arches typical of the Romanesque style. On the second floor above the Madison Avenue entrance is a large circular window. The precinct house contains a small attic that houses the central air-conditioning system added in 1989, much to the relief of the officers.

Large, arched doorways separate the windows on the west and south sides. These doorways are the public entrances to the station, one on Madison Avenue and one on 13th Street. Over each of these doorways is a stone archway upon which is engraved the department's motto, To Protect and To Serve.

A third entrance was added on the east wall in 1977, when the city tore down the buildings to the east of the precinct to add a gated and fenced parking lot for the officers. The windows on that side were bricked over when the offices on the first floor were renovated into holding cells on the south and locker rooms on the north wall. Unlike the two public entrances, the parking lot entrance is magnetically locked and requires a numeric code to open, though the desk sergeant can open the door remotely when someone buzzes in at the door.

There is no door on the north side of the building. Instead, there are three arched windows that face on to a narrow alley the station shares with Bailey's Irish Tavern, a favorite watering hole of off-duty officers. All the windows on the first floor have frosted glass and iron bars. The building is elevated about five feet above street level with stone steps leading up to each of the entrances. Only the 13th Street entrance has handicap access. On the corner of Madison and 13th stands a tall, green sign identifying the precinct house as a National Historical Landmark.

To the east of the building, there is a parking lot capable of holding 15 squad cars and about 30 additional vehicles. Also, the spaces in front of the precinct house on the Madison and 13th Street sides are reserved for squad cars. The parking lot is surrounded by a wrought-iron fence and an electric gate that opens when officers enter a code. The desk sergeant can also open the gate remotely. The 13th Street gate is used only for entering the parking lot. Officers who leave the lot must go out through a second gate on Monroe Avenue. This gate opens automatically when squad cars pull up to it, and also can be opened remotely by the desk sergeant when officers are pulling out on patrol at the start of their shifts. Naturally, the parking lot is under video surveillance. There are six cameras in the parking lot, with another four covering two public entrances to the building. All camera views are cycled through the CCTV screens at the desk sergeant's station.

In the parking lot, about 10 feet away from the door, stands a small, open shed that holds the eight TREK 8000 Police Model mountain bikes used by the precinct's bicycle squad. Each bike is equipped with a luggage rack capable of carrying a nylon trunk bag holding standard duty-belt equipment. The bikes are also equipped with rechargeable headlights and specially designed odometers and speedometers. Extra bicycle helmets usually hang from hooks on the shed wall, and in the back is a large workbench with tools and other equipment for repairing the bikes.

Just to the right of the parking lot doorway is a padlocked steel trap door that opens on to a set of stairs leading to the basement. This is the exterior entrance to the basement boiler room that the city struggles to maintain. The entire system should have been replaced years ago, but doing so would have required much more money than the city was prepared to spend and much more damage to the building's architectural structure than the local historical societies could tolerate. Faced with a cash shortage and the threat of an injunction, the city has spent the last 10 years attempting to maintain a 60-year-old boiler system that works intermittently at best. Officers assigned to the 13th Precinct are advised to bring sweaters in the winter.

The First Floor

The 13th Street entrance is the primary civilian entrance. The Madison Avenue entrance allows citizens to access the Evidence Room to recover personal possessions confiscated during arrest. Officers enter through the parking lot entrance on the east side of the building, and arrestees are typically brought in through that door as well, since it opens directly into the booking area and the holding cells.

Main Reception

The primary public entrance is on 13th Street, and the tall, reinforced, wooden doors open in to a small reception room. At the far end of the room is a large bulletproof window with an intercom button. The on-duty desk sergeant sits on the other side, usually accompanied by a civilian receptionist.

The reception area contains 10 rather uncomfortable wooden chairs. The walls, just as those of every other room in the building, are a shade of gray best described as bureaucratic. The hardwood floors and the high ceiling cause a visitor's footsteps to echo menacingly as she approaches the desk.

The walls are adorned with several posters seeking new recruits for the police academy, as well as one containing

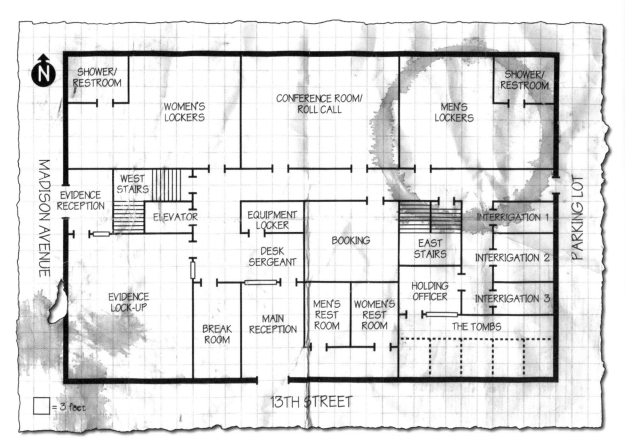

information about the Crimestoppers 1-800 number and another containing information on starting up local neighborhood watch programs. Above the desk sergeant's window are three large, framed pictures of the mayor, the chief of police and the precinct captain. Visitors occasionally remark that none of the three looks particularly trustworthy.

On the left wall is a three- by five-foot handcrafted, wooden display case (made and donated by a former officer who took up carpentry in retirement) that contains police badges collected from all 50 states. On the opposite wall is a framed American flag recently sent back from Iraq by an officer from the 13th called up to active duty and stationed in Baghdad. Also on the right wall is a simple wooden plaque with brass nameplates identifying every officer from the 13th Precinct to have died in the line of duty going back to 1927 — 53 so far. Every 10 years or so, the nameplates are relocated to a progressively larger wooden plaque.

As a visitor comes through the 13th Street entrance, he will see a door marked "restroom" to his right. This door leads to a small corridor with adjacent men's and women's restrooms. To the right of the desk sergeant's window is a magnetically locked steel door that leads to the rest of the station.

Madison Avenue
Entrance and Evidence Lockup

The other public entrance, from Madison Avenue, leads to a much smaller reception area. This area has only three chairs and no decorations at all. There is a glass window and a steel door connecting to the evidence lockup instead of the desk sergeant.

Persons who have been arrested and then released come here to collect their personal belongings. The Evidence Room itself is a fairly large room whose walls are lined with shelves. There are three large sets of storage shelves in the center of the room that run almost the length of the room. The east wall is mostly hidden by filing cabinets.

At the northeast corner of the Evidence Room is another bulletproof window and magnetic-lock door. This window is used by police who come to check out evidence. There is a networked computer at each of the windows for use by the officer assigned to Evidence. While the Evidence Room is fully computerized, the MPD still uses a card checkout system as a redundancy factor, mainly because officers who check out contraband evidence (such as drugs or recovered cash) don't trust computers to register when they have returned the evidence.

The Evidence Room is probably the dirtiest room in the precinct, as the janitorial staff is not permitted to come in except under strict supervision. For the same reason, burnt-out fluorescent bulbs go months without replacement. The shelves are packed with evidence from floor to ceiling, blocking out the beige walls and making the room seem even darker, and the whole design of the room gives it a depressing, cave-like atmosphere.

The Break Room

Both the interior door to the Evidence Room and the door connecting the desk sergeant to the reception area open up into a U-shaped corridor. Between those two doors lies the entrance to a break room for the patrol officers. There are two battered loveseats donated by former officers, soda and candy vending machines, a small refrigerator, a small cabinet with a Formica countertop, an irregularly washed coffee machine and a small TV in the corner.

By tradition, the desk sergeant for each shift is responsible for bringing in several boxes of doughnuts. There is a small jar on the countertop, and officers are on the honor system to put in 25 cents for every doughnut taken. On the wall, there is a small bulletin board to which various cartoons and jokes of varying degrees of political correctness have been stapled. Next to the bulletin board hangs an 11" x 17" framed needlepoint work given to the precinct in 1979 by the mother of a slain officer titled "A Police Officer's Prayer."

A Police Officer's Prayer

Lord I ask for courage
Courage to face and
Conquer my own fears . . .
Courage to take me
Where others will not go . . .
I ask for strength
Strength of body to protect others
And strength of spirit to lead others . . .
I ask for dedication
Dedication to my job, to do it well
Dedication to my community
To keep it safe . . .
Give me Lord, concern
For others who trust me
And compassion for those who need me . . .
And please Lord
Through it all
Be at my side . . .
— Author Unknown

The Desk Sergeant's Station

The door in the north wall of the 13th Street reception room opens into the desk sergeant's station. This station consists of a desk with two chairs, one for the sergeant and one for a civilian receptionist who directs non-911 phone calls. There are three CCTV screens mounted on the desk that cycle through the various security cameras in and around the station. Behind the desk sergeant's station stands a large locked closet, containing extra police equipment such as pepper spray, rifles, extra ammunition and other related equipment.

Locker Rooms and the Main Conference Room

As a visitor continues around the U-shaped hall away from the desk sergeant's station, he will pass the break room, the interior entrance to the evidence lockup, the building's only elevator and the west staircase. In the northwestern corner of the building is a large area that has been converted into a locker room for the female officers. Within the locker room are two rows of gym-style lockers and benches. The locker room also contains a limited amount of exercise equipment, mainly a used Soloflex machine and two treadmills. The locker room also contains a shower room with eight shower stalls and a restroom. The men's locker room is in the northeastern corner of the building and is functionally identical to the women's locker room. However, the men's exercise area consists of free weights instead of the Soloflex. There is occasional tension between the male and female officers over the fact that the two locker rooms are the same size even though the male officers substantially outnumber the female officers.

The locker rooms are separated by a large room with six folding tables and 30 chairs arranged in front of a podium and a blackboard. Roll call takes place in this room. At the beginning of each shift, the shift sergeant will check the roll and advise the officers of any particularly relevant issues (reports of a serial rapist operating in one neighborhood, several convenience store robberies in the same general area, an announcement that the wife of one of the officers gave birth the previous night, etc.). This room also functions as a main conference room, as it is the only room in the building large enough to hold an entire shift. The room contains a single 42" television with a VCR/DVD player on a rolling cart.

Against the south wall of the conference room stands a large wooden mailbox rack. Every officer assigned to the precinct has his own mailbox, and information pertaining to shift assignments and employment-related issues is typically put here.

Booking, First Floor Interrogation and the Tombs

As officers enter through the east parking lot entrance, they first pass a side corridor on the left. This corridor leads to three interrogation rooms and four prisoner holding cells (affectionately known as the Tombs). The holding cells are each eight feet square. The south wall of each cell is brick, and the remaining walls are steel bars. The floors are concrete. Each cell has an individual door, a toilet, a sink and a metal bed bolted to the floor with a thin mattress, pillow and sheets. The doors are all individually locked and open out. On each shift, a single officer (or sometimes a civilian trainee) remains in a cramped office that leads to the Tombs to watch over any inmates via CCTV. It is at best a bleakly dull job, and occasionally a highly stressful one when one or more of the inmates is drunk, high or mentally unbalanced.

The interrogation rooms are each eight feet by 12. Each room has a single wooden table, several wooden chairs and a single light. Each room is accessible by a wooden door. Next to the door is a two-way mirror, and each room contains an intercom system that allows police to listen in on interrogations. Lawyers often meet with their clients in these rooms as well. The east walls of the interrogation rooms are brick, and one can clearly see where the original windows were bricked up. The interrogation rooms are intentionally designed to be small and claustrophobic in order to put suspects ill at ease.

Cell No. 4

An informal tradition holds at the 13th Precinct that prisoners are not placed in the holding cell designated No. 4 unless there is no other place to put them. In 1983, a perp named Harry Moran was arrested on domestic violence charges. His wife Lynda, distraught and codependent, got drunk and tried to drive downtown to free him. She was arrested for DUI and, due to a lack of communication and bookkeeping, was placed in an adjacent holding cell, where Harry somehow got his hands around her throat and strangled her to death. Since then, several rape and domestic violence suspects who've been placed in that cell have required sedation after reporting a nonexistent woman wrapping ethereal hands around their necks.

If an officer continues down the main corridor past the side corridor leading to the Tombs, he will pass the east stairs, as well as a small janitorial closet. Just past the stairs is the booking room. Here, suspects who have been placed under arrest are photographed and fingerprinted. The room contains a sink and a table, which is used as a station where the suspect's fingerprints are applied. The suspect is then permitted to wash his hands in the sink after his prints have been taken.

The south wall is painted white with black lines at one-foot intervals. The booking officer will place the suspect against this wall and take his picture while he holds a slate containing biometric information and other data. Today, booking officers use digital cameras and store all photographs online. In earlier days, booking officers actually had to develop film in this room, and today, long after

the dark room was torn down, the booking room still has an astringent chemical smell.

The Second Floor

The second floor of the station is home to the detectives and to the supervisory officers. As a visitor comes up the west staircase, she first notices an open area with offices on each side. On the west wall, there is a large circular glass window looking down on Madison Avenue. To the east, a visitor will observe men's and women's restrooms and, beyond them, the east staircase. Against the east wall is a large conference and multipurpose room used primarily for coordinating manhunts and task force activities.

Field Investigations and Task Force Offices

At the southwest corner of the second floor lies the Bullpen, a large office used by those detectives who serve in the 13th Precinct but are not assigned to any task forces. There are nine full-time field investigators, generally three per shift, though sometimes an investigator may choose to work odd hours in order to pursue leads in a particular case. In this room is a total of 10 desks, each with a computer and phone. On the north wall is a large chalkboard that identifies ongoing investigations and which officer is assigned to each one.

On the west wall stands a large metal filing cabinet containing extra equipment such as rubber gloves, evidence kits, legal pads and the like.

A large metal cabinet on the south wall remains unlocked. Many detectives keep spare clothes in this cabinet in case their regular clothes get dirty at a crime scene.

Each desk has at least one drawer with a strong lock in which evidence is kept while the detective has it checked out of the evidence lockup. Individual detectives usually keep limited numbers of personal items on their desks, such as family photos, mementos or even small plants. Pauline Reed's desk is in the southwest corner, which traditionally belongs to the senior detective as it has a view of both the west and the south.

Moving east from the Field Investigations office, a visitor will find four 12-foot-square rooms along the south wall. Each of these rooms is assigned to one of the department-wide task forces. The office next to Field Investigations is reserved for Homicide Investigations and is the domain of Sid Routman and his protégé of the moment. The next room is used by the five officers assigned to the Narcotics Task Force, most of whom work the night shift. Gena Buehler invariably works nights when she comes into the precinct house at all (as an undercover officer, she is rarely required to come into the office). The next office is used by the Vice squad, which includes four officers. Vice detectives generally work either Second or Third shifts. Finally, the southeast corner is reserved for detectives in

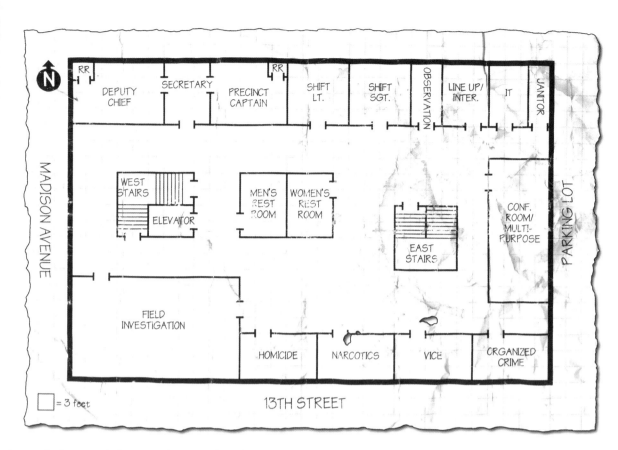

the city's Organized Crime Task Force though currently there are none assigned to the 13th Precinct. Sid Routman schemes half-heartedly to swap offices with the OCT so that he can have a corner office for himself, but he has taken no concrete steps to move.

Senior Staff Offices

To the quiet annoyance of most of the station, the northwest corner of the second floor is reserved for the deputy chief of Field Operations, who maintains an office in every precinct in the city. This office is also used by the police chief or other high-ranking city personnel when their presence is required at the precinct.

In practice, however, the office is rarely used, and this waste of space is galling to many of the personnel who must share tiny offices. The deputy chief's office has other amenities: the best television set in the precinct, a better computer than most of the detectives or any of the patrol officers, and even a liquor cabinet (which is kept locked at all times when the deputy chief is not in residence).

To get to the deputy chief's office, a visitor must first pass through a secretary's office that separates the deputy chief's office from that of the precinct captain. The secretary works primarily for the captain, but also fields calls and does typing for the deputy chief when he is there. The secretary's office contains a computer, fax machine and several filing cabinets, as well as the secretary's personal effects. The filing cabinets primarily contain personnel records, budget

records and personal correspondence from the captain. The secretary at the moment is Mavis Gregoire, a short, heavyset, African American woman in her late 50s who still types a good 70 words a minute and who is virtually indispensable to the captain.

As a visitor enters Mavis' office, the deputy chief's office is on the left and the captain's is on the right. The layout of the captain's office is identical to that of the deputy chief, though the captain's is much more lived-in. The captain is extremely neat and efficient in his office management. On the south wall of the captain's office is a bookshelf reaching up three feet off the ground. The captain's reading habits are eclectic, ranging from Cormac McCarthy to Dave Barry. Sitting atop the bookshelf are a number of personal pictures, including wedding pictures, graduation pictures of the captain's children and a picture of the mayor congratulating the captain upon his assignment. Above them is a large piece of expressionist art, an abstract depiction of the engine block of a 1957 Chevy painted by the captain's son, Derek, who is a promising young artist in Midway. There is a very comfortable leather chair along the north wall. Both the captain's and deputy chief's offices have small private bathrooms.

Continuing east from the captain's office, the next office is shared by all three of the shift lieutenants. The room contains three separate desks, each covered with personnel reports, budget requests and exhaustive lists of outstanding cases.

Next door is the office of the shift sergeants. There are two sergeants assigned to each shift. The office contains two desks, each with three large, locked drawers, and each shift sergeant has a key for one drawer. The office is almost intolerably cramped considering the number of people who use it and the amount of paperwork they must collectively maintain. Outside the sergeant's office, three large calendars are stapled to a bulletin board, one for each shift. Any officer who wants to use a personal leave day can simply write her name on the calendar on the day she wishes to take off. Up to two officers can sign up for leave in this way. If a third officer wishes to take off on the same day, he must have express permission from one of the shift sergeants. In such a case, the sergeant will typically wait until about an hour before the shift begins to see how many officers have called in sick before granting or denying the request. Officers do not require permission to use accumulated sick time, but absent extraordinary circumstances, they must notify a shift sergeant at least two hours before roll call.

Just past the sergeant's office, there are two connected rooms. One is an observation room, while the other is a police lineup room. There is a large two-way mirror on the wall connecting the two rooms, and police typically station eyewitnesses in the observation room for lineups. The lineup room has a small table and chairs that are pushed to the side during lineups. The room is also sometimes used as an additional interrogation room.

Next door is a small office used for the precinct's civilian information-technology staff. All of the IT staff members are city employees hired to maintain official computer systems and technology. At the 13th Precinct, a single IT staff member remains on site for each shift, with additional personnel floating between precincts during the day. The IT room has two small desks, and is otherwise covered with cannibalized hard drives and other technological widgets that are largely incomprehensible to most of the officers.

In the northeast corner of the second floor is a small, narrow office that is used to hold supplies for the janitorial staff, including cleaning supplies and large boxes of toilet paper and trash bags. There is also a mini-fridge and a couple of chairs for the use of the janitorial staff. Emmet Pritchard can often be found here at odd hours. Officially, he comes to spot check the onsite janitors on behalf of G&V Janitorial Services, which has contracted with the city to provide cleaning staff for most city offices.

Chapter Two: The Ride-Along

This chapter presents a general overview of police organization and operations within the fictional Midway Police Department. Space considerations prohibit a truly comprehensive examination of these issues. In addition, policies and procedures vary between departments, and some information in this chapter is deliberately vague or incomplete to avoid compromising officer safety. Do not assume that any police department with which you come in contact operates in the same manner as the MPD.

A Word on Live-Action

Reading this book does not make you a cop. While police officers are dramatically appropriate characters for a World of Darkness LARP, all players should exercise the utmost caution in their portrayals and only do so in LARPs that do not take place in the public eye. Pretending to be a cop in public can result in charges of impersonating an officer, which may be either a misdemeanor or a low-grade felony depending on the jurisdiction in which you play.

As always, we strenuously recommend against weapons (real or fake) in LARP situations. Your prop badge will not save you from real bullets when an armed officer mistakes your toy gun for the real thing.

From the Top

The MPD employs about 7,200 sworn officers and 1,100 civilian staff, making the MPD the fourth largest police department in the United States. The bureaucracy that governs the daily activities of these thousands of personnel is fairly representative of the departments of major cities across the United States.

The highest official in the MPD is a political appointee, the Midway Commissioner of Police. The commissioner serves at the pleasure of the mayor, and, consequently, the MPD's leadership changes just about every time a new party takes over the city government. The commissioner is not required to have been a sworn officer prior to his appointment, which can put someone with no prior law enforcement experience in charge of the department. The commissioner's duties consist primarily of providing political representation for the department at all levels from local to federal, and he is a non-voting member of the city council.

Directly under the commissioner is the Chief of Police. The commissioner appoints the chief, but the city council confirms the appointment before a new chief can take office. The chief is the department's operational commander, responsible both for defining policy that governs law enforcement functions and for directing the execution of that policy. He must personally approve the promotion of all sworn officers above the rank of lieutenant. The chief has his own personal staff of administrators, media liaisons and legal advisors, collectively known as the Office of the Chief. The MPD's chaplains (see p. 77) are also attached to this office.

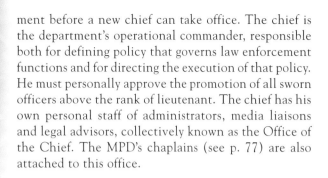

MPD Ranks and Demographics

From highest to lowest, the ranks that an MPD officer can attain are:

- Midway Commissioner of Police
- Chief of Police
- Deputy Chief of Police
- Major
- Captain
- Lieutenant/Detective Lieutenant
- Sergeant/Detective Sergeant
- Senior Police Officer (SPO)/Detective
- Police Officer (PO)

All ranks below that of Chief of Police come via promotion within the department (as noted above, the chief and commissioner are appointees). Promotion through Lieutenant is based on a civil service formula that factors in performance record, time spent in current rank, citations and reprimands, physical fitness exam results, academic degrees and special certifications (e.g., Spanish proficiency, flight training). Promotions to Captain or Major occur only to fill existing vacancies and are largely political.

As an officer rises in rank, his duties become less enforcement-related and more bureaucratic. Lieutenants rarely see the street (though detective lieutenants still work it regularly). Captains never handle cases unless they're politically sensitive. Majors and above are pure administrators. Consequently, many cops consider themselves successful if they manage to avoid promotion above SPO or Sergeant for their entire careers.

A uniformed officer who's eligible for (or who has already achieved) SPO rank can move from patrol duty to plainclothes investigative work by passing the detective's exam. The rank of Detective is equivalent to that of SPO in terms of authority and pay, but the duties of a detective are markedly different (see p. 46). Higher-ranking detectives

prefix their ranks with "Detective." Captains and majors, being administrators more than investigators, abandon the title when promoted from Detective Lieutenant.

Civilian employees (aside from the commissioner, of course) have no formal place in the rank structure and never command sworn officers. Instead, civilian employees belong to the same complex system of government employee pay scales that the rest of the city government uses. In practice, civilian personnel receive exactly as much authority and respect as their attitudes and job descriptions deserve.

Below the Office of the Chief, the MPD's organizational structure branches out into three divisions: Operations, Support and Administration. A deputy chief heads each division. Majors lead bureaus or other major units within the divisions.

Operations Division

When most citizens think of police work, their mental image mainly includes Operations Division. "Ops" is where the "real police work" occurs. The division contains the Patrol Bureau, the Detective Bureau and the Traffic Bureau, each commanded by a major. Operations Division divides the responsibilities of all three of its bureaus geographically by precincts. Thus, parallel units of patrol officers, detectives and traffic cops all work alongside one another on the same streets. Each precinct's patrol officers work under the command of a captain, as do the precinct's detectives. The department has relatively fewer traffic officers, so assigning one traffic captain per precinct would result in a top-heavy structure; instead, each of the Traffic Bureau's four captains supervises two to four precincts' assets, leaving daily traffic supervision at the precinct level in the hands of subordinate lieutenants.

Traffic and patrol cops are assigned to one of three shifts, or watches. These scheduled watches keep personnel on the streets around the clock. Detectives work irregularly (and generally much more than 40 hours a week) as their caseloads require. In each precinct, the ratio of personnel is approximately 10 patrol officers for every three detectives and one traffic officer.

Patrol Bureau

The Patrol Bureau contains the vast majority of the MPD's uniformed officers. These officers patrol assigned areas within their precincts, known as beats, and are the first responders to calls for service. Patrol cops are the most visible members of the MPD and those with which ordinary citizens are most likely to come into contact. A detailed examination of patrol duty begins on p. 37.

Detective Bureau

The Detective Bureau contains trained investigative personnel who focus their work on gathering evidence to solve open cases. The Detective Bureau subdivides its detectives by units according to the crimes in which they specialize: Homicide, Robbery, Property Crimes (burglaries and auto theft), Narcotics, Special Victims (sexual assaults and related cases), Information Crimes (computer-related incidents) and Vice (non-narcotic controlled substances, gambling and prostitution). In addition, the Intelligence Unit focuses on gathering information on the street and passing it along to all other squads as needed. Detectives are assigned to both a unit and a specific precinct, and the resulting small group of detectives is called a squad (e.g., "9th Precinct Narcotics squad"). Each squad takes charge of all crimes within its provenance that occur within that precinct, even though the resulting investigation may take the detectives anywhere in the city. A closer look at detective assignments begins on p. 46.

Traffic Bureau

The Traffic Bureau has primary responsibility for traffic law enforcement, accident reporting and investigation and traffic routing during signal outages or major events. Most officers regard Traffic as the low point of a uniformed cop's career, as contacts with the public are invariably negative and the work isn't as varied or as interesting as patrol or detective duty. (Patrol officers can and do make traffic stops, but one who runs up a record of issuing trivial speeding tickets while missing calls for service may be threatened with a transfer to Traffic.) The Traffic Bureau is the only one of the three bureaus within Operations to employ a large number of civilian field personnel: meter readers, roadside assistance technicians and tow truck operators. All sworn officers in the Traffic Bureau work independently within their precincts, and will often back up nearby patrol officers responding to service calls to break the monotony of their duties.

Other Departments: Division of Assets

The Operations Division structure as described above is rather dated. Most modern departments centralize detective assets, assigning detectives to cases across the city as required rather than pinning them down to individual precincts. Traffic assets tend to work highways and major surface streets that may cross three or four precinct lines. We've deliberately structured the MPD in this manner to facilitate stories focusing on the 13th Precinct that involve officers from

multiple bureaus, but Storytellers who want a different feel should feel free to reorganize the MPD along more contemporary lines.

In Play: Crossing Bureau Lines

The fact that all three bureaus within Operations Division use the precinct system makes it easy for a Storyteller to throw a disparate group of uniformed officers and detectives together: they're all assigned to the 13th Precinct. Several plot hooks can allow cops from different bureaus to work together officially without straining plausibility for players who know something about police work — or allow characters to coordinate efforts against the paranormal without arousing too much suspicion from their superiors.

Same Watch: One easy way to introduce characters to one another and give them reason to work together is to assign all of them to the same watch (preferably the third watch, which tends to be the most sought-after in veteran officers' eyes), then give them a series of service calls that require all of them to respond together. A Storyteller who's good at juggling multiple plot threads may choose to have two or three calls running simultaneously, requiring some characters to investigate an apparent ritual killing while others deal with an armed and barricaded suspect. This plot hook also allows the inclusion of characters who aren't MPD personnel but enjoy friendly regular cooperation with them, such as paramedics or crime reporters.

Task Force: Task forces are both investigative and political tools for the MPD. They bring together officers and civilian personnel from different specialties to work on specific high-profile crimes. Task force assignments usually are temporary, but some task forces run for years, switching out personnel as veterans retire and new officers receive promotions. Detective lieutenants are most likely to be in charge of task forces, recruiting a couple of subordinate detectives to assist with investigations and pulling in patrol and traffic cops for extra muscle, fresh undercover faces or neighborhood familiarity.

Tacit Approval: A slightly more contrived option is to give all of the characters the same commander (such as a precinct captain) who knows just enough about the things in the shadows that he's willing to obfuscate the activities of officers who bend procedure to investigate strange occurrences. Storytellers should be careful that players don't take this as license for their cops to wantonly violate civil rights and engage in shootouts in crowded shopping malls. A little bit of looking the other way is likely for a veteran officer who wants to see justice done, but going over the top and into blatant cover-ups would make LAPD's Rampart corruption scandal look like a playground scuffle.

Support Division

The Support Division collects all of the MPD's assets who work in the field to assist Operations Division officers. Support breaks down into several bureaus and independent units as follows.

Analysis Bureau

This bureau has seen a sudden surge in funding over the past few years as television shows have brought forensic science into public (and thus city council) awareness. The Analysis Bureau handles evidence collection and analysis for MPD detectives and traffic accident investigators as well as Midway Fire Marshal arson investigators. The Analysis Bureau also works closely with the Washington County Coroner's Office, sharing both data and office space. The $15 million Midway Forensic Science Center, completed in late 2004, is a state-of-the-art facility whose only limitation is staffing. The average backlog for time-intensive procedures such as DNA analysis or ballistic profiling is currently seven months.

The Analysis Bureau includes the Evidence and Property Unit (EPU). This group maintains the department's impound yard for confiscated vehicles, as well as an adjacent secure warehouse for low-value seized property. High-value seizures, including all drugs and weapons, go into the evidence rooms of individual precinct headquarters, which the EPU periodically and randomly audits. Particularly large seizures go to the EPU's main evidence lockup in the basement of the city jail's adjacent parking garage.

Most Analysis Bureau personnel are civilian employees of the department, with only a few sworn officers who liaise with the Detective Bureau and ride herd on the staff. Cowboy attitudes are a sure ticket out of the Analysis Bureau — crime scene technicians (CST) are strictly barred from unsupervised investigative work in the field. This is a constant source of low-level friction between the technical personnel and the detectives whose cases the technical personnel support. Some senior Analysis Bureau staff have recently begun lobbying the department to hire anthropologists and sociologists and allow those personnel to actively investigate cases in which their professional knowledge can be considered expert testimony. However, the MPD's leadership is fiercely resistant to the idea of allowing civilians to take point on department investigations.

"Well, It's Another Vampire Murder . . . ."

Savvy supernatural characters who commit crimes may realize that the Analysis Bureau and its counterparts in the Coroner's Office are the mortals in the city most likely to stumble upon the characters' true nature. Any attempts to engage in cover-ups within the Analysis Bureau will reveal a startling truth: any Bureau personnel who are aware of the paranormal are already doing their best to suppress knowledge of it. Medical examiners and crime lab technicians must maintain impeccable credibility if their evidence is to stand up in court. Even hinting in a report that a victim's head might have exploded from a magical blast of energy instead of a .308 caliber hollowpoint would undermine public confidence in the entire justice system. No district attorney ever wins a capital murder case by claiming werewolf involvement. When processing evidence of such weirdness, the lab declares the evidence impossible to analyze or just misfiles it and hopes no one remembers it. Any attempt to reveal The Truth would, at best, earn the reporting officer or technician a psychiatric evaluation.

Law enforcement characters who turn to the Analysis Bureau for assistance in supernatural cases will run afoul of the same recalcitrance. Most Bureau personnel don't want to get involved in actively investigating the paranormal for fear that it'll come back and investigate them. They're smart enough to be afraid of what might have left that blood sample or broken through that fire door.

Surveillance Bureau

With the advent of the War on Drugs and its influx of federal funding, the MPD established the Surveillance Bureau in 1986. The unofficial motto of Surveillance is, Hurry up and wait for the warrant, reflecting the fact that most of Surveillance's mission is illegal without a judge's approval. Surveillance handles all approved electronic information-gathering efforts, including wiretaps, audio and video bugs and computer intrusion. In addition, Surveillance has several unmarked vehicles for use in stakeouts or in monitoring large crowds at public events.

Unlike the Analysis Bureau, the Surveillance Bureau is composed mainly of sworn officers due to its heavy reliance on proper and legal procedure. However, Surveillance does employ a fair number of civilian technicians specializing in audio and video analysis and electronic hardware, as well as at least one interpreter for every major language spoken by ethnic groups within Midway. Also, unlike Analysis personnel, Surveillance personnel enjoy comfortable relations with both their uniformed officers and the detectives whose investigations the personnel support.

Aviation Squadron

The Aviation Squadron is considered a bureau-equivalent unit within the MPD for purposes of funding, despite having fewer personnel than any precinct house. Aviation flies and maintains the MPD's fleet of seven Bell 206 observation choppers and two Cessna Skyhawk light airplanes. All of these aircraft are based out of the MPD compound in the general aviation section of Midway International Airport. The regular operational schedule, subject to maintenance and crew rest requirements, keeps one helicopter in the air at all times and another on five-minute standby to assist ground units in pursuits or searches as needed. The Cessnas see irregular use for surveillance and wide-area searches, most commonly in support of anti-drug task forces. One of the helicopters is equipped for aeromedical evacuation of a single patient and an attending paramedic in the event that no air ambulances are available from area hospitals. The other helicopters can carry up to three passengers in addition to a regular two-officer crew. Every few months, the Emergency Response Unit (ERU) renews its request for a larger helicopter that can carry a full assault team, but money in the budget hasn't turned up yet.

At present, the limiting factor in Aviation operations is crew availability. Few existing patrol officers have the aptitude and desire to become pilots, even though flight school falls under the department's education reimbursement program, and even fewer civilian aviators want to take a pay cut to city rates and endure the MPD Academy. The military has traditionally been Aviation's largest source of recruits, but current U.S. commitments have reduced the number of pilots exiting service.

Character Options: Air Cops

While "police pilot" is an interesting character concept, the nature of aviation duty will keep such an officer separated from the rest of the characters in a police story. Doing nothing but flying around and observing from a safe height can quickly grow stale, and the value (both financial and tactical) of a police helicopter prohibit its crew from landing and participating in ground operations. For this reason, it's best if Storytellers keep the Aviation Squadron out of the hands of players, using it as real cops do: an extra set of "eyes in the sky" that provides observational assistance but doesn't directly do the jobs of the officers on the ground.

K-9 Unit

MPD's canine assets and their human handlers and trainers fall into their own independent unit, housed at the MPD kennel in the 8th Precinct. Few senior officers in the department are sure how to manage non-human assets, so the lieutenant commanding the department's K-9 officers finds herself operating without much attention or oversight from her nominal chain of command. To speed response time when a patrol officer calls for a K-9 unit, the dogs and their handlers are parceled out to individual precincts rather than staging from the kennel. This allows handlers to regularly work with the same patrol officers, building mutual respect and confidence — but it also makes patrol commanders possessive of "their" dogs, which creates occasional conflicts when a K-9 officer responds to a call in a neighboring precinct.

K-9 duty is regarded as one of the more enjoyable field assignments within the MPD because of the relaxed uniform standards and the relatively low number of service calls in which an officer has to be the first responder. Typically, a handler and his dog receive the call after other officers realize they need to search for evidence or suspects. The unit has a long waiting list of applicants, allowing the unit to pick and choose from the best available potential handlers.

It's a Dog Cop's Life

Police dogs are not pets, and misconceptions to this effect occasionally prove painful. Police K-9 training promotes a certain degree of aggression, which is necessary for a dog that is going to be sent after armed suspects. Dogs are trained to defend their handlers and aren't always selective about what constitutes a threat. When a dog comes off the leash during a violent incident, the dog goes after moving targets — which may include other officers who don't heed the handler's warning to let the dog do its job.

Although handlers refer to their dogs as "partners," unit policy advises a certain emotional distance. The dogs are tools for their handler to wield and are less valuable assets than human officers. Handlers are allowed to take their dogs home with them when off duty if they live in Washington County, but dogs that don't live with their handlers stay in large cages inside the MPD kennel. At least one handler is always on duty at the kennel to attend to their needs or handle emergencies. Dogs don't go home with their handlers at the end of the shift, though officers may apply to adopt them when the dogs retire (usually around eight years old).

In the World of Darkness, K-9 officers face unique challenges. Animals are sensitive to many aspects of the paranormal, from the presence of ghosts to the scent trail of the walking dead. Police dogs are trained to defend their handlers from threats, and this training can combine with a dog's natural fear reaction to the paranormal to produce unexpectedly aggressive behavior. On the plus side, due to the extreme loyalty trained into a police dog, any attempts to directly influence or dictate its behavior with supernatural powers suffer a penalty equal to the dog handler's Charisma (unless, of course, the handler is the one using those powers). A police dog's game traits are identical to those of a typical dog (see the **World of Darkness Rulebook**, p. 203), with the addition of a Grapple Specialty for Brawl.

Emergency Response Unit

ERU is the MPD's tactical response team (popularly known by the more common acronym SWAT). The ERU is an independent command within the Support Division. For detailed information on the ERU, see p. 58.

Administration Division

The Administration Division is the smallest division in the MPD and contains the majority of the department's civilian employees. "Admin" handles the bureaucratic workload necessary to keep an 8,300-person government organization functioning smoothly.

Community Relations Bureau

The primary function of the Community Relations Bureau (CRB) is to maintain the department's public image with Midway' citizens. This includes advertising and marketing work, organizing press conferences, conducting community studies, holding citizen forums, and providing much-dreaded sensitivity and multicultural awareness training for officers. The CRB trains all new police lieutenants on public speaking and press management, and the best find themselves rotated into the CRB for several months of duty as public affairs officers. The CRB also runs high-visibility outreach programs such as DARE (Drug Abuse Resistance Education), the department's Police Explorer post and scholarships and grants.

Training Bureau

The Training Bureau's primary focus is the MPD Academy, which manages the conversion of new civilian recruits to sworn uniformed officers. Most of the academy's instructors are SPOs and sergeants transferred from Operations Division for six months to a year, but some higher-ranking officers and civilian specialists do lecture on their fields of expertise. The Training Bureau has the final say as to whether any cadet is hired and sworn as an officer, which occasionally entangles Training in department politics.

Training also handles the continuing education of experienced officers. The academy holds regular in-service training days on subjects ranging from the latest in street-level concealed and improvised weapons to pidgin Vietnamese. Training keeps promising a tuition reimbursement program for officers who want to continue their college educations, but has never been able to secure the budget for such an expensive proposition.

Internal Affairs Bureau

Charged with institutional accountability, the Internal Affairs Bureau (IAB) is the bureau that polices other cops. All citizen complaints against MPD officers come through IAB for review, regardless of the complaints' apparent validity. In addition, IAB also handles the routine procedural investigations that department policy requires of certain incidents involving officers, such as traffic accidents, weapon discharges and injuries or deaths of suspects in custody. IAB's most significant task, however, is watching the watchmen — managing disciplinary and criminal cases against other MPD officers who violate laws or the MPD's ethics guidelines (see p. 75).

All sworn officers assigned to IAB are detectives, mostly drawn from the Property Crimes, Vice and Intelligence Units. Such an assignment is a black hole for most careers. Once in IAB, it's hard to ever completely regain the trust of other officers, regardless of how much of a reputation an IAB detective tries to cultivate for just and fair behavior. IAB also employs the MPD's four department psychologists who perform evaluations on applicants to the MPD Academy, officers under investigation and personnel who've been involved in a "critical incident" (such as a shooting).

As might be expected, many other MPD officers view IAB as a collection of Judases. Common wisdom among street officers holds that Internal Affairs is the refuge of the cowardly, corrupt and petty members of the department's ranks. With that being said, part of the selection process for IAB is a rigid fair-mindedness, and IAB investigators can determine when a citizen complaint is so much *pro forma* bullshit. Rampant charges of vampire patrol officers on the night shift or seizure-inducing mind-control lamps

mounted in cruisers' light bars will not have any effect on a cop's career. More subtle accusations, however, such as an officer being hooked on heroin or taking a few more kicks than necessary to break up a fight, can result in an investigation if sufficient suspicion exists.

Most formal IAB investigations into misconduct become public knowledge as soon as they begin (though standard legal protocol prevents IAB from releasing any information on an ongoing investigation). The modern news media's love-hate relationship with police departments demands nothing less. Savvy lawyers representing alleged victims of the MPD release press statements simultaneously with filing suit against the department in order to keep influential officers from sweeping anything under the rug. Depending on the nature of the case and the immediately available proof, the targeted officers will be suspended either with or without pay for the duration of the investigation. (Midway's civil service regulations require proof of misconduct for unpaid suspension.) If the case, which proceeds little differently from any other detective work, uncovers sufficient evidence for criminal charges, IAB detectives have the unpleasant duty of arresting their fellow officer.

Covert IAB investigations occur only in cases in which officers are suspected of criminal conspiracy or widespread crimes that haven't become public. IAB's first task in such cases is to gather enough evidence to convince a judge to issue warrants for wiretaps and covert searches. Investigations then proceed into several weeks of surveillance of the target's personal and professional activities. If IAB accumulates sufficient evidence, officers then make the arrest, preferably while catching the subject red-handed at whatever he was involved in. If the case doesn't pan out, however, IAB shuts down its investigation. The case never touches the officer's personnel file, though IAB maintains its records in case allegations arise again later. A cop who's been the subject of such intense scrutiny may never know he was under investigation unless he's an expert at counter-surveillance.

In Play: Internal Affairs

For a Storyteller running a chronicle featuring one or more MPD characters in the hands of players, IAB is the ultimate control rod in the reactor of player irresponsibility. A dedicated group of cops may be able to cover up subtle extracurricular activities, but it's hard to keep anyone from noticing rampant vigilantism or wanton abuse of authority. No matter how careful characters are about leaving no witnesses or evidence, a single slip-up is all a Storyteller needs for IAB to uncover forensic evidence or receive an anonymous report

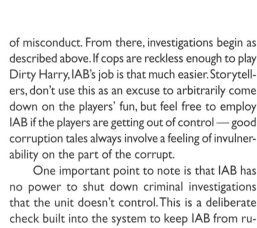

of misconduct. From there, investigations begin as described above. If cops are reckless enough to play Dirty Harry, IAB's job is that much easier. Storytellers, don't use this as an excuse to arbitrarily come down on the players' fun, but feel free to employ IAB if the players are getting out of control — good corruption tales always involve a feeling of invulnerability on the part of the corrupt.

One important point to note is that IAB has no power to shut down criminal investigations that the unit doesn't control. This is a deliberate check built into the system to keep IAB from ruining valid criminal cases due to the involvement of a crooked cop. If an IAB investigation reveals that a few officers or a detective squad are all in violation of the law, their superiors will reassign their cases to other personnel.

World of Darkness: Infernal Affairs

Supernatural power players who wish to cultivate influence in a city's police department often turn toward that department's Internal Affairs Bureau for leverage over troublesome officers. This can be effective for isolated individuals whose conduct actually does violate laws or department ethics (or can be made to appear thus via falsified evidence).

Subtlety is the key, however. Too much use of IAB resources to pressure troublesome officers can generate patterns that savvy observers will notice. IAB recruits superior detectives and trains them to investigate cops who already know all the weak points of police procedure themselves. If IAB officers realize they are being manipulated to harm the department — particularly if someone points them at too many honest cops who haven't done anything wrong — IAB can easily shift its focus to a sting investigation designed to catch the manipulators in the act. For that matter, if outside officers discern a pattern of questionable actions on IAB's part, they may go straight to union representatives or the Office of the Commissioner, bringing heat back on possible corruption within IAB itself.

Facilities and Property Bureau

Any tendency to label the Facilities and Property Bureau (FP) "janitorial staff" would be misleading at best. FP does have responsibility for custodial work on the MPD's buildings and grounds, but FP also manages and maintains all of the department's other hardware, from traffic barricades to the motor pool. The MPD's armory and its full-time gunsmith also fall under FP's chain of command.

Communications and Records Bureau

"Comm" runs the department's information technology assets, 911 call center ("Dispatch") and radio networks. This bureau maintains not only the databases of all MPD cases and calls within living memory but also the physical archives and logbooks stretching back to the department's inception in the 19th century. Computer crimes are technically the responsibility of the Detective Bureau's Information Crimes Unit, but the civilian information technology experts in Comm spend up to half their time assisting these detectives.

Central Dispatch

Midway's 911 call center ("Central Dispatch") is also Comm's responsibility. Central is a 28-desk facility in the subbasement of the city government's annex building. Designed to function even through large-scale natural disasters (or a nuclear attack, having been built at the end of the Cold War), the building has independent diesel generators and air filtration systems sufficient for 72 hours of continuous operation at full capacity. All 911 calls made in Washington County come here, where operators ascertain the nature of the emergency. If a police response to a call is required, the operator keeps the caller on the line while using the department's computer network to route the report of the call to the appropriate precinct's dispatcher. Fire and medical emergencies are handled similarly, using the MFD's own separate computer network. This system is cumbersome and occasionally causes breakdowns in communication, and the city government is putting mounting pressure on the emergency services to phase out precinct dispatchers. The MPD and MFD both prefer the current system, however, as it keeps personnel at the precinct houses and fire stations in the loop on all calls. The current system also provides a convenient place to stash older or physically disabled officers who can't work the streets any more but deserve jobs until they retire.

Learning the Beat: The MPD Academy

Similar to any other job, law enforcement requires training before a new employee can perform her expected duties. In the case of new Midway Police Department recruits, this training occurs at the MPD Academy. Before training starts, though, a prospective officer has to prove that she can make the initial cut.

Getting In

The MPD's minimum qualifications for applicants are fairly typical for academies. The minimum age is 21 and the maximum is 40. An applicant must have a driver's license and a high school diploma or GED. No felony convictions are allowed, or misdemeanors or illegal drug use within the past 12 months — and, in practice, *any* criminal record more significant than a couple of speeding tickets may disqualify the applicant. Other disqualifying factors include an job firing within the past year (or at any time if the job was a law enforcement position), any legal prohibition on ownership or use of firearms, a questionable driving record, a dishonorable military discharge and any brands, tattoos or body or facial piercings that would be visible in uniform.

Assuming the applicant meets all of these requirements, she must then undergo preliminary testing. This begins with a multiple-choice exam on reading, grammar and math skills. Following this comes a physical fitness exam requiring the applicant to bench press 65% of her body weight, do 18 sit-ups in a minute, run 300 meters in 65 seconds or less and run 1.5 miles in 17 minutes or less.

The next stage in the application process is an oral examination administered by a board of four sworn officers and one community member, all of whom independently score the candidate on her suitability to become an officer. Success in the oral exam leads to a background check, including criminal, financial, employment and education history, followed by a polygraph screening.

The final steps in entering the academy are medical and psychological screenings. If an applicant is still interested in the job after jumping through all these hoops, her performance on all of the tests determines her ranking in the current register of applicants. The top 90 applicants and 10 alternates receive employment offers two months before the next biannual class begins. These offers are conditional. That is, if a candidate washes out of training or her instructors recommend against making her an officer, her MPD employment ends when she exits the academy.

The Curriculum

Upon accepting the MPD's offer of employment, an applicant becomes an officer trainee and begins earning her starting salary. For the next 28 weeks, her full-time job is to attend the MPD Academy. The academy is a comprehensive training program designed to meet state and federal certification requirements for law enforcement officers. The curriculum breaks down into several phases, each of which concludes with written and oral exams on the subject matter. A trainee who fails any phase's exam has two weeks to bring her grades up or wash out of the academy.

Phase One (four weeks): Orientation

Trainees learn the organizational structure, policies and bureaucracy of the MPD and the Midway city government while filling out innumerable forms. This phase also includes instruction on professional ethics, basic computer literacy, public and media relations and local geography.

Phase Two (three weeks): Legal

Officers must know the law before they can enforce it. The majority of this phase focuses on the mechanics of the criminal justice system, the state penal code, city ordinances and the legalities of arrest, search and seizure. Other topics include controlled substances, interrogation, domestic violence, the use of force, the limits of an officer's authority and individual and department liability.

Phase Three (six weeks): Patrol Operations

This phase begins the hands-on instruction in police work. Trainees learn how to handle the common incidents and infractions they will encounter during the course of patrol duty. They receive instruction in dispute mediation, hazardous materials response, missing persons handling, care of EDPs, building searches, radio communication protocol and the use of MDTs and NCIC terminals. This phase also includes cultural diversity lessons, 40 hours of law enforcement-oriented Spanish and the first of several ride-alongs that trainees will conduct with patrol officers during their academy education.

Phase Four (seven weeks): Patrol Skills

Phase Four builds on Phase Three, moving toward less lecture and desk learning and more practical work. Much of Phase Four involves field exercises and hands-on simulations, with instructors, sworn officers and civilian volunteers playing the parts of victims and suspects. Trainees learn tactical driving, traffic and DUI enforcement, traffic stop tactics, manual traffic control, accident investigation, body and vehicle searches, civil disturbance handling and evidence handling.

Phase Five (four weeks): Investigations

Moving the trainees back to the classroom, the academy teaches them the basics of investigating crimes so that they don't necessarily interrupt investigations in progress as part of their patrol work. Phase Five begins with crime scene examination and processing (with a reality-check lecture on how the crime lab's capabilities fall short of what the trainees have seen on television). Following these lessons comes instruction on police report writing, case preparation and court testimony, gang and organized crime activity, controlled substances, auto theft, burglary, robbery, domestic violence, sexual assault — in short, a guided tour of the things the trainees signed on to prevent. They also hone their interpersonal communication, interview and interrogation skills and learn special considerations for communicating with children and the elderly.

Phase Six (three weeks): Certifications

This phase covers state-mandated courses on the proper operation of breathalyzers and radar and laser speed sensors. Phase Six also includes Red Cross first aid and CPR certification and additional instruction on airborne and blood-borne pathogens.

Ongoing Training

Throughout the academy curriculum, trainees undergo continuous physical conditioning, as well as a total of 150 hours of "defensive tactics" training in the use of batons, pepper spray and bare hands. Another 98 total hours of firearms training with handguns and shotguns, including safe weapon handling, marksmanship and shoot/no-shoot simulations, begins during Phase Three and continues throughout the program. Instructors are constantly watching and evaluating the trainees, compiling six-month histories of their performances and characters that will be as important as their final exams in determining whether or not the department hires the trainees as full-time police officers.

Finals Week

The last week of the academy includes a brief lesson on ceremonial drill, which will be important for the trainees who pass their final exams, and dress uniform fitting. The final exams themselves comprise most of the last week. In addition to written and oral exams, trainees must also pass their final physical fitness tests, defensive tactics tests and marksmanship qualifications.

Graduation and Hiring

By the end of finals week, the instructors and their superiors know which trainees passed and which didn't, and which of the passing students the instructors intend to recommend not be hired. The majority of successful trainees, however, have demonstrated what it takes to become sworn MPD officers. At academy graduation, the officers — no longer trainees — receive their badges from the chief, who then administers their oath of office:

I, (officer's name), do solemnly swear that I will support and defend the Constitution of the United States and the Constitution of the State of (the home state) against all enemies, foreign and domestic; that I will bear true faith and allegiance, to the Constitution of the State of (the home state); that I take this obligation freely, without any mental reservations or purpose of evasion; and that I will well and faithfully discharge the duties of the office of Police Officer of the City of Midway, acting to the best of my ability.

The Real Final Exam

The academy teaches a wide array of practical skills, but some lessons come only through experience. When an officer graduates, her first patrol assignment is a probationary one that pairs her with a field training officer (FTO), an SPO or sergeant who's passed the department's qualification course to serve as a field instructor. This assignment lasts a minimum of 90 days, during which the FTO shares his own experience with the probationary officer while evaluating her competence. After three months, the FTO formally reviews the rookie's performance. Performance during this initial period is crucial, as the department considers a rookie who can't meet standards to be a serious liability.

Even if the rookie passes her FTO's evaluation, she most likely won't be assigned to normal duty for another 90 days. Most evaluations include harsh (but hopefully fair) criticism of the rookie's shortcomings, areas in which she must improve in order to survive and succeed as a street cop. Depending on the skill sets and personalities, the FTO may continue to train the rookie himself, or he may request that the department assign her to another FTO who's better suited to instruct her. A rookie remains on probation for one full year after graduating from the academy, and any infraction during this time can lead to dismissal, even after she's out from under FTO supervision.

Character Options: Earning the Badge

In game terms, a character who wants to enter the MPD Academy must have no Attribute lower than 2 except Manipulation, which may be 1. Furthermore, she must have a minimum Morality of 6, a minimum Willpower of 5 and no derangements. All of the other requirements described above fall under character history and Flaws.

The MPD Academy's training and final exams guarantee that any graduate has at least the following *minimum* traits (thus, any MPD character must meet these criteria) in addition to the minimum scores required to enter the academy in the first place.

• Mental Skills: Investigation 1, Medicine 1 and either Academics 1 or Politics 1.

• Physical Skills: Drive 1, Weaponry 1 and a total of five points between Athletics, Brawl and Firearms with at least one point in each.

• Social Skills: Intimidation 1, Persuasion 1 and either Empathy 1 or Subterfuge 1.

These aren't "free dots." They reflect the training period and, thus, the experience gained during that training period. Be sure to keep a running tally of how many experience points worth of new dots the character acquires, as you would with any other experience point expenditures.

An officer with prior experience and training from another department who wants to transfer into the MPD must also meet these requirements.

Other Departments: Employment and Training

Entrance requirements vary among departments, but those described on p. 34 are typical for law enforcement agencies throughout the United States. The most variable requirements are the academic ones, as some departments mandate that candidates must have completed an associate's degree or 60 hours of college coursework, or, alternately, have two years of active-duty military or other law enforcement experience.

The MPD training described above is likewise fairly typical for large city and state police departments that run their own academies, though precise training times vary. Smaller departments lack the size and funding necessary for such operations, and, instead, send their recruits to academies run by their state police.

Hitting the Streets: Patrol Work

Every new officer begins his career in Operations Division, the backbone of the MPD, and spends at least two years on patrol duty before being eligible to apply for other positions within the department. Patrol and traffic work are the most visible jobs in the MPD, and the Division's uniformed officers feature prominently in the average citizen's mental image of "cop." These cops are the first responders to the majority of 911 calls, giving them a clear, if grim, picture of daily events on the city's streets.

The Basics

MPD patrol officers work five days a week. First Shift reports for duty at 6 A.M. and works through 2 P.M. Second Shift works from 2 P.M. to 10 P.M., and is the busiest and heaviest-staffed shift. Third Shift ("midwatch" or "mids") comes on duty at 10 P.M. and goes home at 6 A.M. Shift assignments change every three months, with selection order determined by seniority. Many married officers prefer First Shift so they can maintain some semblance of a normal family life, while the adrenaline junkies like Second Shift. Third Shift is the refuge of the tenured, wise and independent cops because the brass never works Third and the end of the shift is usually slow enough for an officer to get caught up on paperwork. Conversely, on First and Second Shifts, activity increases as the shift draws to an end, leaving officers less likely to be able to finish their paperwork and go home on time.

Each precinct's patrol officers fall under the command of a captain, who typically spends First Shift in his office at the precinct house, handling the administrative side of the precinct. If the captain shows up during another shift, there's trouble on the wind. Rank-and-file officers can go a year without exchanging words with him if they avoid extremes of performance.

Within each precinct, patrol responsibilities are subdivided among squads. Each squad consists of eight to 20 officers, one or two sergeants as field supervisors and a lieutenant. Most squads are assigned geographically by parts of the precinct ("2nd Precinct North squad" or "8th Precinct Docks squad"), but some receive assignments based on specific areas of their precincts that need special attention, such as housing projects. Precincts form other squads either temporarily or permanently for special duty — a good example of the latter is the mountain-bike squads that the downtown precincts deploy for additional mobility in pedestrian-heavy areas. Each squad further breaks down its area into individual beats, which are the default patrol areas of individual officers when they aren't responding to a call for service.

Partnerships

Street cops' partner system is more than a convenient mechanism for Hollywood to produce buddy movies. As illustrated throughout this chapter, the partner system has immense practical and safety value. Statistically, lone officers run a much higher risk of being attacked by single aggressors or small groups — the mere presence of a second cop stops many confrontations before they begin. During patrol work, having an extra pair of eyes to scan sidewalks and alleys is invaluable. When the team is in their car, one officer drives while the other handles paperwork and radio

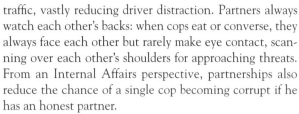

traffic, vastly reducing driver distraction. Partners always watch each other's backs: when cops eat or converse, they always face each other but rarely make eye contact, scanning over each other's shoulders for approaching threats. From an Internal Affairs perspective, partnerships also reduce the chance of a single cop becoming corrupt if he has an honest partner.

Patrol sergeants and some SPOs — usually those also certified as FTOs — have no assigned partners. If an FTO with a partner receives a probationary officer to polish (see p. 36), his partner works alone or with the solo senior cops, depending on whether the squad has a spare car available for him.

Partner assignment in the MPD is the responsibility of each squad's lieutenant. Typically, leaders try to create teams with complementary skill sets or put younger officers in need of guidance and experience with veterans who can offer those resources. Partnerships have to function well for eight hours a night, with both officers occupying the same car and struggling with the same suspects. Consequently, many cops compare partnership to marriage, and may be more willing to confide in their partners than in their spouses. A good partnership can last for a decade or more, so long as both cops stay in the same assignment or apply for all transfers together.

Unwritten rules of cop etiquette say that what happens in the car stays in the car. Conversations take on the sanctity of the confessional, never to be spread around the locker room or the local cop bar. Officers expect their colleagues to work interpersonal problems out on their own without bringing the rest of the squad into it.

When a partnership isn't working out, the first stage of correction comes from the squad's sergeant, who applies an impartial ass-chewing to both parties. If this doesn't have the desired effect, the lieutenant steps in and reassigns the officers to other partners within the squad. In extreme cases, one partner may be transferred out of the unit, usually as part of disciplinary action.

Ride-Alongs

The MPD's ride-along program allows private citizens to spend a shift with patrol officers to see what the job is really like. To apply for a ride-along, a prospective observer submits a written application through the Community Relations Bureau, indicating the reason for her request and any preferred shift, precinct or officer. The department runs a background check to ensure that the observer has no felony record and no misdemeanors more recent than three years. If the department approves the application, the CRB contacts the

appropriate shift commander and schedules the ride-along with him. FTOs without partners or probationary officers are the most likely officers to take an observer, as they're the most able to explain the job while doing it (and the open seats in their cruisers allow observers to sit up front and not take up prisoner transport space). The most common observers are relatives of cops who want to see "a day at the office," prospective recruits who want to know more about the job and reporters.

Observers must sign waivers absolving the department of any liability for anything bad that happens to them during their ride-alongs. They are under "their" officers' orders at all times; failure to obey can result in the observers being sent home or, in extreme cases, charged with interference with an officer. Officially, they cannot carry weapons or engage in violence for reasons of department liability, though officers who personally know their observers' weapon skills and judgment do sometimes overlook violations if it means they'll be a little safer that night.

Other Departments: Rolling Solo

Again, we've deviated from modern police practice for the sake of game play — in this case, not splitting characters up any more than necessary. Almost all contemporary departments assign officers to solo patrol work (with the exception of FTO/rookie pairs). In such cases, two to four cops are designated as beat partners and independently work the same beat or set of overlapping beats. When one officer is on a call, the others usually gravitate toward that area if they aren't handling anything at the moment, just in case their beat partner needs help. This occasionally results in three more bored cops showing up for a single, low-threat traffic stop, but it's better to have the help and not need it than to need it and not have it.

Checking In

A patrol officer's duty shift begins when he reports to the precinct house for roll call. The daily roll call briefing starts at the official beginning of each shift and lasts 10 to 15 minutes. On a quiet shift, this is the only time at which officers will interact with their commanding lieutenant. The lieutenant (or the sergeant, if the lieutenant is unavailable, aloof or lazy) starts the briefing by taking roll, ensuring that each officer under her command is present and ready for duty. She presents any special precinct information for the squad, then switches to a computer for a citywide shift briefing prepared at MPD Headquarters during the previous shift and distributed over the department's data network in streaming video format. Most briefings include lists of upcoming special events, construction that may disrupt traffic, descriptions of recently stolen vehicles and suspects in recent crimes and precinct- or department-wide advisories.

The MPD no longer holds regular formal inspections of officers' uniforms and equipment during roll call. The assumption is that officers are responsible enough to keep their gear and themselves in proper order. Sharp-eyed sergeants, though, do take note of the condition and appearance of each subordinate as he leaves the briefing room, and a threadbare uniform or five o'clock shadow will earn discipline for the unfortunate officer. Occasionally, a particularly motivated or bored lieutenant also will hold a surprise inspection to keep the troops on their toes.

Once roll call is over, officers head out to their vehicles, which they inspect to ensure that all equipment is available and in working order. They then sign in for duty on their MDTs, notifying Dispatch that they're ready to take calls for service. (Officers not assigned to vehicles sign in by radio instead.) This officially begins the shift.

On the Job

Some prospective officers enter MPD Academy expecting wild nights of car chases, shoot-outs and heroic derring-do. By the time they receive their badges, their instructors have subdued these expectations (or washed out those students who couldn't settle down), but many newly hired officers still secretly harbor such visions. The actual nature of patrol work, as they soon learn, is far from cinematic. Two mundane elements dominate their daily routines: paperwork and simply talking to people.

The common police motto, To Protect and Serve, means *public* service, and this, in turn, requires a large amount

of contact with individual members of that public. Many calls simply involve an irate citizen wanting someone to whom he can vent or two disputants who need an impartial third party to decisively settle a minor issue. From a disagreement over payment for lawnmower repair to a teenager whose parents don't approve of the gang members with whom he's starting to associate, people want police attention to forestall a possible crime or just to make themselves feel better. In such instances, the officer's primary job is to make the citizens feel that someone in authority is listening to them — not necessarily agreeing, just listening — and then issue a statement or decision backed by the weight of that authority. Verbal warnings, stern talkings-to and dry humor are all tools a cop can use to resolve such situations without resorting to citations or arrests.

This isn't to say that such service calls are always without incident or danger. Seemingly trivial incidents can open up larger cases. That lawnmower repairman might have an outstanding warrant for methamphetamine possession three states away, or the budding gang member might have been intimidated into silence regarding something he saw. Cops learn to treat every call, no matter how minor it appears, as a potential source of intelligence.

Burglar Alarms

Alarms in Midway don't report directly to the police. Instead, the alarm company maintains a central monitoring center for all of its alarms in the city, and notifies the MPD only of alarms whose owners have paid an annual license fee to the city. When an alarm goes off (an "alarm drop"), the minimum-wage monitor on duty decides whether or not to request a police response to the alarm, based on the information he has available to him. For residential and business alarms, standard procedure requires a telephone call first. If no one answers, or if someone answers who doesn't give the correct "all clear" pass phrase that the alarm company has on file for that location, the alarm company requests a police visit to the scene. If an alarm's "panic button" feature is activated, the alarm company calls the police first and asks questions later, assuming that some rich client is undergoing a home invasion or medical emergency. Likewise, if a video surveillance system shows that a business is being broken into, the police get a call, even if someone with the correct pass phrase answers the phone. If the person answering the phone gives an incorrect pass phrase, the monitor acts as if it were correct, then calls police — the assumption being that either a burglar answered the phone, or the homeowner has a gun to his head and needs help without alerting the criminal.

Alarms without an indicator of a threat to a citizen are low-priority tasks, more so if the location has a history of false alarms (which more than 99% of alarm drops are). More than one false alarm in a one-year period results in a citation and fine for the property owner (not the alarm company). In circumstances that are more likely than normal to trigger false alarms, such as thunderstorms or nearby construction, alarm calls may go unanswered for hours — if the monitoring center passes the calls on to the MPD at all. Even in a home invasion or other urgent threat situation, the call filters through the monitoring center before police become involved, adding several minutes to response time.

Building Clearance

Officers answering an alarm drop or burglary report, or chasing a suspect fleeing on foot, frequently must explore the unknown contents of a darkened building. In this, the first rule of horror movie survival — never go in alone — is an excellent guideline. Procedure calls for summoning enough backup to cover every exit in case a suspect attempts to flee, as well as contacting the building's owner to acquire a description of the building's interior and permission to enter it (though the latter isn't legally required if the officers are in pursuit of a violent felon).

Once the perimeter is secured, a search team of two to four officers enters the building. Multiple teams only go in for very large structures, as the potential for blue-on-blue encounters is high when clearing a building. The team spreads out to reduce the chances of a stray shot penetrating one officer to strike another, and to allow more than one officer to scan ahead. Noise discipline is also vital, and all team members should turn off their radios and cell phones before going in. In a building entry or search, doorways are referred to as "vertical coffins" because they restrict movement and make excellent chokepoints for criminals to ambush officers. To minimize this risk, an officer moves through a door while keeping low, rotating around the edge of the door in a "slicing the pie" motion that allows her to scan one narrow section of the room at a time.

Anyone the team finds while clearing a building is considered a suspect until the officers have time to establish his identity — outside, with him in handcuffs for safety. While the laws of evidence and privacy restrict officers to searching places that a suspect could reasonably hide, any evidence they uncover during such a search is still admissible in court, so long as they conducted the initial search legally.

Domestic Disturbances

Police officers claim to hate domestic disturbance calls ("domestics" for short) because of the unpredictable and violent emotions of those involved in the situation. Family members may suddenly take or switch sides, escalating an almost-controlled situation into a chaotic melee. Sudden reversals of perspective are common as a battered spouse suddenly realizes that this isn't just a minor event any more and a partner is about to go to jail: the victim can turn on the arresting officers in such an event. For these reasons, such calls are among the most dangerous of the incidents to which officers respond on a regular basis. Domestics also frequently involve the same people — it's not uncommon for cops to know exactly whom they're going to have to deal with as soon as they hear the dispatcher announce the address.

With all this being said, many officers secretly don't mind domestics as much as they claim to. These calls are both interesting (especially in terms of the personalities encountered) and challenging, and involve less paperwork than alarm drops. In a domestic, multiple officers always respond in order to get the situation under control as quickly as possible. The first priority is to separate the disputants and get statements from each of them out of earshot of the others. After that, though, officers often have limited options. Unlike some jurisdictions, Midway lacks a law that requires officers to make an arrest if any disputant levies an accusation of domestic violence. If there's no evidence of an actual assault, all they can do is try to calm down the children and offer the apparent victim transportation to a women's shelter. Experienced officers develop a frustrating gut feeling for when a given household is about to experience a murder.

Family Services

After domestic disturbances, police often work with social workers from Midway's Department of Family Services

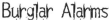

(DFS). DFS personnel's primary responsibility that brings the department in contact with the MPD is child protection. If DFS receives a report that indicates possible child neglect or abuse, the department initiates an investigation within 24 hours. If an initial contact with the family doesn't conclusively indicate that the report was unfounded, the investigation continues. State law requires DFS to make a final recommendation within 30 days. If clear evidence exists that a child is at immediate risk, DFS doesn't have to wait for a formal investigative process — the department has the authority to intervene immediately.

If DFS finds that a case of neglect or abuse does exist, the department has the legal right to move an endangered child into foster care immediately. This usually occurs concurrently with MPD officers arresting one or both parents. DFS maintains a list of households that have volunteered to serve as emergency foster homes and have undergone MPD background checks to ensure their suitability.

Paperwork

Cops have to do a *lot* of writing. Every incident, no matter how minor, must be documented in detail in case the incident becomes relevant in a future case. With the advent of MDTs, the department has eliminated much of the actual paper in "paperwork" in favor of electronic forms, but veterans complain that the ready availability of such options has actually increased the total amount of writing they have to do. The average police report for a minor service call or traffic incident or a misdemeanor takes about 20 minutes to complete. It's the rare officer with a gift for detailed writing who can get an arrest report written in under 45 minutes. The ability to write clearly and concisely is one factor that detective squads use when trolling for new recruits from patrol units.

Welfare Check-Ups

One type of low-threat service call that still can end poorly is a "check welfare" call. These typically start when a citizen's family member, friend or neighbor hasn't had contact with her for a lengthy period of time and calls the police to check up on her. Check welfare calls are low priority for MPD patrol officers because of the low likelihood of any actual crime being involved, but high priority for administrators because they're high-visibility, non-confrontational public service.

When an officer takes a check welfare call, the first course of action after getting all of the subject's information (name, age, medical conditions) from the complainant is to run a check on the address, just in case. A history of domestic violence calls or ambulance runs at the same address may indicate that something more than a simple missed phone call is at stake.

As a welfare check-up doesn't involve a violent felony in progress, the responding officer isn't entitled to kick in the door if no one responds to his knock. If the residence is a rental property, he can contact the landlord for a spare key and legally gain entry in that manner if the landlord feels cooperative. Otherwise, the officer's only recourse is to file a report indicating the lack of answer — unless his check of the residence's exterior gives him a view (or a smell) of a cadaver inside. Tragically, a significant number of check welfare calls do end in such fashion, as most subjects of such calls are elderly citizens living alone.

Emotionally Disturbed Persons

Using terms such as "nut job" or "fucking loon" in official reports is impolitic, so the bureaucratically correct term for a mentally ill individual is "Emotionally Disturbed Person," or EDP. EDP calls are a unique variety of frustration for cops. In most cases, an EDP isn't an active threat to the public, but he is a nuisance, especially if he's one of the large number of homeless individuals suffering from mental illness. The guy knife-fighting with an imaginary god on the sidewalk outside the restaurant is bad for business.

An EDP often isn't doing anything illegal when the cops arrive. There's no law against not bathing for months on end or whispering broken Latin verses into a statue's ear. If an EDP isn't committing an arrest-worthy offense, a responding officer's first task is to evaluate the EDP's mental condition. Statutes providing for the involuntary commitment of the mentally ill require that the individual be a danger to others, a danger to himself or incapable of providing for his basic human needs. If the subject fits one of these criteria, then it's the officer's responsibility to take him into custody and transfer him to a local hospital for evaluation by medical professionals. Otherwise, the officer's only recourse is sweet reason, knowing that even if he resolves the immediate situation, a colleague will get another call about the same EDP the next night.

EDP calls involve drugs on a regular basis. Some EDPs acquired their unfortunate conditions through drug abuse, while others have gone off their prescriptions or added street drugs to their normal treatment regimens. Being an EDP does not absolve a suspect of criminal charges for possession.

If an EDP is committing a crime, the arrest should proceed like any other. However, the subject's irrationality often complicates this matter, as he may not understand who the officer is or that an arrest is even taking place. Officers treat such arrests as potentially dangerous for these reasons and often approach in overwhelming numbers in case the EDP suddenly turns violent. Once the cuffs go on, the arresting officers are thankful to turn him over to the custody of the jail, which is only marginally better equipped to deal with him than they are.

In Play: Exceptionally Deranged Persons

The concise list of derangements on pp. 96–100 of the **World of Darkness Rulebook** should never allow players to diagnose the mental health problems of EDPs whom their characters encounter. Irrational behavior can have many sources, ranging from psychological problems to drug abuse to, in the World of Darkness, super-natural influence. Storytellers should ensure that EDP calls to which characters respond are as unpredictable and unnerving as the horror genre warrants.

Vehicle Stops

Traffic stops almost always occur when an officer notices something about a vehicle or its occupants that calls for further action. Traffic stops are a common instance of proactive (in response to something the officer sees) rather than reactive (in response to an outside report of an incident) police work. To make a stop, an officer must have an immediate reason to pull over the vehicle. Equipment violations (burnt-out headlights, mufflers or stereo systems louder than allowed by noise ordinances, expired license plate) and traffic law violations (speeding, running a red light or stop sign) are the most common reasons. Signs of recent violence (bullet holes, blood splatters) or theft (broken windows, missing trunk lock or license plate) are also valid. The appearance of the vehicle's occupants, however, is not a legal reason for a stop, no matter how much they might look like stereotypical drug dealers — this falls under profiling, an activity in which officers are not legally entitled to engage.

If an officer has a reason to make a stop, she looks for a safe location to pull over the vehicle *before* turning on her lights and siren. Many motorists drive in an oblivious haze and may panic as soon as their rear-view mirrors are full of blue, pulling over right into a curb or parked car. The ideal site for a stop is a well-lit area with a shoulder

wide enough for both vehicles to completely exit the road. Bridges, curves, hills and other chokepoints or areas of low visibility are all bad options because of the increased risk of another driver striking a vehicle. While the officer driving the cruiser is doing this, her partner is running its license number through the MDT (see p. 74) and notifying Dispatch of the vehicle's description, the number of occupants and the reason the officers are making the stop.

Once the officer finds a safe area, she activates her lights and siren. This is the point at which most pursuits (see the following section) begin. Assuming that the driver does comply, the officer parks her own cruiser about 20 to 30 feet behind the stopped vehicle, angled outward toward the roadway. This provides some measure of protection from oncoming traffic that might otherwise strike the officer.

If neither the computerized search nor Dispatch indicates any reason for the officers to consider the stop a high-threat situation (see below), both officers approach the vehicle on opposite sides. The officer on the driver's side will handle all interactions with the driver. This requires the driver to turn over his shoulder to speak to her. The other officer has a better view of the passengers and the vehicle's center console (a common storage place for weapons or contraband). While moving forward, the officers check that the vehicle's trunk is secure (or that the bed of a pickup doesn't contain any additional passengers or other threats) and scan all of the vehicle's occupants. The offside officer stays near the rear corner of the vehicle and continues to observe while the one on the driver's side approaches the driver's window. To keep the driver from striking her with the door or exiting the vehicle rapidly, the officer stands behind the rear edge of the driver's door, outside its arc but close enough to step in and block an attempt to exit. The primary objective at this point is to keep all of the vehicle's occupants under observation while controlling their movements to minimize their chances of attacking the officers or attempting to flee.

When the officer on the driver's side of the vehicle approaches, she initiates a conversation with the driver to discuss the reason for the stop and to observe his reaction and behavior. At the officer's discretion, she may ask the driver to get out, bringing his license, vehicle registration and proof of insurance with him to the rear of the vehicle. This is a matter of preference and varies by situation. Bringing the driver out allows him to save face in front of his passengers, gets him away from any weapons in the car and isolates him if his behavior indicates that the situation may involve more than the initial traffic violation. But bringing the driver also gives him more opportunity to fight or to flee on foot.

If the officer determines that she needs to issue a citation, she leaves the driver where he is and returns to the cruiser to enter the information on the MDT. Her partner remains at the stopped vehicle, keeping an eye on all of its occupants. Once the paperwork is complete, the officer returns to the driver to issue him the citation and send him on his way. Both officers then return to their cruiser, wait for the vehicle to safely pull out into traffic and notify Dispatch that they are done with the stop and are back in service.

Opposite Extremes

Motorcycles present a significant flight risk during a traffic stop because of their high acceleration. A skilled rider can wait until the officer is approaching him, then launch in a spray of gravel and be a quarter-mile away before the officer can sprint back to her vehicle and notify Dispatch that she's in pursuit. For this reason, officers stopping a motorcycle use their cruiser's loudspeakers to ask the rider to step off the bike before they exit their own vehicle.

Larger passenger vehicles such as buses and motor homes are also problematic because of the number of hiding places they offer for passengers or contraband. Unless some sort of emergency situation demands it, lone officers never approach or board such a vehicle. The MPD's preference in such situations is at least two officers. One enters the vehicle while the other stays outside to observe the passengers and intercept anyone who tries to flee through an emergency exit. Vans are much smaller than buses but present many of the same hazards, and most MPD officers prefer to call for backup when stopping vans as well.

DWI

When police traffic enforcement began, drunk driving, or driving under the influence (DUI), was the only enforceable factor of driver impairment. Today, however, the state legal system recognizes the wider category driving while impaired (DWI), which also includes prescription drugs, illegal drugs, sleep deprivation and medical conditions, all of which can affect judgment and reaction time. An officer has reason to suspect DWI if she observes erratic driving or signs of alcohol or drug use. Factors such as slurred speech, inconsistent vehicle operation and unsteady reactions may all lead her to conduct a field sobriety test on the driver. MPD policy requires an officer to conduct at least three of the following tests:

• **Alphabet:** Does the suspect have enough concentration to correctly recite the alphabet only between two specific letters, or backwards?

• **Walking:** Can the suspect walk along a straight line on the road, one foot directly in front of the other, then turn 180 degrees without stumbling or falling?

• **One-leg balance:** Can the suspect stand on one leg for 30 seconds?

• **Finger-to-nose:** Can the suspect, with both eyes closed and both arms out, touch his nose with one fingertip?

• **Horizontal gaze:** Can the suspect follow a moving object with his eyes?

If the suspect fails a majority of these tests and the officer believes him to be under the influence of drugs or alcohol, she then arrests him. Arrests are left to the officer's discretion in cases of sleep deprivation or medical issues. Upon arrival at the city jail, the suspect receives an opportunity to take a breathalyzer test and repeat the field sobriety tests.

Vehicle Searches

To conduct a search of a vehicle during a traffic stop (or at any other time), an officer must have probable cause to believe that contraband or other evidence of a crime is inside the vehicle. Such probable cause generally comes from the officer's observations or the statement of witnesses to a crime involving the vehicle or its occupants. A large body of case law exists with regard to probable cause in vehicle searches. MPD officers generally operate on the following principles.

• Owners and occupants of a vehicle have a reduced expectation of privacy due to the vehicle's mobility and the visibility of its interior. All rights to be free of unreasonable search and seizure are contingent on having a reasonable expectation of privacy. You have no realistic expectation of privacy for the contents of your car if you leave them plainly visible within the car and leave the car parked in a public area, so keep that crack pipe locked up in the glove compartment.

• Probable cause requires some definable factor for the officer to believe that the vehicle contains evidence of a crime. Generally, searches require the officer to have probable cause, which means that the searching officer has a reasonable basis for thinking that the area being searched has evidence of criminal activity.

• Officer safety can occasionally serve as substitute for the traditional interpretation of probable cause. More accurately, an officer can perform a Terry search (see p. 63) on anyone if the officer can articulate any rational basis for thinking the person being searched represents a danger to him. Terry searches are limited to pat-downs. (The officer can't make the suspect empty his pockets just on a Terry search.) However, if the officer feels something suspicious, such as a bag of crack or a weapon, he then has probable cause to order the suspect to empty his pockets. Terry searches do not extend to the interior of a vehicle, though the officer could ask someone to step out of the car and submit to a pat-down. On the other hand, and this is the linchpin, if a cop arrests the driver or a passenger of a car, the cop can immediately search the reachable area of the car — any place in the car the suspect could have reached and used to hide evidence before apprehension. Also, if the police impound the car, they are authorized to search the car entirely, ostensibly for the purpose of verifying the car's contents in case the suspect later claims that the police stole something from the car. Anything found pursuant to this type of search is admissible.

• An officer can always ask a vehicle's operator for permission to search the vehicle without probable cause. However, if the driver refuses, different circumstances apply. The Fourth Amendment forbids search and seizure absent a warrant issued by a magistrate and supported by probable cause. In theory, the cop has to swear out an affidavit attesting to what he's looking for, where he expects to find it and why he thinks it's there. A magistrate judge then reviews the affidavit and the proposed warrant and either signs off on it (insulating it against most Fourth Amendment challenges) or does not (on the grounds that the magistrate does not consider probable cause to exist). Legally speaking, absent a search warrant, all expressly denied searches are presumptively unconstitutional.

If an officer conducts an unconstitutional search without probable cause, any evidence she obtains through that search can be thrown out of court.

That said, there are numerous exceptions to those general rules that almost swallow up the Fourth Amendment whole in some liberal political opinions.

• An officer who has probable cause can search a car without a warrant under the exigent circumstances doctrine if he believes that there is a great likelihood that a criminal will escape or that evidence will be destroyed before he can obtain a warrant.

• He can search if he has the permission of the car's owner or the permission of anyone else who indicates that she owns the car and has apparent authority over the car. This is called the Good Faith exception.

• He can search the immediate reachable area around anyone he arrests without a warrant in order to ensure that, for example, the arrestee didn't hide evidence or contraband under a seat.

• In some cases, even warrant-less searches that have no rational basis for probable cause or that have not fallen under any other exceptions have been upheld under the inevitable discovery doctrine, which states that if the evidence would have been discovered soon by some other means (such as the vehicle being impounded and subjected to an impound search), then the warrant-less search in the field was not unconstitutional.

High-Threat Stops

The MPD defines a high-threat stop as any traffic stop in which the officer has reason to believe that the suspect vehicle's occupants pose a significant risk to the officer or to others. This includes a display of weapons, a report that the vehicle is stolen or was involved in a serious crime, identification of any vehicle occupant as a violent offender or aggressive actions on the part of the vehicle's occupants. In any such situation, MPD policy is to assume that all occupants of the vehicle pose lethal threats to the officers and are better-armed.

When a stop moves into the high-threat category, the officer who made the initial stop (the primary officer) calls for backup and uses her cruiser's loudspeaker to order the vehicle's occupants to stay in it. Secondary units always pull in behind the vehicle, never in front of it, to avoid the possibility of a crossfire if the incident devolves to a gunfight. Once more officers than suspects are present, all officers exit their vehicles, using them for cover. The primary officer is responsible for giving all commands to the suspects during the incident. She orders the driver to remove his keys from the ignition and toss them out the window, then exit the vehicle facing away from the officers, kick the door shut, pull up his shirt to reveal his waistband and make a slow 360-degree turn. She then has the suspect walk backward toward the officers, drop to his knees and lie facedown with his arms spread and ankles crossed. Two other officers move from behind cover to handcuff the suspect, move him back to cover and search him. The officers then repeat this process for every occupant of the vehicle.

Vehicle Pursuits

A traffic incident changes from a stop to a pursuit when the driver fails to pull over for an officer. Due to the high risk to both bystanders and involved parties, MPD has rigid regulations governing when an officer can initiate or continue a pursuit. For a legitimate pursuit to occur, the risk posed by allowing the suspect to escape must be greater than the risk posed by continuing the pursuit. This usually means that officers (reluctantly) let car thieves go, but will run violent offenders to ground.

Once a pursuit starts, the first thing the officers do is call for backup, describing the vehicle they're chasing and giving as many tactically relevant details as possible about its occupants. The driver keeps her attention entirely on the road and the suspect vehicle while her partner stays on the radio, calling the turns that the quarry makes. If a single officer is involved in the pursuit, she only stays on the radio until a backup unit arrives, at which point she concentrates wholly on driving and lets someone in a car behind her do the radio work.

As an officer's field supervisor, her sergeant usually scrambles to join any pursuit as quickly as possible. The ranking officer on the scene has the final call as to whether to break off pursuit at any time. This depends on the aggressiveness of the individual supervisor — and, in many cases, the availability of an aviation unit to continue the chase without the immediate pressure that ground units put on a suspect.

Terminating the Pursuit

MPD officers are entitled to use force to terminate a pursuit only if the suspects are too dangerous to be allowed to escape and the pursuit has to be stopped immediately to prevent significant risk to officers or civilians. MPD policy considers pursuit termination to be lethal force due to the hazard of serious injury or death involved in a crash at pursuit speeds. Because of uncertain backdrops, gunfire during a chase is officially prohibited, though officers who have no other option are unlikely to be up for disciplinary action if they don't cause any inadvertent injuries or property damage. Officers have two approved options for terminating a pursuit: Pursuit Intervention Maneuvers (PIT) and spike strips.

A Pursuit Intervention Maneuver is a controlled ramming technique that breaks the traction of a vehicle's rear tires, forcing it to spin out. To perform a PIT, the officer brings the front of his car even with the rear quarter panel of the suspect vehicle, steers over to make gentle contact, then shoves hard sideways. This shove forces the target into a spin while hopefully leaving the officer some degree of control to recover from the maneuver. Ideally, a PIT occurs with other units in close proximity, ready to move in before the suspect can recover and get moving again.

A spike strip is a segmented plastic ribbon about 15 feet long. When stored, it coils into a container the size of a small briefcase. To deploy a spike strip, an officer removes it from its case and tosses it to unroll it across the road he wants to block. The end of the strip closest to the officer is attached to a 20-foot control cable. When the officer yanks the cable, three-inch spikes spring upright from the strip until the officer releases the tension on the cable. In a pursuit, an officer with a spike strip sets it up ahead of the route the pursuit is likely to take, triggers it as the suspect approaches and then lets the spikes retract before the pursuing units hit them as well.

In Play: PIT and Spikes

To perform a PIT, a pursuing character must have caught up to the target vehicle (see "Vehicle Pursuit," p. 69 of the **World of Darkness Rulebook**). The two drivers make opposed Dexterity + Drive rolls. If one vehicle is smaller, it suffers a penalty to this roll equal to half the difference of the two vehicles' Sizes, rounded down. If the pursuer loses the roll, he misses or falters and the pursuit continues, with the quarry gaining the number of successes by which he won the roll. If the pursuer wins the roll, the quarry's vehicle suffers a damage roll equal to 1 + the number of net successes the pursuer received. In addition, the quarry must make a second Dexterity + Drive roll, suffering a penalty equal to the number of successes by which the pursuer won the roll to PIT. If the quarry fails this second roll, he spins out and comes to a halt. In any of these cases and on any of these rolls, a dramatic failure results in a crash.

If a vehicle strikes a spike strip, each tire suffers a separate five-die damage roll with the Armor Piercing 1 effect (thus, a normal tire's Durability of 1 does not protect against this damage). A spike strip has Durability 3, Size 2 and Structure 5, but does not suffer damage from being run over.

Code Eight: Officer Down

The worst thing any MPD officer can hear over his radio is "Code Eight." This call indicates that another cop is in trouble and needs immediate assistance. Upon receiving a Code Eight call, all officers in the precinct who aren't involved in other incidents immediately converge on the subject officer's last known location (as may some who are engaged in citing trivial misdemeanors or minor traffic violations). Until the dispatcher cancels a Code Eight call, the assumption is that the officer in need of assistance is fighting for his life or critically injured. Because cops' families, criminals and news reporters all have police radio scanners, the department never broadcasts an explicit "officer down" call — such situations always go out as Code Eight.

In Play: Cop Killers

Many World of Darkness stories suffer players who believe that their characters can assault and kill cops and escape all consequences of their actions because of their superhuman powers (or simply because they're the protagonists). Players who believe this often move on to even more gratuitous in-game violence, and suddenly a horror game whose protagonists once avoided public attention for fear of public vengeance comes to more closely resemble *Grand Theft Auto* with silver bullets. Police officers become no more threatening than any other ordinary mortals, whole squads falling to the twin Desert Eagles and laser katanas of characters run amok.

We strongly encourage Storytellers to avoid minimizing the consequences of such actions. Although characters may be possessed of supernatural capabilities that enable them to kill one officer, or even a handful of cops, they are neither omnipotent nor infallible. Killing cops generates a manhunt unsurpassed by anything within the average character group's capabilities. Officers will stop at nothing to find and bring down the individuals responsible for the deaths of fellow officers.

Once characters are cornered, some players will want to shoot it out to the bitter end, refusing to believe that their characters can be taken down by "mere mortals." In such an eventuality, we encourage Storytellers to, quite simply, kill those characters. The following are some tactical points to consider:

• Cops have considerably more tactical sense than the average group of characters in that cops fight in a coordinated fashion. They also know when to pull back and set up a perimeter rather than

fighting to the death like blue-garbed mooks. If the officers are responding to a situation with a known high threat level, they'll set up a perimeter to establish containment rather than going in at all. That's what the ERU guys get paid to do.

• Cops can and will call for backup. Police procedure calls for overwhelming force when confronting armed suspects. This entails a secure perimeter, snipers, helicopters and a tactical entry team. Such a turnout invariably brings a massive media response.

• If characters are somehow able to kill and escape from an entire police tactical response, such a display puts the characters on the level of national terrorist threats. This will involve a federal, and eventually military, response. The question is not if the characters will die, but when.

Mitigating circumstances of course apply. If one of the key antagonists of the story is a crooked cop, only a sadistic Storyteller would punish his players for delivering such a foil to his final reward. On the other side of the coin, a character whose moral code punishes killing might suffer greater pangs of remorse for killing a cop — the cop isn't just an average citizen, he's a symbol of the law and order that exists to protect people.

We're not asking you to jeopardize your story for the sake of realism, we're just suggesting that the police be played intelligently and given genuine respect for their position.

On the Trail: Detective Work

Once an officer passes the detective's exam, he starts learning an entirely new aspect of his job. Patrol officers see the immediate results of crimes, but detectives have to clean up the mess afterward. Detective work is much slower than patrol work, with little of the immediate satisfaction of rolling up on a crime in progress and making a timely arrest. The controlled aggression that served a patrol cop well can result in an impatient detective who doesn't take the time to let cases play out.

Detectives are rarely the first responders to calls for service unless they happen to be in the neighborhood and are the closest available units. Instead, the MPD's detective units receive their cases from patrol or other uniformed officers who are the first responders, take initial statements, file preliminary reports and move on to the next calls for service. Accordingly, detectives appreciate patrol cops who take the time to get all the details of a call written down, and will occasionally try to recruit the more meticulous ones for the Detective Bureau.

As noted previously, the MPD divides its detectives into individual units, each focusing on a particular type of crime. Special training in a unit's area of expertise is available, and graduate degrees are not uncommon for detectives who choose to make whole careers of their assignments. Many detectives become specialists, never transferring out of their units or cross-training. It's rare to find a detective who's spent a significant amount of time in more than one unit unless he's trying to position himself for department politics or has a sufficiently abrasive personality that his bosses keep bouncing him rather than continue to work with him.

On Duty

Similar to patrol officers, detectives in units that deal with violent crime or violent criminals work in partner teams. Those in the Property Crimes and Information Crimes Units, however, usually work alone due to their staffing levels and lower risk during investigations. Partnerings tend to be more flexible than in the Patrol Division, with assignments changing out depending on caseload and individual areas of expertise. Schedules are likewise flexible as detectives work around their cases, contacts and court appearances.

Running Investigations

Detective work in the MPD bears a closer resemblance to *Law & Order* than to *CSI*. A detective doesn't sift every square inch of a crime scene with multi-million-dollar laboratory equipment to track down a culprit via DNA sampling and behavioral profiling. The MPD doesn't have Hollywood's budget (not even in the Analysis Bureau), and cannot rely on every case coming together with perfect synergy in 42 minutes of exciting investigation. Instead, investigators deal with a job that's 99% routine and 1% adventure, relying on the same basic resources that their predecessors used for decades.

• **Interviewing.** Even more so than a patrol officer, a good detective must be able to talk to people. Victims, witnesses, suspects, contacts and their relatives, friends and coworkers all may possess vital information related to a case. The trick is getting them to give it up and recognizing when they do, in keeping with the police aphorism of "everyone you meet in this job will lie to you." Being a hardass gets a cop only so far — small concessions and a display of understanding for even the most loathsome individuals can build a rapport that eventually leads to a case-breaking tidbit told in confidence. A solid instinctive understanding of human behavior allows a good interviewer to tell the difference between truth, evasiveness, outright fabrication, misunderstanding, memory lapse, lies of omission and the myriad other ways in which a subject can consciously or unconsciously distort the truth. Repeat interviews are vital, as human memory isn't infallible. Witnesses can recall seemingly trivial facts that hold vital importance when placed alongside other evidence, or liars can introduce telling inconsistencies into their stories.

• **Paperwork.** Every officer should write every report with the assumption that the Supreme Court will review the report in a constitutional case. Such a possibility is roughly as likely as winning the lottery, but both events do actually happen. The vast majority of reports, however, fall under the scrutiny of detectives who have to piece together a case from someone else's observations of scenes, witnesses and physical evidence. The introduction of computer databases into police work has reduced the physical amount of paper that investigators have to shuffle while processing a case, but increased the total amount of information available. A detective must be able to filter the irrelevant parts of records and isolate the significant details. Particularly when working a case that spans multiple crimes, repeated review of witness statements, crime scene reports and lab results can gradually lead to an emerging pattern, which gives the investigator something else on which to build his case.

• **Instinct.** No experienced cop will deny the value of instinct in police work. However, personal bullshit meters and sixth senses are inadmissible in court. The trick is for an investigator to recognize what part of her training or street experience is triggering her well-developed cop instincts, then act on that. Animals rely on natural instincts, but cops — and the criminals they hunt — develop their instincts through subconsciously learning to synthesize seemingly trivial facts that don't individually mean anything. A detective can't testify in court that she spontaneously knew that a suspect was lying, but she can point to specific training she received regarding the telltale physiological signs of deception.

As a matter of policy, the Detective Bureau puts its highest priority on violent crimes such as homicide, assault and sex offenses. Property crimes rarely receive high levels of attention — unless a rash of crimes suddenly targets Midway's upper crust. In general, the cases most likely to be solved, or that most need to be solved as a matter of public safety, are where the MPD's focus lies.

Character Options: Detectives

To pass the MPD's detective exam, a character must meet the following minimum criteria:
- Attributes: Intelligence 3, Wits 3, Composure 3 and either Presence or Manipulation 3
- Mental Skills: Academics 1, Investigation 3, Politics 1
- Social Skills: Five points among Empathy, Intimidation, Persuasion and Streetwise

This ensures that the character possesses the basic skills necessary to become a detective. In addition, assignment to some detective units requires the following additional expertise:
- Homicide: Medicine 1 or Science 2
- Robbery: None
- Property Crimes: None
- Narcotics: Streetwise 3
- Special Victims: Medicine 1, Empathy 3, Willpower 6
- Information Crimes: either Academics 2 with an Accounting Specialty, Computer 3 or Crafts 2 with an Accounting Specialty
- Vice: Socialize 2 and Streetwise 2
- Intelligence: Contacts Merit 4
- Organized Crime Task Force: Politics 2
- Gang Task Force: Streetwise 2

Networks

After a few weeks on the streets, a patrol officer begins to recognize certain "regulars" on his beat. These may be gangstas who always loiter on the same corner, nosy old ladies who call in complaints on their neighbors like clockwork or just familiar faces who always seem to be in the area when an alarm drop comes in. Some of these citizens may become familiar suspects, even nemeses. Every experienced Midway cop has a few stories about the girl he's arrested a dozen times for brawling in Fat Sam's pool hall, or the guy whom he's been trying to catch stealing cars for years. An equal number of frequent encounters, however, can form the start of a cop's network of informants. Lonely old ladies

with nothing better to do than watch their neighborhoods really do have useful information on occasion.

The lists of criminals and observers aren't always mutually exclusive. Nonviolent Midway street regulars such as prostitutes and petty thieves can develop a certain measure of trust toward a specific officer who treats them with more courtesy than they're accustomed to receiving, even if he does so while arresting them again and again for the same offenses. The principle of officer's discretion often comes into play, particularly in cases in which the initial relationship is already established: "Suzie, what we're gonna do is confiscate these rocks and send you home, but I need to know what you've heard about the drive-by the Cobras did over on Eighth Street." While not wholly reliable in any regard, these "regular clients" can be some of the best sources of information for an investigator who's looking for a break in a case. However, every officer must remember that such sources aren't the most reliable ones — working from a single piece of sketchy information provided by a twitchy heroin addict is an invitation to disaster. The Reagan-era arms control motto of "trust but verify" is particularly applicable to street information.

A Midway detective has considerably more latitude in cultivating his networks than a patrol officer does. A detective operates in plainclothes, which enables him to conduct informal meetings that would ruin his sources' reputations and alert observers if the detective were seen talking to them in uniform. A detective also has more influence to get an informant off the hook for minor offenses if her information helps break a larger case — though he should remember to never actually make any promise that he can't keep, lest he lose credibility. Generally, a detective's network focuses on the crimes he most frequently investigates. Property Crimes detectives know a lot of used car dealers and pawnshop owners, while those on the Narcotics squad know dealers and junkies. The officers with the largest and most varied networks often wind up in the Intelligence squad, which doesn't take point on any given crime but rather focuses on information-gathering to support investigations across the Detective Bureau. Such collections of contacts are rarer than they used to be — in today's mobile society, no more than one in 10 officers is able to develop and maintain effective networks. Insular ethic communities, such as indigenous natives (Native Americans, in the United States) or recent immigrants, are particularly difficult places to cultivate and maintain connections, especially when an investigation focuses on an event that vindicates or avenges the community. In the World of Darkness in general, and Midway in particular, such crimes are likely to include paranormal events with connections to the community's belief system. These groups often see the justice system of white, English-speaking Anglo-Saxon males as useless at best, particularly if it's previously failed to solve and prosecute crimes against the community. If such minorities have been scapegoated in past unsolved crimes, their reaction to cops meddling in their neighborhoods and affairs may turn overtly hostile. Unless an officer comes from such an ethnic group, undercover infiltration is doomed to failure. Social workers and local charity organizers may serve as bridges to an isolated minority group, but such people are often hesitant to jeopardize their own credibility by seeming too sympathetic to the MPD.

World of Darkness: Networks

Even cops who are aware of the supernatural don't investigate paranormal events with the regularity of Mulder and Scully — not if those cops want to keep their badges for long, anyway. Accordingly, the Storyteller should carefully moderate most characters' use of a Contacts Merit devoted exclusively to the supernatural. This goes double for Contacts who actually are supernatural themselves, as the idea of a narcotics detective who has half the vampires in the city on speed-dial is dubious without extenuating circumstances. At most, a character with no supernatural capabilities himself should have one supernatural entity as a major contact, and the character shouldn't even be aware of the nature of his associate.

This being said, a cop's network can be the means by which the Storyteller introduces the character to the world of the supernatural. If one junkie reports a werewolf sighting, an officer will most likely shrug it off as a drug-induced interpretation of a random feral dog encounter. Once people start turning up dead from large animal maulings and eight separate street informants report the same rumor, the character may start paying more attention.**Confidential Informants**

The Intelligence Unit of the MPD's Detective Bureau maintains the department's Confidential Informant (CI) database. Information sources who've proven themselves to be consistently accurate, or who are critical to an ongoing high-priority investigation, can go on the list for a set period of time at the discretion of any detective. When an officer runs an identity or background check on a CI (such as during a traffic stop), the MPD's computer system flags the suspect's status. Being on the CI list grants a source limited immunity from misdemeanor charges, though habitual offenses will void this agreement unless the detective in control of the informant states that the offenses were directly relevant to solving a felony investigation.

CI status also grants an informant a degree of protection from publicity. This isn't just a privacy concern — being known as a snitch on the street can be a terminal reputation. In open court records, an officer never identifies one of her CIs by his real name. If patrol officers pick up a CI, the proper procedure is to release him with a plausible reason for not arresting him, such as "insufficient physical evidence" or "the complainant couldn't identify him."

Unlike federal authorities, the MPD rarely provides financial incentives to compensate CIs for the risks they run and the services they render. Detectives running CIs must pay for tips out of their own pockets, and pay surprisingly little: some detectives have bought intelligence on major felonies for $50. The most common method of "payment" is to convince the district attorney's office to cut a favorable plea bargain deal for the CI or one of his loved ones. In such negotiations, the going rate is three-to-one — information that helps solve three felonies will get one felony charge reduced.

In Play: Contacts

In game terms, the Contacts Merit (see the **World of Darkness Rulebook,** p. 114) represents an officer's network of informants and snitches. This Merit is arguably one of the most important ones available for a detective or an experienced patrol officer. Traffic cops, administrators and those on other specialized assignments such as the Bomb squad are least likely to develop networks, as their jobs keep them from hitting the streets and talking to the locals on a nightly basis.

Remember that Contacts is a Merit that requires cultivation and upkeep. Characters who intend to sit in the comfort of their own offices and crack cases with a few hours of phone calls probably won't be very effective for long. Storytellers should remember that Contacts exist to provide information, not to lift and carry for a lazy investigator or substitute for half-assed police work.

Rather than generating answers, such Contacts should generate possible leads an investigator can follow up to find answers. Any detective who declares a case solved and makes an arrest without doing a significant amount of his own legwork will be torn to shreds when a competent defense attorney puts him on the stand and shows the jury the detective's complete lack of evidentiary credibility.

Optional Rule: Pushing and Burning Contacts

A character sometimes needs more information than her contacts will provide willingly. In dire straits, she may choose to put pressure on her network rather than nurture it. If she uses coercion to gain information, the player may roll Manipulation + Intimidation in place of the usual Contacts rolls. This is a calculated gamble: the roll gains the 9 Again effect, but 1s also subtract successes, and a failure permanently reduces the character's Contacts trait by the appropriate dot as part of the network decides the relationship isn't worth it any more. For example, if Erik

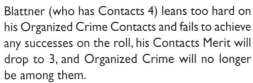

Blattner (who has Contacts 4) leans too hard on his Organized Crime Contacts and fails to achieve any successes on the roll, his Contacts Merit will drop to 3, and Organized Crime will no longer be among them.

A character may also go even further, deliberately endangering or directly threatening contacts. If she decides to burn a contact in this manner, the roll gains the 8 Again effect, but 1s also subtract successes, *and* she *automatically* loses one dot of Contacts after making the roll.

Homicide

Murder is one of the highest-priority crimes for the MPD as a whole, with Midway averaging 410 murders a year out of the 16,000 murders committed annually in the United States. (Storytellers may wish to inflate these real-world figures to account for the World of Darkness' much higher rates of violent crime.) Most murders, detectives know, are crimes of passion or opportunity committed by someone who already knew the victim, frequently a domestic partner. Premeditated murder is rare, no more than one in 15 or 20 cases, and frequently tied to organized crime. The premeditated killings, however, are often the most difficult to solve, as killers who do their homework know how to avoid the obvious mistakes. The amount of physical evidence left in most murders sets up significant leads — often pointing directly to the killer, if not narrowing the field — and provides strong support for detectives' other findings when a case goes to court. Overall, the MPD's clearance rate for murders is 40%, below the national average of 50%.

Given the above factors, most homicide investigations begin with a close examination of the victim's family and associates, looking for someone with a reason to kill the decedent. The Latin adage *qui bono?* — "Who benefits?" — is a common thread throughout police work, but never more so than in homicide investigations. Many murders occur for reasons that outside observers find to be the height of stupidity: who gets the last beer, or which football game to watch.

Organized Crime Murders

Contrary to the view popularized by Hollywood, killings arranged by organized crime aren't usually intricate or poetic. Most of these killings target members or associates who betrayed the organization, whether by agreeing to testify in court or by skimming profits. Unless the organization has a clueless junior member it wants to rid itself of, the organized crime group will take one of two paths: either have a trusted friend of the victim take him out when he's at ease and expecting no threat or subcontract the hit to a petty street criminal (and keep an eye on him in case he

starts bragging). "Professionals" from out of town only come into the picture if the organization knows that it's under such heavy surveillance that the members can't arrange anything on their own.

Starting the Investigation

A homicide investigation usually begins with the discovery of a body. Patrol officers are almost always the first MPD personnel to see the corpse. Their responsibilities, if no murder suspect is present in the immediate area, are to secure the crime scene and begin recording statements from witnesses. Unless the officers need to secure a weapon or otherwise move to preserve physical evidence, they're to disturb the scene as little as possible. If a suspect is present, however, the obvious arrest happens.

It's also possible to start a homicide investigation without an actual dead person. If an individual is reported missing and sufficient evidence — physical or circumstantial — exists to indicate that foul play was involved, the case becomes a homicide investigation. Few such investigations end in a conviction solely on the basis of some bloodstains and the lack of a body. However, a sufficiently large body of evidence is justification for an arrest warrant (see p. 63), and detectives have obtained many convictions on the basis of confessions.

The Victim

Every homicide scene is unique and unnerving. Veteran homicide investigators and crime scene technicians can handle indescribably gruesome visuals, but the stench of violent human death is an indescribable miasmatic combination of blood, piss, shit, fear sweat and decomposition. Many detectives take up smoking to deliberately destroy their senses of smell, going for the foulest cigars they can find. Others rub mentholated muscle balm under their noses or, if the body is near a kitchen, burn a pan of coffee grounds on the stove.

Every victim holds a story for the trained eye. The best piece of evidence in a case is the guy at room temperature. Crime scene technicians know that every physical contact leaves a trace on the corpse and objects, and accordingly examine the victim and his surroundings to build the chain of clues leading back to the murderer. Passionate murders committed out of rage against the victim usually involve far more strikes or shots than necessary to kill. Severe facial injuries to a female victim often point to a jilted or unfulfilled romantic partner.

Three-quarters of murder victims are male. Over the past two decades, a trend has emerged in homicides: many victims are criminals themselves. Drug involvement is a particularly common circumstance for murder. Homicide Unit detectives now notify their Narcotics Unit counterparts whenever they find drugs on or near a victim, and many Narcotics investigations have ended with the death of the primary suspect.

The Killer

As with victims, the majority of murderers are young adult males. FBI statistics show that more than a quarter of the murderers in the United States are black men between the ages of 17 and 50 who come from low-income communities. Murderesses make up no more than one-tenth of cases. (Disturbingly, mothers or other female relatives commit most child murders.)

As previously noted, many victims knew their killers. Searches of victims' address books, calendars, phone records and photographs can all point to close acquaintances, maybe unknown to other associates, who are likely suspects. "Where were you that night?" should be heard in every interview in the case. Suspicion also focuses on the last person to be seen with the victim, or the one who reports discovering the body.

Murderers talk. It's the rare killer whose conscience and self-control allow him to keep his mouth shut. Sooner or later, a proud murderer brags to share his triumph, or a guilty one confesses for absolution. A suspect's acquaintances notice changes in behavior. If arrested, an innocent suspect stays wired until he crashes, but a guilty one involuntarily relaxes or even goes to sleep as he realizes his wait is over.

Assault

Due to familiarity with the many means by which people inflict violence on one another, as well as the many reasons for doing so, Homicide squads also receive assault cases that require detectives' attention. Midway had just under 12,000 simple (as opposed to sexual) assaults last year, but only a small fraction of those were severe or puzzling enough to warrant detectives' attention. The severe cases are prosecuted as attempted murder, which is Homicide's justification for dealing with them.

Some Homicide detectives find these cases harder to deal with than actual murders, as the detectives have to confront the attack's psychological impact on the victim. Other detectives, with typical cop gallows humor, privately refer to assaults as "murders that the killers fucked up." Assault investigations proceed much like murder investigations, but typically are much easier because the victim can still speak. On the other hand, assaults are comparatively lower-priority investigations unless the suspects are involved in other murder cases.

World of Darkness: Serial Killers

Serial killers — murderers who repeatedly kill in a specific preferred manner for psychological thrills rather than personal gain — are an unfortunate fact of life in the real world, with FBI statistics suggesting that approximately 35 are active in the United States at any one time. In the World of Darkness, serial killer scares are much more common, and no major city goes more than three years without hosting one. When a pattern of evidence in three or more separate homicides points to a serial killer's involvement,

Homicide Unit detectives invariably take point on the task force created to manage the ensuing investigation.

Following the trail of a serial killer can be one of the most frustrating and unnerving experiences an officer can face — but it also makes for great dramatic storytelling. Fear can paralyze an entire city, particularly if the killer appears to be choosing his victims at random rather than by a particular profile. The resulting media frenzy places the department and the task force under a microscope. Officers find themselves operating under paranoid circumspection, as unthinking or uncaring reporters can easily compromise an investigation if they get their hands on sensitive information.

Serial killers commit their acts compulsively. Once they start, most are incapable of stopping for more than a year, usually much less. When they learn that the police are on to them, they begin to view the investigation as a game they can win by making more spectacular headlines and frustrating investigators.

The typical serial killer is an adult, white male acting alone, though all ages and ethic groups have been seen, as have women. Serial killers derive their motivation from a wide array of psychological compulsions, mainly those toward physical or sexual power or the assertion of their own superiority. Many serial killers faced abuse of one or more forms during their childhoods, leading to deep-seated desires to "prove" themselves in order to escape those memories.

In game terms, serial killers almost always suffer from one or more derangements (most likely Megalomania, Paranoia, Schizophrenia or Irrationality) that they've gained while descending to Morality 2. This degeneration occurs during childhood and adolescence, over the course of a sequence of experiments with lesser acts such as arson and animal torture that eventually leads them to human subjects. See the **World of Darkness Rulebook**, pp. 91–94 and 96–100, for the appropriate derangement and Morality rules.

All of these factors make serial killers compelling and challenging adversaries for MPD characters, even without bringing the supernatural into the mix. A serial killer who does possess paranormal capabilities is an even more difficult foe. Such a case is unlikely to end in an arrest. Once officers close in, bringing to bear an amount of force commensurate with the killer's demonstrated capabilities, he will probably either escape or die in the attempt.

Supernatural characters who overtly and wantonly commit murder often do so in a significantly recognizable fashion. Vampires drain their prey, werewolves eat human flesh, mages conduct ritual sacrifices. Although these acts don't fit the traditional definition of serial killing, as all are motivated by factors other than normal ones, from the perspective of investigating officers, such acts are the same, who view the events through a lens of human criminal behavior. An unknown number of serial killers in the World of Darkness are actually such beings who fail to consider the consequences of their actions (which may

include the players' characters). Once the MPD launches a public investigation, a character who repeatedly leaves his messes lying around for others to find becomes a target not only for the police but for his own kind as well. Smart supernatural beings know that a successful investigation of one of them may result in all of them being exposed, and they have neither laws against nor qualms about permanently taking down a rogue who threatens their collective existence.

Robbery

The MPD's Robbery squads stay busy, with 8,700 robberies reported last year. These crimes range from simple muggings — the vast majority — to carjackings, home invasions and complex armed robberies of businesses and banks.

Muggings

A large number of muggings occur to provide funding for petty criminals' drug habits. Robbery detectives consequently keep in touch with Narcotics squads to stay on top of the locations of local shooting galleries and crack houses, periodically going along on raids to see if any of the detectives' suspects turn up. Many mugging victims become targets because they break their usual patterns, going away from their accustomed neighborhoods and making themselves obvious victims. Muggers choose targets, preferably female, who appear to be outsiders and oblivious to their surroundings. Similar to predators, muggers hunt the weak and infirm. Many mugging victims were in the wrong place at the wrong time for reasons they'd rather not reveal, such as drug deals or prostitution, and may give less than fully accurate statements to officers.

Carjacking

Few carjackings are premeditated — a car thief who thinks ahead steals the vehicle when the owner isn't around. Because the victim can simply drive away if she retains presence of mind, no more than half of carjacking attempts are successful. Most occur when a vehicle stops at an intersection, with the assailant ambushing a complacent driver with overwhelming force. Many carjackings with multiple assailants begin as a staged minor collision, with the assault occurring when the victim exits his vehicle to check the damage. Some carjackings inadvertently turn into kidnappings if passengers fail to abandon the vehicle before the carjacker drives away.

Unlike well-planned auto thefts, carjackings are immediately obvious to the victims, resulting in much more rapid notification of the MPD. Patrol and traffic cops can and do intervene in carjackings shortly after their commission, which frequently results in high-speed chases.

Home Invasion

Home invasions are the Robbery Unit's least favorite crimes within its bailiwick. Most home invasions involve small groups of two to four suspects, and many quickly escalate into sexual assault or homicide. The same groups, frequently gang members, tend to commit multiple home invasions in the same area in succession. Some use confederates in repair industries or package delivery companies to gain information on homes that are likely targets.

Armed Robberies

Although few armed robberies go down like the cinematic example in *Heat* or the infamous North Hollywood shootout, the most successful ones do benefit from a wide array of technical talent and extensive planning. Successful armed robbers — those who aren't killed or caught at the scene or in the ensuing pursuit — know their targets, local police response time and escape routes well in advance.

Many well-executed armed robberies are traceable to organized crime. Premeditated armed robberies are rarely gang-related, as few street gangs have the organizational skills or subtlety necessary to put together a successful high-end operation. However, armed robbery of businesses in low-income areas is a classic gang activity. These incidents are more likely to result in victims being shot due to lack of restraint on the part of the criminals.

Starting the Investigation

In most robbery cases, detectives begin working the case after the incident occurs and the victim has filed an initial report with patrol officers. The first step is to begin with a follow-up interview of the victim for additional details about the suspects and the items taken. However, sometimes the Intelligence Unit or the Organized Crime Task Force receives a tip on a major heist being planned. In such a case, detectives have the opportunity to work proactively to identify possible high-value targets and forestall the attempt.

Property Crimes

The Property Crimes Unit (PCU) focuses on non-violent crimes that involve the loss or destruction of property: theft, burglary or breaking and entering, auto theft and vandalism. Property crimes are legally and logistically distinct from robberies in that the thieves in property crimes never directly confront their victims. A PCU case begins with an initial crime report, invariably filtered through the patrol officer who showed up to the complainant's call, wrote down a description of the missing items, made a few reassuring comments and left to a more interesting call. PCU has the thankless task of following up with the distraught property owner a week later.

Most of the arrests that PCU detectives finally make are of career criminals against whom the detectives gradually accrue a body of evidence over months or years. Burglars, safecrackers and car thieves tend to be career criminals who establish patterns, such as similar methods of entry to dwellings, always targeting vehicles in parking garages in a small area and so on. Once PCU becomes aware of a pattern, the detectives can start focusing investigations on likely suspects (the unit maintains a file of career burglars and annotates it with their preferred patterns) or advising precinct commanders to shift patrols to targeted areas. Few PCU cases end with the suspects being caught red-handed unless witnesses call in and patrol officers arrive in time.

A truism in PCU is that thieves target other criminals, who are less likely than the average citizen to report thefts or to be credible witnesses if the cases do go to court. A large number of anonymous tips come from criminals who feel they didn't get their fair share of the take from a joint effort or who want the cops to take the competition off the streets.

One of the best breaks PCU detectives can get is when a suspect tells detectives how he's disposing of his stolen property in exchange for reduced charges. Busting a fence or chop shop can be a major undertaking requiring weeks of surveillance. Confident detectives may allow an operation to run unmolested for weeks in hopes of picking up more thieves before shutting down the "business." Such tips sometimes lead PCU to work hand-in-hand with the Narcotics Unit or the Gang Task Force. Similar to robberies, many thefts on today's streets are drug-related. Career thieves avoid drugs, however, and tend to be some of the smartest and most cautious criminals on the street — making them PCU's most adept adversaries.

Property Recovery Squads

The first assignment for new detectives in PCU is one of the three Property Recovery squads. Each of these specialized squads covers multiple precincts in its area of responsibility (as opposed to the "regular" one-per-precinct Property Crimes squads). The squads' duties involve legwork of the most mundane sort. This consists of checking pawnshops, used car lots, jewelers and thrift stores in a never-ending attempt to match lists of stolen property against current inventory. The detectives also liaise with the Analysis Bureau's Evidence and Property Unit to check incoming evidence and seizures against these same lists.

Narcotics

Prior to the 1980s, Homicide was the place to be if a detective wanted upward mobility and publicity. However, since the explosion of cocaine two decades ago, police estimate that up to 75% of violent crime is somehow drug-related, either directly (drug wars and rivalries) or indirectly (junkies needing fast money to fuel their addictions). Consequently, the MPD's Narcotics Unit is the largest and best funded in the city's Detective Bureau. Narcotics personnel do much of the department's undercover work, and the narcs are always looking at patrol squads for fresh faces to put on the street. Patrol cops with the right look can expect

to be "borrowed" by their precinct's Narcotics squad for temporary duty as backup for buy-bust operations. Narcotics work is some of the most dangerous work in the Detective Bureau. Undercover officers must stage drug transactions alone and in the open, without the benefit of body armor or other equipment that would mark them as cops. The glamour of the undercover narc lifestyle promoted by every cop show and movie since *Scarface* and *Miami Vice* is a far cry from the squalid, roach-infested, piss-stained reality of street-level drug trafficking. Extended undercover assignments are rare at the local level, as operations in even the largest cities lead to officers being well known in the local criminal community within a few years. Some officers (and even more federal agents) have to use the substances they pursue at some point in order to maintain their covers. Even those narcs who never find themselves in such a situation can count on environmental exposure to both drugs and processing chemicals. Policy requires officers to notify their supervisors as soon as possible after any such occurrence, but this doesn't always happen. Internal Affairs keeps a close eye on narcs and the results of their department-mandated drug tests, and clashes between Narcotics supervisors and IAB investigators are legendary. Officers who succumb to addiction and retain the presence of mind to seek help find that their department medical coverage doesn't cover the cost of rehabilitation; even if they complete it successfully, they'll rarely be trusted to work the streets again.

Experienced Narcotics detectives are legendary for their ability to find *anything*. Drug dealers are infinitely creative with means of hiding their stashes, and narcs have to be one step ahead of the dealers. On the street, dealers don't always keep their drugs on them. Some dealers may work curbside with one or more associates holding their drugs in alleys or building entrances, shuttling the drugs to and from the curb as needed. If the dealer on the street is busted, the guys with the cash and drugs fade into the background before the officers can get to them. Solo dealers similarly establish drop points nearby, under loose bricks, in apartment mailboxes, inside electrical outlets or on the collars of their pit bulls. Those who do keep their merchandise on them put it in empty shells of personal electronics, inside hats or in their underwear. Many package their goods in balloons, condoms or plastic baggies so they can swallow the evidence.

The drug business runs on word of mouth and networks. Officers begin by cultivating informants, then use the most reliable of those to gain introductions to dealers. From there, the officers work the small transactions, building credibility until the dealers show them their systems and introduce them to their business partners. The best undercover detectives are those who can forget their uniformed backgrounds and stop subconsciously acting like cops — and be likable to their targets, because it's harder for even a drug dealer to kill a friend.

Active pursuit of drug users is a relatively low priority for the MPD. Most arrests for narcotics possession are made incidental to other offenses, such as traffic violations, and

Trait: Exposure, which ranges from 0 to •••••. Every cop starts with Exposure 0. For every six months the cop spends on the street, her player rolls Composure + Streetwise. With a failure, the cop's Exposure increases by 1. In addition, whenever the officer appears in a headline news story, her Exposure automatically rises by 1. Once acquired, Exposure can never be removed.

When a cop attempts to go undercover, her Exposure works against her. If she has Exposure, the first time she meets any major Storyteller character, the Storyteller rolls the character's Wits + Fame + the cop's Exposure. On a success, the character recognizes the cop for what she is.

The Merit Occultation (see **Mage: The Awakening**, p. 86) partially counteracts Exposure. A character's effective Exposure is reduced by her Occultation, so a character with Exposure ••• and Occultation •• functions as if she had Exposure •.

users can often negotiate in exchange for information about their suppliers. The department's real targets are the dealers and their distribution networks. Once a Narcotics squad gathers enough evidence to obtain a search warrant for a crack house, meth lab or distribution hub, the squad calls in overwhelming force. The MPD assumes all such warrants will involve violence, as virtually every drug dealer is well armed. Thus, the warrant entry usually forms around an ERU assault team (see p. 58). Every available uniformed officer in the area converges to establish a perimeter. If the warrant is being executed on a suspected lab, the Fire Department also turns out in case chemicals necessitate a HAZMAT response.

Exposure

After several years on the street, a Narcotics detective's face becomes too well-known to the area's denizens. As a result, Narcotics assignments are fluid, and officers transfer to different precincts' squads on a regular basis. When a narc finally becomes too well-known to safely work undercover anywhere in the city, he typically goes to a desk job or transfers to another detective unit. The Intelligence Unit actively recruits overexposed narcs so the police can exploit those officers' well-developed networks.

Optional Rule: Exposure

Players and Storytellers can track characters' street visibility as cops with an additional

Special Victims

Special Victims Unit (SVU) duty is one of the most emotionally demanding assignments in the MPD. SVU is tasked with cases involving rape, child molestation and child abuse, all of which inflict severe emotional suffering on the victims in addition to the physical trauma. Officers assigned to SVU must have both emotional fortitude and strong self-control.

While SV squads are assigned to each precinct, their desks at the precinct houses collect a lot of dust. Most Special Victims detectives keep mobile offices in their cars and work primarily out of the hospitals and women's shelters in their precincts. This speeds the detectives' response time when victims are brought in for medical treatment — often the first point at which the department is notified of the crime — and enables the detectives to conduct interviews in settings less intimidating than police facilities. Most SV partner teams are composed of one officer of each gender.

A rape investigation almost always begins when the victim reports the crime. Due to the intimate nature of the crime, few rapes have witnesses who can reliably report them, and doctor-patient confidentiality prohibits physicians from disclosing rapes involving adult victims if the patients don't want the stigma of an investigation. Once SV detectives are called, their first action is to gather statements from both the victim and the medical personnel who treated her (if any). With consent, the detectives also have a physician gather physical evidence from the victim's body and, if possible, dispatch a CST to gather additional evidence from the place where the rape occurred. SV investigations require an immense amount of paperwork, sometimes even more than homicides.

Information Crimes

The smallest and newest detective unit in the MPD is the Information Crimes Unit (ICU). Established in 2001, the ICU focuses on computer crimes and identity theft, though the unit does include a few veteran detectives who pick up the occasional forgery or counterfeiting case; locally committed fraud also falls into the ICU's bailiwick. Due to the decentralized nature of computer crime, the ICU is not broken up into squads by precinct. The whole unit is based at the Midway Forensic Science Center, going into the field only when necessary to execute warrants or interview complainants. In addition to being skilled at computer security and research, many ICU detectives also function as financial auditors and are capable of uncovering money laundering in business bookkeeping or suspiciously vague transactions in personal checking records.

Investigation of information crime at the local level is difficult at best. A hacker can steal a credit card number from half a world away, well outside the jurisdiction of federal authorities, let alone the MPD. Accordingly, the ICU finds itself in a liaison role far more than its leadership would like. The ICU maintains open lines of communication with the FBI and Secret Service, the federal law enforcement agencies that handle the majority of computer crime investigations within the United States.

Local fraud investigations almost always involve someone with whom the victim had business contact. Likely suspects include checkout clerks, loan officers or other people who misused legitimate access to the victim's financial information. For example, in 2003 MPD broke a major credit card theft ring involving a group of college students who'd all taken jobs at gas stations near campus and were stealing the store copies of the credit card receipts left by customers who paid at the pumps. In the case of locally occurring identity theft, family members are among the most common suspects. In such instances, juveniles often misappropriate their parents' identities to make illegal purchases.

Vice

Until the late '80s, the Vice Unit's responsibilities included drug investigations. When the War on Drugs heated up, Narcotics split off from Vice to become a separate unit, taking the lion's share of the funding and the best investigators. Today, Vice's responsibilities include so-called victimless crimes such as prostitution, unlicensed gambling, gunrunning and smuggling of non-narcotics contraband. On the other hand, many cops assert that there's no such thing as victimless crime.

Permanent Task Forces

As mentioned on p. 30, the MPD periodically assembles task forces from several bureaus to target specific crimes or criminals. Two task forces in particular have become permanent cross-disciplinary additions to the MPD Detective Bureau. Technically operating under the aegis of the Intelligence Unit, they are large and busy enough to serve as separate units in their own right.

Organized Crime Task Force

Traditionally, "organized crime" has meant "Mafia." In modern Midway, though, the category encompasses a wide array of formalized criminal organizations. Organized crime operations are involved in many illegal activities, including extortion and protection rackets, money laundering, insurance fraud, property crimes of all stripes, unlicensed gambling, smuggling, identity theft, prostitution, drug trafficking — in short, virtually any criminal enterprise that can be organized for greater efficiency. In addition, mid-ranking figures in these organizations are heavily involved in legal businesses such as licensed gambling, pornography and shipping.

Criminal organizations operate in the same manner as any other business. They identify (or create) a need that a segment of the population has, then provide goods or services to fulfill this need. At the high levels, most organized criminals are not assassins or leg-breakers but savvy businessmen and political deal-makers. The involvement of organized crime in many aspects of legitimate business leads detectives to refer to the hidden cut of profits that goes to organized criminals as "street tax." In investigations, one of the foremost rules is "follow the money." Thanks to the asset forfeiture provisions of the Racketeer Influenced and Corrupt Organizations Act (RICO), successful investigations allow the MPD to seize all property gained through criminal activity, hitting the organizations where they feel it the most.

These organizations exist to do business, but thrive on corruption. Most organized crime groups could not function effectively without bribing or threatening parts of the criminal justice system to look the other way. From uniformed cops and city prosecutors to judges and legislators, all levels of the government can be turned. Most officers on the task force have personal lists of individuals whom they know to be dirty but don't have the evidence to touch.

As organized crime operations cut across the lines that divide Detective Bureau tasking, the OCTF does likewise, recruiting talent from every detective unit as well as the Surveillance Bureau. Operations target street-level activities, but can rarely touch the upper echelons of the organizations, as captured junior members know the high price of loose lips. Most OCTF detectives believe that the best way to get to high-level organized criminals is through intensive investigation of murders performed under their orders.

This Thing of Ours

The Organized Crime Task Force has identified the following criminal organizations operating within Midway.

- **Gelati:** Small (20–30 members) Georgian organization split from the Russian Mafiya. Involved in extortion, gunrunning and trade in sex slaves kidnapped from Eastern Europe.

- **Black Cherry Blossom Society:** Mid-sized local chapter of a yakuza organization out of Hiroshima, formed around recent immigrants. Making inroads into virtually all organized crime areas of interest.
- **Mafia:** Primarily Italian with a few Greek and Irish members. Upward of 400 full-time personnel whose sole sources of income derive from illegal activities. Known or suspected to be involved in virtually everything under the sun except drug trafficking, but this may be changing.
- **Four Coin Triad:** Mid-sized (~100) chapter of global triad based in Hong Kong. Operations include shipping theft (especially tobacco products) and distribution of counterfeit consumer goods from China.
- **Redfellas:** Russian, 75+ members, many ex-Red Army. Brutally violent. Primary businesses include smuggling and heroin distribution.

Gang Task Force

The Washington County justice system defines a street gang as any group of three or more individuals with a common identifying name or symbol who jointly engage in criminal activity. Commonly, but not always, gangs are both ethnically and geographically based, drawing membership from a particular neighborhood. The most successful gangs are national or international in scope with chapters in multiple major cities.

Gang activity bears a superficial resemblance to organized crime (see previous), but on a smaller and often more violent scale. The most common gang offenses include vandalism, armed robbery (particularly home invasion), auto theft, narcotics trafficking and homicide. Typically, most gangs have a small core of experienced leaders, a larger group of junior members and an additional body of local associates, allies and hangers-on. The Gang Task Force's focus is the disruption of gangs' organizational structure by identifying leaders and arresting and prosecuting them for violent felonies or on drug charges. This task force also uses RICO statutes to seize gangs' financial and property assets, which occasionally brings the Gang Task Force into conflict with the OCTF.

In addition to law enforcement operations against gangs, the Gang Task Force engages in gang prevention in conjunction with the Washington County School District. This partnership provides sponsored after-school and summer programs, school presentations from teens who've been permanently disabled by gang violence, graffiti removal projects and community outreach efforts.

Streets of Midway

According to some estimates, Midway has twice as many gang members as police officers. The Gang Task Force lists the following gangs as the largest and most dangerous in Midway, but numerous other examples exist:

• **Los Tigres:** Hispanic gang composed solely of Mexican and Central American immigrants who (accurately or not) claim partial Aztec descent. Initiations incorporate poorly researched fragments of rituals based mainly on elements portrayed in Mexican pop culture. Partial to marijuana and natural hallucinogens, both distribution and use thereof, as well as armed robbery and auto theft. Tags depict a stylized snarling jaguar's head and colors are Jacksonville Jaguars athletic wear.

• **Shield of Thule:** Primarily white gang that originated in federal prisons, originally focused on mutual protection against black and Hispanic gangs. Now heavily tied to the Ku Klux Klan and various neo-Nazi and white supremacist groups. Some members are involved in Ásatrú (Odinism), a neo-pagan attempt at modern revival of Norse faith. Recently began recruiting white-collar criminals, offering protection from prison violence while providing white supremacist indoctrination.

• **Gold Blood Dragons:** Southeast Asian (primarily Vietnamese, Cambodian and Laotian) gang, heavily involved in home invasion and carjacking. Colors are red, black and yellow.

• **Seventh Street Set:** Exclusively black offshoot of a well-established nationally active gang that originated in Los Angeles. Strict codes of behavior delineate a rigid hierarchy with rigid discipline. Colors are a black and red bandanna, though members prefer to use tattoos for identification to frustrate police.

• **Midway Gangsta Front:** Multi-racial gang organized around Midway's inner city public schools. Average membership is considerably younger than that of most other local gangs. Started as a youth fad but rapid recruiting and juvenile peer pressure have catapulted the gang into full-scale criminal enterprises. Believed to have formed around a core of leaders whose elder siblings had been jailed for gang activity. Colors include logos of any of the city's professional athletic teams worn with a black bandana.

Evidence Analysis

When investigating major cases, detectives work closely with the crime scene technicians and criminalists of the Analysis Bureau. Although the Detective Bureau does train its sworn officers in evidence gathering, in-depth analysis is specialty work every bit as intensive as police investigation techniques. Virtually every violent felony investigation, as well as major property crimes investigations, calls on the resources of the Analysis Bureau. When a crime scene goes active, the detectives handling the case call the Analysis Bureau and request a crime scene technician. (MPD CSTs don't work the same schedules as patrol officers, but instead have four-day work weeks and additional on-call duty schedules.) If the crime scene involves a body, the Washington County Coroner's Office also sends a coroner's assistant to take custody of the decedent once the CST is done with her job.

Contrary to entertainment media presentations of crime scene technicians, crime scene technicians working for the Analysis Bureau spend enormous amounts of time compiling data and looking for clues. Television shows depicting one-hour, case-closed forensics have become a major hindrance for prosecutors, as jurors have unrealistic expectations of the amount of physical evidence that should be available for most crimes. Furthermore, even with the opening of the city's new crime lab, technicians are still sufficiently backlogged that detectives may have to wait days or weeks for a given piece of evidence analysis.

Chains of Custody

In order to defend the accuracy of evidence in court, prosecutors must be able to account for the evidence's entire history, starting at the crime scene and continuing forward through the actual introduction of the evidence in the courtroom. This history is known as the chain of custody, or the evidence trail. The first step in dealing with a crime scene is to take detailed photographs from every possible angle to establish the initial positioning of all evidence, including corpses.

Once the photographic record is complete, CSTs and detectives move in to catalog every piece of physical evidence. Sterile slides, swabs and plastic baggies are used for the secure collection of the smallest items. Once a piece of evidence is bagged, the CST or detective labels it with a unique identifier. This is where the chain of custody begins. From this point on, anyone taking or relinquishing possession of the item must record this transfer in the department's computerized evidence tracking system. An extensive set of rules govern where and how evidence must be stored at the crime lab or in an evidence lockup. This allows investigators to establish the whereabouts of each piece of evidence at any time during the investigation, as well as the identities of everyone who had access to the piece of evidence.

Task	Skill	Work	Turnaround
Autopsy/determine cause of death	Medicine	8 hours	3 days
Ballistic matching/identify firearm	Science	8 hours	1 month
Blood toxicology/list substances in bloodstream	Medicine	8 hours	3 days
Cast/identify footprint or tire track	Investigation	2 days	1 month
Catalog computer data	Computer	12 hours	2 weeks
Chemical analysis/identify unknown substance	Science	3 days	2 months
Decrypt Computer data	computer	12 hours	2 weeks
Dental identification of body (confirming a suspected identity)	Medicine	8 hours	2 days
Dental identification of body (victim totally unknown)	Medicine	2 months	1 year
Detect chemical residue at scene	Investigation	4 hours	8 hours
DNA matching	Medicine	2 weeks	7 months
Fiber/trace matching	Crafts	4 days	3 months
Fingerprint matching	Investigation	30 minutes	2 hours
Fingerprinting at crime scene	Investigation	2 hours	6 hours
Verify authenticity of possibly forged item	Crafts	1 week	3 months
Voice analysis/voiceprint matching	Computer	1 day	2 months

Evidence Analysis Mechanics

Preliminary evidence work can take place at a crime scene, but intensive analysis has to happen in a well-equipped crime lab. If the characters don't have the leverage to bump up the lab's priority on a given procedure or the skills and access necessary to do the work themselves, they'll have to wait for test results. Presented here are the skills and working time required for various evidence analysis tasks, as well as the average turnaround time for lab work that characters don't handle themselves. All rolls use Intelligence plus the indicated Skill (see chart)

In addition to the detailed work listed above, cops can perform some preliminary field tests themselves. Every patrol and traffic vehicle's standard equipment includes a field drug test kit. Checking a given substance sample to see if it contains narcotics takes about five minutes and a Wits + Investigation roll. Also, every officer is trained to take a suspect's fingerprints as part of the booking process, requiring a Wits + Investigation roll to generate useful fingerprints. (A field fingerprinting kit imparts a +2 modifier to this roll, while the more sophisticated desk arrays at precinct houses or in jails offer a +4 modifier.)

issued weapons (any MPD CST who carried a gun while working a crime scene would be fired for allowing chemical contamination of evidence), and they are empowered to make arrests. In a Storytelling setting, CST characters can expect to sit back and watch sworn officers do a lot of the work.

With that being said, CSTs are still viable characters, as their varied technical skills can grant them access to clues that sworn officers may not have the training to find or the knowledge to recognize as significant. Most of the arguments for putting together officers from different branches of the department work equally well for CSTs. To be hired as an MPD CST, a character must meet the following minimum standards:

• Attributes: Intelligence 3, Wits 3 and Composure 3
• Mental Skills: Academics 1, Computer 1, Investigation 3 and a total of 3 points between Medicine and Science
• Psych Profile: Morality 6, Willpower 5 and no severe derangements

Character Options: Crime Scene Technicians

The success of forensic science television shows makes CSTs popular character choices. As described above, the reality of CST work is somewhat different from Hollywood's portrayals. As civilian employees of the MPD, CSTs are not

When Cops Call 911: ERU

The MPD Emergency Response Unit (a kinder, gentler name for SWAT) is built around four 12-man tactical squads (Red, Green, Gold and Blue). Each squad is divided into two five-man assault teams and a pair of sharpshooters. In addition, the MPD's three bomb technicians and their technical support personnel are attached to the ERU as the EOD (Explosive Ordnance Disposal) squad, though they most frequently find themselves working with the Midway Fire Marshal's office to investigate arson cases. The ERU's non-combat assets include the Negotiation squad, which includes three psychologists specializing in crisis negotiation and their administrative staff, and the Surveillance squad, which collects a half-dozen electronic intelligence specialists who can wire an entire building for sound and video in under an hour. The MFD also provides a half-dozen paramedics, all cross-trained or former cops, who deploy with the ERU to provide combat medical support. Other attached personnel include a department lawyer and a public affairs officer from the Administration Division.

Culturally, the ERU is one of the most tightly knit groups in the Midway Police Department; the unit has its own traditions and special events (cookouts, bowling nights, etc.). The commanders demand frequent cross-training from sworn officers and civilian employees, and it's not unusual to see a bomb technician studying behavioral profiling or a psychologist engaging qualification targets with a submachine gun. Outside observers whose images of gun-toting maverick cops comes from movie portrayals of SWAT operations are surprised at the restraint and professionalism of ERU personnel. Much of this comes from the unit's high degree of readiness and constant training. Despite having some of the most hazardous duty in the department, the ERU has a lower rate of serious duty-related injuries than the Patrol Division. Training injuries are another story, and it's rare for a tactical squad to have all 12 members completely healthy. The psychological screening process to join the ERU heavily favors officers with stable marriages, as such domestic situations provide an additional degree of emotional support and act as a brake on wanton risk-taking.

Selection

The ERU holds tryouts in May of every year. An officer who wants to apply for the unit must be in peak physical condition. He must have a clean service record (citizen complaints are acceptable, but significant disciplinary actions can disqualify him) with at least three years of experience in the Patrol Bureau. In addition, he must pass psychological screening to ensure that he is capable of making life-or-death decisions in a combat situation and knows not only when to shoot but when *not* to shoot.

The tryout process itself is a comprehensive evaluation of the applicant's physical fitness, marksmanship and judgment. Tryouts begin with the "ERU Pentathlon," an obstacle course beginning with a two-mile run, followed by a 120-foot vertical rappel, an obstacle course, a timed test of pull-ups, push-ups and sit-ups and a handgun marksmanship course. Candidates wear 40 pounds of body armor and tactical gear through the entire course.

Callouts

In ERU parlance, a "callout" is any event that requires deployment of a tactical squad or a bomb technician. At least one assault team is on duty at any time, training and analyzing intelligence on high-threat criminals and locations, and the rest of the tactical squad to which that team belongs must be able to assemble on-site within 45 minutes of receiving a callout. Commanders regularly stage drills to check officer readiness, and missing one callout deadline puts an officer on probation for six months, during which time missing a second one puts the officer back on the streets.

When a callout occurs, the ready assault team deploys to the callout location in ERU vehicles that contain the entire squad's weapons and specialized equipment. The initial squad sets up a rally point a few blocks away from the incident, and the rest of the ERU responders converge on this point to gear up and assess the situation. If the callout is in response to an immediate threat such as a bomb or a barricaded hostage-taker, the ranking ERU officer has the authority to take command of all patrol assets on-scene until a precinct or bureau captain arrives.

Most callouts do not end in shootouts. During the last calendar year, the ERU had 62 callouts, only three of which required responding officers to discharge their firearms. Four other incidents required the use of tear gas or distraction devices (flash-bang grenades), and eight were bomb threats. The remaining incidents were resolved through negotiation or the display of force.

Regular Deployments

After responding to callouts as needed, the ERU's next most common activity is providing muscle for detectives who need to serve high-threat warrants or otherwise kick in doors. In such an operation, which occurs about twice a week, a full tactical squad deploys to provide overwhelming strength (and to break the monotony of training).

The high-tech equipment and armament of the ERU can be a potent recruiting tool for the department as a whole. Currently, Gold Team's Second Squad is the most photogenic group of Midway ERU officers, and these five men find themselves the target of jokes from the rest of the unit when they're assigned to make an appearance at a local career fair.

During major sporting events, parades and political rallies, all of the ERU is on the streets — or on the rooftops, or in helicopters or ready to roll from hiding spots in parking garages. The unit's intensive study of possible trouble spots in the city enables the ERU to play a coordinating role in any event that requires heightened security. The unfortunate side effect of this is the need for ERU commanders to liaise with federal agents.

One downside to long-term ERU duty is an officer's loss of contact with the street. To counteract this, ERU policy requires every tactical squad member to return to a patrol assignment for a three-month stretch after every two years with the unit. This is the least popular provision of the unit for patrol officers who joined the ERU to get off the streets, many of whom argue that they lose proficiency in ERU-specific skills while chasing shoplifters and stopping speeders.

Equipment

The ERU has a wide variety of equipment not available to a patrol officer or detective. Most of these items have several pages of department regulations governing their use.

Weapons: Similar to virtually every police tactical team in the United States, the ERU has adopted the Heckler & Koch MP5 submachine gun as a general-purpose weapon. Colt M4A1 assault carbines supplement the MP5s for situations in which longer range may be necessary. Snipers use Remington Model 700s. Tear gas and flash-bang grenades are available for use against barricaded suspects, as are 37mm tactical launchers for firing smoke or tear gas canisters.

Armor: Tactical officers on a callout start suiting up with a Nomex undersuit, gloves and hood, similar to those worn by firefighters, to protect against chemical splashes and flames. Over this goes heavy Type III body armor with ballistic plates, providing protection for the torso against most rifle bullets and covering the thighs and upper arms against shrapnel and pistol-caliber ammunition. A ballistic helmet with a clear polymer face shield completes the ensemble. Most support personnel wear standard-issue vests (see p. 69), but the unit's attached paramedics don the full loadout in case they have to go into a firefight to save someone's life.

Vehicles: Each of the four tactical squads has two unmarked, large SUVs of varying models to transport its personnel, as well as a large panel van to haul gear. In addition, the unit as a whole has a large RV set up as a field command post for extended operations. All vehicles have undergone full security upgrades with concealed ballistic protection and bullet-resistant polycarbonate windows.

Communications: The ERU is the only group in the MPD with fully encrypted radio communications. The military-grade Motorola systems are a relatively new addition to the unit's inventory, acquired in 2002 after a failed raid on a suspected cocaine distribution ring turned up radio intercept equipment that the gang had used to monitor the ERU's preparations. Following successful field use of these radios, the Police Commissioner is trying to acquire Department of Homeland Security funds to secure and modernize the rest of the MPD's communications.

Character Options: ERU Characters

Realistically speaking, ERU duty is not something that a starting character can enter due to the physical demands of the job. To apply for the selection process, a character must meet the following minimum standards:

- Attributes: all Mental 2, all Physical 3 and Composure 2
- Physical Skills: Athletics 2 and Firearms 3
- Initiative Modifier: 6
- Psych Profile: Morality 5, Willpower 5 and no derangements that affect decision-making or combat capability

The isolated nature of the unit makes integrating an ERU assaulter or sharpshooter difficult — the team roles most likely to appeal to players — into an MPD story. The ERU operates as a entity unto itself and doesn't do a lot of investigative work or regular patrol duty. The best way to plausibly add a lone ERU operator to a mixed group of characters is to assign him to his periodic rotation back to regular patrol duty. Another option is to make such a character one member of an ERU tactical squad that's frequently called on to support a task force to which the rest of the characters belong.

By the Book: Policy and Legality

Police work is governed by a massive body of regulations and case law. While it's not an officer's job to be aware of every major federal case, smart officers who don't want their arrests thrown out of court do try to stay on top of the latest significant rulings. In addition, MPD policy is a constantly evolving collection of department decisions that govern every aspect of a cop's professional conduct and tactical decisions. The following high (or low) points are the major considerations that an officer has to take into account during the course of his duties.

Officer's Discretion

It's a physical impossibility for police officers to enforce every law in existence simultaneously. The MPD recognizes this, as well as the fact that its personnel spend much of their time operating independently and making decisions on their own. Accordingly, the department allows officers to exercise their own discretion in issuing misdemeanor citations or making arrests for non-felony warrants. (Felony warrants always require an arrest.) Most officers base their decisions on whether to issue a citation, make an arrest or just issue a verbal warning on the following criteria regarding the subject:

- the subject's demeanor and politeness to the officer
- the subject's history of prior offenses
- how much of a danger the subject appears to be to the officer or the public

• whether the negative effects of an enforcement action would outweigh the positive ones

In practice, officer's discretion allows a cop to waste neither city time nor taxpayer dollars in arresting a vagrant for sleeping on a steam grate or citing a driver for going 47 mph in a 45 mph zone. Abuse of this privilege, however, can lead to an IAB investigation, particularly if an officer were to blow off the arrest of a subject who is later involved in a felony. Also, officer's discretion doesn't extend to outstanding arrest warrants. Unless a suspect has an immediate medical emergency, he's going to jail once the officer runs the subject's identification.

Professional Courtesy

Broadly stated, professional courtesy is the principle of exercising officer's discretion in law enforcement involving other cops or emergency personnel. The general rule of thumb in the MPD is that "cops don't write other cops," reflecting that professional courtesy most often comes into play in traffic enforcement against off-duty officers. Police officers stopped for minor violations within the MPD's jurisdiction rarely receive citations if they hand over their department IDs with their driver's licenses.

Professional courtesy also comes into play outside actual law enforcement. The nature of the Job makes for something of a closed society (as described on p. 78), and professional courtesy plays into this in the form of openness and honesty for "insiders," even if they aren't members of an officer's own agency. For example, MPD policy officially prohibits passengers, but few patrol sergeants will discipline officers who offer a lift to out-of-town cops who flag them down for directions.

Professional courtesy does have its limits. Officer's discretion ends at arrest-worthy offenses. If cops have to intervene in a domestic violence assault against an officer's spouse or pull him over for DUI, that officer is going to jail regardless of professional courtesy. In addition, most cops' willingness to extend PC ends if the officers they pulled over have lousy attitudes. "Courtesy" goes both ways.

Other Departments: PC

Professional courtesy is not a constant, and it's a hot-button issue for many cops. Few departments have written policies on it, and standards vary widely depending on local law enforcement culture. Generally speaking, the MPD's PC culture portrayed above follows the point of view most common in the northeastern United States.

Cops in southern and western states are less likely to exercise PC toward officers from other jurisdictions.

Constitutional Issues

Several provisions of the Bill of Rights address the rights of a suspected criminal. The MPD educates all officers on these issues as part of their academy training, out of concern for both department liability and the validity of all arrests.

First and foremost in the public eye are the rights commonly referred to as Miranda rights, after the Supreme Court case of *Miranda v. Arizona*. In this case, Ernesto Miranda was arrested in 1966 for stealing eight dollars in cash from a Phoenix bank. After two hours of police questioning, however, he confessed to the kidnapping and rape of an 18-year-old girl. The Supreme Court decision reversed his conviction on the grounds that he had not been advised of his constitutional rights to counsel and to avoid self-incrimination. The initial decision was controversial, but the ruling has since become an integral part of the American criminal justice system. Subsequent to Miranda, all arresting officers must advise suspects of these rights as soon as the arrest occurs *if the officers intend to question the suspects about any criminal activity, and before any such questioning takes place*. In practice, virtually any arrestee will be subject to questioning at some point, so most departments require their officers to Mirandize all suspects as a matter of policy.

The Miranda Card

No legal ruling exists regarding the exact phrasing of a Miranda warning, so the precise wording varies between jurisdictions. The MPD has standardized the following phrasing, which is printed in English and Spanish on a laminated card issued to every officer:

You have the right to remain silent. If you give up that right, anything you say may be used against you in a court of law. You have the right to consult with an attorney and to have one present during questioning. If you cannot afford an attorney, one will be provided for you. If you choose to talk to a police officer, you have the right to stop the interview at any time. Do you understand these rights as I have read them to you?

The Miranda warning does not include the "right" to a phone call. However, MPD policy grants every arrestee the right to two monitored phone calls, each no more than 10 minutes in length, once the arrest paperwork is complete.

The Right to Remain Silent

The Fifth Amendment of the Constitution guarantees the right to remain silent via the provision that "no person . . . shall be compelled in any criminal case to be a witness against himself." More than 200 years of judicial precedent states that not only does this prevent a defendant from being forced to testify at his own trial, but this provision also prevents prosecutors from admitting the defendant's illegally obtained confession as evidence. The Miranda ruling clarified that this right is not limited to forced confessions but extends to fully voluntary ones made while in police custody. Unless police inform a suspect of his right to remain silent and the possibility that anything he says may be used in court, any incriminating statements he makes, no matter how voluntary, are inadmissible evidence. This extends not only to suspects who have been formally arrested and charged but also to individuals police are detaining for questioning. However, circumstances in which a suspect is obviously free to leave, such as interviews in a suspect's own home, do not fall under this right.

In addition, this right excludes statements made only to law enforcement personnel during the course of questioning. Statements made to other individuals, such as reporters, friends or cellmates, are admissible unless the witness was actively working with police to elicit a statement against the suspect's own interest. Likewise, statements not made in response to actual police questioning (such as the suspect encountered near a downtown murder scene who blurted out "I didn't kill anyone" to officers who had pulled him aside for questioning when he had not yet been told that a murder occurred) are generally admissible.

Regardless, the legal effect of violating a suspect's right to avoid self-incrimination is that any statements she makes prior to being advised of her rights cannot be admitted in court. Violations may also fall under the "fruit of the poisonous tree" doctrine, which requires evidence acquired as a result of violations of this right to likewise be excluded. For example, if a suspect who has not been informed of his rights tells police where a murder weapon is hidden, the weapon itself may not be introduced as evidence.

The Right to an Attorney

The right to consult with an attorney falls under the Sixth Amendment, which states that an accused "shall enjoy the right . . . to have the assistance of counsel for his defense." Similar to the right to remain silent, the right to counsel applies from the moment of a suspect's arrest. From that point on, the suspect may invoke this right, and any questioning must cease until the attorney arrives. However, this request must be unambiguous. Legal precedent holds that vague statements such as "maybe I shouldn't say anything until I talk to a lawyer" do not constitute requests for a lawyer. Once an attorney is present, officers may no longer interrogate the suspect on her own unless she voluntarily waives this right by specifically requesting to speak to them without counsel. In addition, a suspect's statements made outside the presence of her lawyer may be admissible if they are not in response to actual questions or are not directed toward law enforcement officers or those working for them.

Where Miranda Ends

As noted above, violations of a suspect's Miranda rights only have the effect of excluding her statements (and evidence derived from those statements) from trial. Contemporary courts generally interpret this rule in a fairly technical manner. Thus, police may obtain a confession from a suspect before reading her rights to her, then ask her to repeat the confession after they've Mirandized her. The second confession is admissible, along with all evidence derived from it, unless the defendant can prove that the police coerced her into it.

An officer cannot arrest someone for refusing to answer a potentially incriminating question on the basis of his Fifth Amendment rights. However, an officer can arrest a suspect who refuses to comply with a lawful order (such as demanding identification from a driver stopped for a suspected traffic violation).

Officers are not required to inform suspects of constitutional rights not covered by the Miranda warning. For example, in a traffic stop, an officer may request to search a vehicle without informing the driver of her right to refuse (see p. 43). If the driver consents to the search, any evidence found is admissible. The fact that the driver gave consent to the search without being told she could refuse does not transform her permission into any sort of "implied confession" in violation of the Fifth Amendment.

Outside the Bill of Rights and the Miranda warning, cops are free to use a wide variety of (sometimes questionable) tactics to manipulate suspects out of relying on their Miranda rights. The Miranda case's unspoken assumption is that once a suspect has been advised of her rights, she is held to fully understand them, and police may use almost any non-violent means to induce her to forego those constitutional protections. For example, an officer may read a suspect her rights, then urge her to "come clean," warn her that asking for a lawyer may make her "look guilty" or even lie outright to her (such as telling her that a witness has identified her or an alleged accomplice is about to accept a plea bargain).

Search and Seizure

The Fourth Amendment governs the right to security against unreasonable search and seizure. The key word in this situation is "unreasonable," and Fourth Amendment case law focuses on the legitimacy of a given search or seizure. Generally speaking, an officer may not legally search any area in which a suspect has a reasonable expectation of privacy unless the officer either has a search warrant or obtains permission to search from someone with the authority to grant that permission.

To acquire a search warrant, the officer must sign an affidavit stating that he has reason to believe that items for which he wants to search can be found at the target location. The affidavit must be specific and must articulate the officer's basis for his belief (though this basis can come from an unnamed or anonymous informant, so long as the officer can swear to facts supporting the source's reliability). The warrant itself authorizes a search only within the scope of the affidavit. For example, an MPD officer who wanted to search a house for a shotgun used in a murder could not search in containers that are obviously too small to contain a shotgun. Thus, detectives tend to draft warrants to target the smallest possible relevant evidence — in the above case, shotgun ammunition — so they have a legal basis for as intensive a search as possible.

Warrant-Less Searches

An officer may still search without a warrant if someone with authority to permit a search (or even *apparent* authority to do so, such as an adult guest in a house) consents to the search. If such consent is given, any evidence found is admissible. Even if the individual who gave consent didn't actually have a legal basis for doing so, the search is constitutional if the officer had a reasonable belief to the contrary.

Searches of publicly accessible items are always legal. One excellent example is garbage. So long as a garbage can is on its owner's property, officers can't search the can without consent. However, as soon as the owner takes that can to the curb, he places the garbage can in the public eye (and implicitly relinquishes the can's contents to sanitation workers), and it's a fair target for a warrant-less search.

Wiretaps and Surveillance

Police surveillance falls under the same general rules as searches. In order to conduct surveillance operations inside a target's home or anywhere else where he has a reasonable expectation of privacy, officers must obtain a warrant on the basis that they believe the target will discuss criminal acts in a specific location. However, conversations held in public — including at pay phones — do not have this expectation of privacy. Likewise, if a target leaves his blinds open, "anyone" could see inside, and police may legitimately observe and photograph through that window.

Personal Searches

One exception to warrant and consent requirements is the Terry search, known after the Supreme Court case of *Terry v. Ohio*, which definitively legitimized a type of personal search. The Terry case held that an officer is legally entitled to frisk anyone the officer meets for weapons if the officer has any reason to believe that he might be in danger or that the suspect might be armed. If such a search leads the officer to discover other evidence, such as a vial of crack that he feels in the suspect's pocket, the officer can then order the suspect to empty the contents of his pockets. Any evidence discovered through this inventory is then legally admissible.

An officer is also legally entitled to make a search incident into an arrest, which permits him to thoroughly search an arrestee. This is advisable to both preserve evidence and maintain officer safety. During the arrest and booking process, a suspect can expect to be searched multiple times: during the

initial arrest, during the processing of the arrest paperwork at the precinct house and upon transfer to the city jail.

Vehicle Searches

If an arrestee was in a vehicle immediately prior to the arrest, the officer may search the area of the vehicle immediately accessible to the arrestee. This search is intended to be primarily for weapons, but any other evidence in that area is also admissible, even if the suspect isn't the vehicle's owner or operator.

When the department impounds a vehicle, the officer is also authorized to itemize its contents. This is ostensibly for the purpose of ensuring that none of the owner's possessions disappear while the vehicle is in police custody. However, despite the fact that this search is not primarily occurring for the purpose of finding evidence, any evidence uncovered is admissible.

Arrests and Probable Cause

The Fourth Amendment also governs seizure of a person, which must also be reasonable. In this case, reasonable arrests depend on the principle of probable cause. This means that a sensible person (such as an average adult) in the position of the arresting officer would have reason to believe that a crime had been committed and that the arrestee was the person who committed it.

An officer may make an arrest under one of two circumstances. First, a judge must sign an arrest warrant finding that probable cause for the arrest exists. This occurs when officers conducting an investigation present that judge with sufficient evidence against the subject of the requested warrant. Second, the officer personally observes the arrestee committing a crime or arrives soon enough after the crime's commission to believe that the arrestee is the guilty party.

No minimum severity of crime exists to govern when officers may or may not arrest a subject. Theoretically, police may arrest a suspect for committing a misdemeanor as insignificant as eating on a subway in violation of a municipal code forbidding such actions. Once the arrest occurs, police may conduct a standard search to ensure officer safety, and may question the suspect regarding activities other than the crime for which she was arrested.

MPD Arrest Procedures

As with every police department, the MPD requires arresting officers to Mirandize suspects as soon as the officers place the suspects under arrest if the officers intend to interview the suspects. The suspect then goes to the precinct house and into a holding cell until his arrest paperwork is complete, at which point officers fingerprint him and give him a second reading of his Miranda rights. If the arrest involved DWI, the suspect has the opportunity to take a second breathalyzer test at this time.

If officers have probable cause to believe that a blood sample will provide material evidence of a crime — usually

sexual assault — they may obtain a search warrant for a suspect's blood, then call a paramedic or nurse to extract a blood sample. If anyone has been exposed to the suspect's blood or other bodily fluids, the suspect must be tested for HIV. In the latter event, an involuntary blood draw is permissible pursuant to court cases that classify such exposure as attempted homicide.

The holding cells are only a temporary solution, as precinct houses aren't set up for long-term storage of prisoners. If a prisoner's arrest was for a minor offense, he has proper identification and he has no outstanding warrants and doesn't appear to be a flight risk, officers will release him with a Court Appearance Ticket, which is a summons to appear in court at a future date. However, most arrestees have a destination other than home. If they aren't being held for interrogation or additional paperwork, they're bound for "downtown."

A prisoner who remains in police custody for more than a few hours after his arrest paperwork and background checks are complete is loaded into a prisoner van and taken to the city jail. Here, the MPD hands him over to the custody of the Washington County Department of Corrections. State law requires that the prisoner to be brought before a judge within 24 hours for arraignment, after meeting with his attorney. At this point, the prisoner is out of the department's custody, though an investigation against him is just beginning if he's been arrested for a serious crime.

If a prisoner requires medical attention (or claims to require it), MPD policy requires officers to transport him to an emergency room and keep him under guard until a physician releases the prisoner to police custody. The death of a suspect while in custody is guaranteed to have civil rights groups up in arms about police brutality, regardless of the amount of evidence the department has of his offenses and prior medical condition, so proper medical care is a significant liability issue. In practice, this also gives officers the ability to grant a suspect the enjoyable experience of a stomach pumping if he claims to be experiencing medical complications after swallowing crack rocks. A suspect who believes he'll have an easier time escaping custody at a hospital is disabused of this notion once he finds himself handcuffed to a stretcher.

In Play: Obtaining a Warrant

Even if an officer feels that he has overwhelming evidence against a suspect, the officer is not always assured of getting a warrant. Some judges take an adversarial view of requests for warrants without what they consider probable cause, which may not always agree with the officer's own belief in probable cause.

Acquiring a search or arrest warrant requires at least 30 minutes and a Manipulation + Politics roll. The degree of evidence the character possesses may affect this roll: only hearsay from unreliable sources (−4), flimsy circumstantial evidence (−2), extensive circumstantial evidence (−1), testimony from a reliable witness (+1), testimony from multiple reliable witnesses (+2), significant physical evidence such as video footage (+2) or incontrovertible physical proof such as DNA evidence testing (+3).

The arresting officer doesn't have to be the one to request the warrant. It's perfectly acceptable for one detective to go find a judge while the others wait around a fax machine for a copy of the signed paperwork.

Use of Force

Similar to all departments, the MPD has a use of force policy that regulates the degree of force that an officer can use in response to varying threats. The policy establishes a continuum of force that proceeds from minimal to lethal force. An officer is legally entitled to use one level of force greater than that used or threatened by an opponent. The MPD's continuum of force, from lowest to highest, is:

• Verbal commands
• "Soft hand": compliance holds (arm locks, pressure points)
• Chemical irritant: pepper spray
• Non-lethal armament: electrical stun weapon
• "Hard hand": punches, kicks
• Impact weapons: batons, electrical stun weapons

• Lethal force

Thus, if a suspect refuses to comply with an officer's commands, the officer is fully within his rights to put the suspect in an arm lock to gain that compliance. Likewise, if a suspect is brandishing a baseball bat, the officer may draw his sidearm and threaten to shoot the offender if he doesn't put down the large, blunt implement.

In addition, officers are entitled to use deadly force to stop fleeing violent felony suspects, even if the suspects aren't using force at the time. The legal issues for this decision revolve around the suspect's potential to commit additional violent acts if not immediately stopped.

A large body of legal precedent has established that police officers are never under any obligation to sustain injury, and the threat of imminent violence is sufficient for them to act preemptively with appropriate levels of force. MPD trainers drill this into new recruits as the "no fair fights" principle. Nothing requires an officer to drop his pepper spray and engage in a fistfight, or to put his baton up against a knife. Officers have access to different weapons so they can calibrate their responses to the situation at hand.

Liability for improper use of force is an ongoing concern for all police departments, and MPD officers do have some reservations about how far the department will back them up on their decisions in the field. In addition, the mandatory IAB investigation into any firearm discharge during the line of duty (see below) is an intimidating prospect.

Twenty-One Feet

The MPD teaches the Tueller Standard, named for the police officer who first articulated the principle that a subject armed with a melee weapon is capable of covering 21 feet and striking a killing blow in the 1.5 seconds that it takes a trained officer to draw a handgun and fire in self-defense. This is the standard for use of lethal force against suspects armed with knives, clubs and other potentially lethal hand weapons. Practically speaking, MPD instructors teach that strong or fast adversaries are dangerous at much greater ranges, and a blood-drenched suspect swinging a fire axe in the middle of the street is likely to be shot at greater ranges if he doesn't surrender.

Drawing Down

FBI statistics say 40% of police officers will never have to draw their sidearms against other people, but most MPD cops believe that those 40% all live in small towns or have desk jobs. In the MPD, displaying a gun is a weekly, if not nightly, event for patrol officers who need the threat of deadly force to gain compliance from a suspect. Officers who work the rural fringes of Washington County may have to use their weapons on a weekly basis to put down injured or dangerous animals — and policy requires a crime report for any shots an officer has to fire, which leads to some interesting death scene sketches.

Practically speaking, unholstering a gun preemptively is a survival technique for cops on the street. The MPD doesn't teach gunslinging quick-draw techniques, which would be vastly less effective with retention holsters anyway. Instead, officers are expected to anticipate threatening situations whenever possible. A common tactic used during traffic stops that aren't high-threat but nevertheless arouse an officer's suspicion is to draw and hold the gun behind the thigh while approaching the suspect vehicle.

Warning and Wounding

MPD policy states that officers are entitled to use lethal force "to eliminate the threat of lethal force." No mention is specifically made of killing a suspect, but department instructors teach their students that any firearm is deadly and any shot fired has to be fired with the understanding that it will kill. Officers learn to always aim for the center of a target, and going against this deeply seated muscle memory in the middle of a gunfight takes more concentration and forethought than most can muster. The idea of blasting a gun out of an opponent's hand or putting a round through a fleeing felon's calf is best reserved for the silver screen, not the streets of Midway. Likewise, the MPD considers warning shots a violation of policy and a waste of ammunition. If a cop feels the need to fire a warning shot, the suspect is already sufficiently dangerous and non-compliant that the bullet should have gone into him instead of into the air.

After the Shooting Stops

Any use of lethal force by an MPD officer requires an Internal Affairs investigation to determine whether the officer acted properly and the extent of the department's liability, if any. IAB detectives conduct a preliminary interview with the officer as soon as possible, either at the scene of the event or at his precinct house. He then goes on paid suspension while IAB further investigates. The mandatory minimum length of such a suspension is three days to give the officer time to deal with the emotional aftermath of the event, even if IAB absolves him of any wrongdoing after a cursory review of the evidence. If he acted legally but outside the department's use of force policy, he may be subject to disciplinary action. If IAB's review indicates that the officer violated the law, he can expect to be arrested once the investigation generates enough evidence for a warrant.

Prisoner Restraint

Similar to many MPD policies, the one on restraint of prisoners attempts to strike a balance between officer safety and department public image. At present, officer safety is winning this fight, despite public outcry over the occasional handcuffed grandmother. MPD officers are entitled to handcuff anyone they're detaining for questioning, even if only for a few minutes, and routinely do — just because someone acts compliant doesn't mean he won't stab the officer in the neck with a pencil. Once a suspect is arrested, handcuffing is mandatory until he's booked into the jail and leaves the officer's custody.

If handcuffs aren't sufficient to restrain a particularly violent prisoner, patrol sergeants also carry four-point locking restraints in their cars. These allow officers to hog-tie a suspect, securing both wrists and ankles behind his back. Most sergeants also carry "spit bags," hoods with locking necks for prisoners who insist on spitting saliva, blood, tobacco juice, etc. at officers. As both pieces of equipment present suffocation hazards, officers must be able to document the need for their use.

Unless a suspect has an obvious medical reason to be cuffed in front, cops always put the cuffs on behind his back. As instructors put it, if someone's hands are cuffed in front of him, the only things he can't do are jump rope and wipe his ass, and cuffs make a good improvised garrote. The only other time a prisoner is fortunate enough to have his hands cuffed in front is for court appearances when he will have to sign paperwork.

Standard-Issue Equipment

The MPD's equipment policies are rigid due to liability reasons. All department-issued gear has gone through extensive evaluation to determine suitability for street use. An officer who replaces department-issued gear with something he liked in a catalog puts lives at risk if untested equipment fails at a critical moment. Retention holsters need to keep criminals' hands off officers' guns; handcuffs must hold prisoners securely. Although officers may supplement their equipment with personal purchases of additional tools (clipboards, flashlights, digital voice recorders), replacing critical department-issue duty gear is forbidden. This has additional practical considerations above and beyond the legal ones.

Weapons are of particular concern to the department. The MPD's training courses cover all aspects of the use and maintenance of everything officers are supposed to carry, from their pepper spray to the longarms in their cruisers. Officers must be able to testify in court that they acted in accordance with this training. The department also chooses armament with a balance of effectiveness and public safety in mind. If the department suffers a civil suit due to property damage or the injury or death of civilians, the department had best be able to prove that it mitigated risks as best it could. The MPD will not look kindly on an officer who "upgrades" to an excessively powerful weapon and shoots a citizen through a suspect.

Alternate Sidearms

The MPD does allow a few options for certain cases in which the standard-issue Glock may not be an officer's preferred weapon. Many older cops joined the MPD when the Beretta Model 92 was the standard sidearm, and a few cops first shot their qualifications on Colt Pythons. In both cases, an officer whose original service weapon is still in good repair is allowed to carry the weapon on duty.

A backup gun carried on duty must be wholly concealable on an officer's uniform, which limits choices to small-frame handguns with limited ammunition capacity that can go in a pocket, ankle or small-of-the-back holster. The gun must pass inspection with the department armorers before an officer is authorized to carry the weapon, and the officer must pass marksmanship qualification with it. The gun must also be of a caliber that the department considers sufficient for emergency use without being excessive: no smaller than .38 caliber and no larger than .45, with .41 and .44 Magnum excluded and a minimum capacity of five rounds. Off-duty guns carry no such restrictions.

Many officers who aren't particularly interested in guns beyond "does mine work?" buy a single handgun to use as a backup gun while in uniform and a primary one while off-duty. For undercover officers who don't want their Glocks to identify them as cops to their criminal associates, the same caliber and qualification standards apply to personally owned weapons carried as primary sidearms.

World of Darkness: Quality Control

Equipment is one of the two areas in which an ill-funded department suffers the most (the other being training). In the World of Darkness, institutions tend toward one of two extremes: well established and well-off or crumbling and impoverished. The MPD presented in these pages falls under the former, but a Storyteller who wants to make cop characters feel a little more overmatched on the streets can easily flip the switch to present a department that can barely scrape together its annual budget. Replace the high-tech polymer Glocks with aging Beretta Model 92s or Colt Pythons with worn-out barrels and metal fatigue, swap leather duty belts for threadbare and abrasive nylon, add five years and 150,000 miles to every cruiser and take away most of the computers.

Off-Duty Policies

The starting salary for a patrol officer is roughly equivalent to that of any other entry-level government employee — minimal. Recognizing this, the MPD allows its personnel to moonlight during their off hours, so long as the secondary employment neither interferes with their scheduled duties nor reflects negatively on the department's public image. Officers may use department property or wear their uniforms only while working within the department's jurisdiction. Most cops who take extra jobs work security for malls or major events or provide traffic control at highway construction sites.

In practice, the only law enforcement that off-duty MPD cops can do is security work. They aren't on shift and under department supervision, and thus can't conduct investigations, engage in high-speed pursuits or make traffic stops. Officers must also request authorization for any off-duty employment, and a captain is unlikely to allow one of his detective squads to hire itself out as freelance monster-hunters. Getting caught doing unsupervised and unauthorized work is grounds for an IAB investigation into corruption and possible criminal activity.

While professional courtesy gets MPD officers out of most minor traffic violations in the Midway area and surrounding counties, some incidents carry much heavier penalties than ordinary civilians would face. Any DUI, narcotics or domestic violence charge puts a cop on suspension while IAB investigates, and conviction costs him his job. Even if an officer is found innocent, he may be required to attend counseling or substance abuse treatment as a condition of continued employment with the department.

Federal law signed into effect in late 2005 allows police officers to carry concealed firearms nationwide, subject to the limitations that other federal laws impose on civilian possession of deadly weapons in certain areas (such as national parks, post offices, federal courthouses and commercial flights). As a practical consideration, most patrol officers and detectives never leave their homes unarmed, even when attending church or school functions, just in case of encounters with criminals who know them by sight.

The MPD policy for off-duty officers witnessing crimes requires them to intervene only if an immediate threat of a violent felony exists. In all other cases, they're advised to pull back and call for on-duty officers. Two major schools of thought exist on this advice: "cops are always on duty" and "not my problem." Officers generally polarize toward one side or the other depending on whether or not they have families and how close they are to retirement.

Use of other equipment while off duty is left to the individual officer's discretion, but few carry more than their off-duty guns, badges and IDs, and only the most paranoid wear body armor while on their own time. Officers concerned about being identified as cops carry their badges and police IDs separate from their wallets so they won't immediately be made if they have to show ID at a store or hand over their wallets during a robbery.

part of their graduation and swearing-in ceremony from the MPD Academy. Only sworn officers are entitled to wear badges, which the department issues and can revoke as both a practical and symbolic disciplinary act. Badges are department property. Officers who retire honorably are entitled to keep their badges as mementos, but those who quit the force or are drummed out in disgrace must turn in their badges along with all other issued equipment.

When in uniform, officers wear their badges pinned to the left breast of their shirts or jackets. Plainclothes officers have several other options, depending on their duties. Those making public appearances in business clothes use folding ID cases that slip into the breast pocket of a suit, leaving the badge hanging exposed. Detectives who don't want to immediately be recognized as cops prefer badge holders that clip to their belts. Officers operating in physically demanding plainclothes assignments such as drug buy-bust operations tend toward badge holders on lanyards that they can pull out from under their shirts when they need to identify themselves. When operating on extended undercover assignments, cops usually leave their badges in the custody of their supervisors, partners or spouses. If the department is in mourning for a slain comrade, all officers wear a black ribbon across the center of their badges or, more rarely, wear them upside-down.

Each badge bears an individual serial number, which serves several purposes. Officers use their badge numbers as internal identifiers in department records and paperwork. If revealing an undercover officer's name in court records would jeopardize his safety, his testimony and evidence can be recorded under his badge number. Citizens can record a badge number for later reference, usually when complaining to an officer's superiors about perceived or actual misconduct. In some departments, a badge number, if not an actual badge, can be re-issued, allowing an officer a form of symbolic continuation from the same badge that a relative or mentor once wore. Finally, should an officer's body be mutilated beyond recognition, his badge number provides a final means by which forensic examiners can identify his remains.

Tools of the Trade

Cops carry a fair amount of equipment during the course of their normal duties, and have access to even more specialized items as required by specific assignments.

The Badge

A police officer's badge is a symbol of his authority and responsibility, and many consider the badge the most morally (if not tactically) significant piece of equipment they wear. Newly minted officers receive their badges as

Other Departments: Stars and Shields

Badges typically take one of a few shapes, the most common of which are shields (also used synonymously with "badge") and five- and seven-pointed stars. Each design bears deliberate symbolism, much as any other professional or martial insignia does. City and state police departments' badges often bear the seal of their jurisdiction. Many badge designs in American departments incorporate an eagle, wings outstretched across the top of the badge, representing the United States and the Constitution that the officer protects. The shield symbol represents protection and an officer's duty to provide that protection to the citizens he serves. In a star, the points stand for the virtues of a police officer, such as honesty, character, loyalty, knowledge, judgment, courtesy and integrity.

World of Darkness: More than a Tin Star

A badge is a symbol of sufficient power to acquire paranormal properties in several ways. A slain officer's ghost might be anchored to her badge (see the **World of Darkness Rulebook**, p. 209). As a unique physical aspect of one person's occupation, if not her destiny or purpose in the world, a badge can provide a mage with a sympathetic connection to its owner (see **Mage: The Awakening**, p. 114). Conversely, a badge is a symbolically appropriate vessel for spells or spirits intended to enhance, assist or protect the wearer during the course of her duties.

Uniforms

The MPD includes a uniform allowance as part of an officer's annual salary. This invariably defrays, rather than fully covering, the cost of all of the uniform items an officer must own. Uniform standards include Class A, Class B, Class C and full dress.

The Class A uniform consists of blue uniform pants, polished black leather shoes and a long-sleeved uniform shirt with a necktie (clip-on to prevent strangulation). Undershirts must be white, navy blue or black, with no visible markings. As mentioned above, the officer wears his badge on his left breast. The right breast bears the officer's nameplate, with bars for commendations pinned above it. A department patch is sewn to the left shoulder, with an American flag on the right. Polished metal rank insignia are pinned to each collar. In cold weather, officers may wear a navy blue "commando-style" sweater (one with leather shoulders and elbows) over the shirt, bearing the same insignia. A uniform hat is mandatory outdoors. Class A uniforms are required for court appearances, formal department proceedings and high-profile public duty such as security details. Many officers find their Class A uniforms sufficiently expensive that they're reluctant to chase or scuffle with suspects while wearing them.

A Class B uniform is identical to Class A, but with more comfortable (and durable) pants and no tie or hat. A short-sleeved shirt is optional in warm weather, and officers don't have to wear their commendation bars. Class B is the default for patrol and other uniformed assignments — except when the MPD is under public scrutiny, at which point the chief's office usually requires all officers to go to Class A uniforms for a few weeks.

Full dress uniform is worn only for official ceremonies, such as graduations, awards presentations, weddings and funerals. Full dress begins with Class A and adds a uniform coat and white gloves and is typically worn without the full duty belt (see p. 70).

"Class C" is a catch-all term for non-standard uniforms approved for individual units. The most common Class C standard is black combat boots and navy blue BDUs (Battle Dress Utilities, or military fatigues) with embroidered nametags and rank insignia. This is standard for personnel in physically intensive assignments, such as K-9 handlers, cops on a narcotics bust and patrol officers on van duty. Officers assigned to bicycle or Segway patrol are allowed to wear shorts and more appropriate shoes. Aviation crews wear military flight suits and helmets. The ERU wears black or camouflage BDUs, depending on where the unit is deploying.

Some other units are authorized to modify Class A and Class B standards for the demands of their jobs. Motorcycle and mounted officers both wear helmets, black leather gloves and knee-high boots with their pants tucked in.

Other Departments: Uniformity

Uniform standards are a topic of intense debate among and within departments, with the major points of contention being professional appearance, economy, utility and officer comfort. Some departments relax their dress codes to permit BDUs for all patrol officers, or at least the ones on night shifts, while departments with more traditional standards find this the height of sloppiness. The latter departments take great pride in the style of their Class A uniforms, sometimes going to the extent of having specific unique designs commissioned (to the quiet grumbling of the officers whose uniform allowances don't cover these overpriced garments).

Body Armor

Modern body armor is thin and light enough to be worn under a Class A uniform shirt without undue visibility — though even the most modern designs are never comfortable. MPD policy requires armor to be worn only when an officer is engaged in high-risk action such as raids, warrant service and searches, but strongly encourages body armor to be immediately available for all other standard duty. Almost all patrol officers wear armor while on duty. About a third of detectives do.

Patrol officers typically wear vests that the industry classifies as "Type IIIA." This grade of armor protects against most handgun ammunition up to .44 Magnum. Such a vest adds a certain blockiness to the appearance of an officer's torso but doesn't significantly hamper movement. In hot weather, heat dissipation becomes a problem and a sweat-wicking undershirt is common. This does tend to saturate the armor itself with sweat, which requires more frequent washing and breaks down the protective fibers of the armor. Standard policy is to replace armor every three years or after any significant incident in which the armor "took the hit," but officers have to pay for replacements out of their uniform allowances, and many delay this expenditure for as long as they can.

The oldest serving officers still maintain some degree of skepticism about the benefits of armor, but those whose careers began during the 1980s or later are convinced that it's worth the inconvenience. In addition to stopping bullets, armor has been shown to provide significant protection to internal organs in car crashes, which kill three times as many cops as shootings. Still, even the most devout believers recognize the limitations of armor. It only protects the torso, manufacturers insist that it's bullet-resistant and not bulletproof and blades go right through it.

Standard armor's outer shell, invisible under the uniform shirt, is a popular place for officers to express themselves in a manner only visible in the locker room. Some write religious verses or darkly humorous phrases on the armor, while more practical cops stencil their blood types and drug allergies for paramedics' reference.

Type IIIA armor is available for police dogs as well as human officers. The MPD sees this as a health hazard due to overheating and doesn't like to send its dogs into situations in which they're likely to be shot in the first place. However, some handlers have used personal funds to buy sets for their dogs "just in case."

Weapons

MPD officers carry both lethal and non-lethal weapons. The standard array of armament for a patrol officer includes pepper spray (typically referred to as "OC" after the active ingredient, oleoresin capsicum), a polymer PR-24 baton (which officers intensely dislike for its tendency to warp in hot weather) and a department-issue Glock 22 semi-automatic pistol with two spare magazines.

MPD policy forbids carrying knives that are classified as weapons under state law (those with blades longer than three inches), but many officers carry folding utility knives clipped into pockets or inside their body armor. These knives almost never see use as weapons, but officers find the need to cut a wide variety of things such as seat belts, packages of heroin or the clothes of suspects snagged on picket fences. Officers are also forbidden from using any other unapproved weapon, such as a sap, cattle prod or obscure martial arts implement. The main reason for this policy is liability, as the department's use of force policy (see p. 64) takes into account only specific weapons whose effects have undergone careful review.

Backup handguns are allowed, but they're subject to review by the department armorer before being approved — see p.66 for the MPD's policy for backup guns. Glock 27s are popular because they can accept the higher-capacity magazines of the full-size duty sidearms. The most common methods for carrying a backup handgun are ankle or small-of-the-back holsters. Some traffic enforcement officers prefer to carry a small revolver in a pants pocket holster so they can "casually" approach a suspect vehicle with a hand on this hidden weapon.

In addition to the standard array of personal weapons, most officers who work out of cars are issued a Mossberg Model 590 12-gauge shotgun for supplementary use in high-threat situations. This weapon is kept in a locked vertical clamp bolted to the dashboard of the patrol car. A few qualified officers, mostly those with prior military experience, are issued AR-15 or M4 assault rifles instead.

All patrol officers of sergeant's rank and above, as well as all ERU team members, are trained with additional non-lethal weapons for controlling hostile crowds or subduing particularly aggressive suspects. These personnel are also issued pepperball guns and/or ranged stun guns ("Tasers"). Pepperball guns stay in their cases until needed, but Tasers come with holsters that attach to duty belts and are available for immediate use.

Mechanics

A PR-24 baton functions as a tonfa. It's a blunt implement with Damage 2(B), Size 2, Durability 3 and a +1 Defense bonus. A Glock 22 is a .40 caliber light pistol with Damage 2 (9 Again), Range 20/40/80, Clip 15+1, Strength 2 and Size 1. If you have access to **World of Darkness: Armory**, all of these weapons are described in greater detail therein. The tonfa is described on p. 29, and the Glock 22 is on p. 65. Pepperball guns appear on p. 92 and ranged stun guns on p. 93.

Duty Belt

A patrol officer's duty belt holds most of the equipment that he uses on a daily basis. The wide, black leather duty belt goes on over the officer's uniform belt. Belt keepers, small loops with snaps, attach the duty belt to the uniform belt to keep the duty belt from twisting around or sagging. MPD policy requires all patrol officers to arrange the equipment on their duty belts in the same fashion. This leads to some grumbling but makes inspections easier and allows an officer to grab equipment from a partner who is busy wrestling with a suspect and doesn't have a free hand.

An officer uses a retention holster for his duty sidearm. Drawing from a retention holster requires the officer to perform a set of motions unique to the specific holster design in order to make the mechanism release the gun. An MPD officer suffers no slowdown on his draw thanks to trained muscle memory, but an aggressor trying to grab a gun from a retention holster must succeed on a Strength + Firearms roll opposed by the officer's Strength + Brawl.

In addition, the duty belt contains a magazine carrier with two spare magazines for the officer's service sidearm, a personal radio, a handcuff carrier, carrying loops for the officer's baton and flashlight, a pepper spray holster and a case for two sets of surgical gloves.

Noise Discipline

Cops carry a lot of gear, and those with a few years of street experience have learned every possible trick for making the gear as quiet as possible. Noise can get an officer killed when he's searching a dark building for an assault suspect or trying to get into position to tackle a drug dealer. Smart cops take loose change out of their pockets, use earpieces for their personal radios and set their cell phones on vibrate. They also take the time to break in leather duty gear before taking it out on the street so it won't creak at inopportune moments.

Other Gear

Subject to department regulations on illegal substances and unapproved weapons, officers acquire other gear at their own discretion. Every cop has his own short list of indispensable and inexpensive pocket items that he always carries against necessity. While MPD cops use phrases such as "gear queer" to refer to colleagues who are excessively fond of gadgets, most cops are always on the lookout for tools that help them do their jobs better or more safely. Commonly, an officer has a "squad bag," a durable athletic bag full of the little things he might need while on duty that goes in the trunk of his cruiser when he checks in for the night's work.

Many of the people with whom an officer comes in contact are a veritable potpourri of communicable diseases. A box of surgical gloves in the car is a good start, and most officers also carry breath masks (in case they have to administer rescue breathing or CPR) and bottles of antibacterial solution. Sanitizing wipes also come in useful for cleaning off returned handcuffs or wiping down the interior of a patrol car. Some cops who aren't concerned about getting busted for drinking on the job carry a small bottle of vodka or other high-proof alcohol for rinsing out their mouths if suspects spit in their faces.

While surgical gloves do protect against bodily fluids, these gloves are inadequate for many other hazards that an officer encounters during the course of his duties. A good pair of search gloves, leather lined with puncture-resistant synthetic material, is a cop's best friend when he's patting down a suspect with a dirty needle in his pocket. The intimidation factor of wearing black leather gloves doesn't always hurt, either.

Almost every officer in the MPD has a work-only cell phone. This is for both convenience and safety, as no one wants to give junkie snitches his home number. Hands-free accessories are wildly popular for use while driving, particularly in pursuit situations when an officer needs to stay in contact with Dispatch but can't spare a hand for his radio. Cell phones also have the advantage of not being open to monitoring by police-band scanners in the hands of criminals or the media. Older officers, however, tend to disparage cell phones as toys of Generation Y.

MPD authorizes handcuffs in a single standard design, allowing any officer to unlock any other officer's handcuffs. The department issues one pair to each officer, but most patrol cops buy at least one spare set in case a prisoner gets taken away wearing theirs. Spare keys are also popular — for the practical, in case one goes missing, and for the paranoid, in case a cop finds himself taken hostage and restrained with his own cuffs.

Day-shift personnel don't think much about it, but cops working after dark can never have enough illumination. In addition to the heavy department-issued rechargeable light, virtually every second- and third-shift patrol officer carries at least one extra pocket flashlight. After a couple of bad experiences with cheap models, most officers gravitate toward brighter and more rugged tactical lights, either handheld or mounted on the accessory rails of their sidearms.

World of Darkness: You're Carrying What?

Players portraying officers may be tempted to gear up with an array of strange implements, particularly if the characters have had encounters with the supernatural (or aren't entirely human themselves). The Storyteller should feel free to work the details of such "emergency preparedness" into the course of the chronicle. The MPD is not a monster-hunting organization, and a cop who carries wooden stakes and a mallet in the trunk of his cruiser or pins a fresh sprig of wolfsbane to his body armor every night is going to quickly go from being the butt of locker room jokes to the recipient of a psychiatric evaluation. Discretion is the order of the day for such equipment. This can make for strong dramatic conflicts for the officer who knows a little more about what's out there.

Vehicles

The majority of the MPD's fleet is composed of the ubiquitous Ford Crown Victoria Police Interceptors (CVPI) that dominate the law enforcement market in North America. A CVPI differs from an ordinary production vehicle in several respects even before an individual department customizes the CVPI and loads it with issued equipment. A large engine and heavy-duty brakes and suspension facilitate high-speed driving and rough use. An upgraded electrical system provides more power for radios, MDT, lights, siren and other electronic tools (and the distinctive whine from the larger fan and alternator is recognizable to experienced criminals from blocks away). Vinyl and rubber replace cloth and carpet for easier cleanup. Due to a rash of fires involving rear-end collisions with previous models, newer CVPIs have an impact-activated fire extinguisher mounted next to the fuel tank. Ballistic panels in the front doors are also a factory option for new models, and the MPD is beginning to order these in new vehicles assigned to high-threat precincts.

The MPD's preferred modifications are fairly standard for police cars. Searchlights on both A-pillars provide high-intensity illumination. A few older units still have conventional lightbars, but newer units mount high-intensity LED bars. The standard configuration features red and blue strobes for emergency signaling, white "alley lights" for sideways illumination and a strip of rear-facing, yellow signal flashers for use in traffic control. A kill switch under the dash enables the driver to shut off the car's interior and brake lights and its "door ajar" chime for those times when stealth is essential.

The front of the passenger compartment is crammed with the car's radio transceivers and MDT, along with the dash-mounted video camera. The locking clamp for the officers' assigned shotgun or semi-automatic rifle puts the weapon in the middle of the passenger's knee space. In the back seat, two modifications prevent escape. The door handles and lock and window switches are removed, and a clear polycarbonate shield blocks access to the front seat.

The trunk is lined with ballistic protection to minimize the effects of rear-impact damage on the rear occupants (and to forestall escape into the trunk). The recorder for the video camera is mounted here, as are the GPS receiver and wireless network transceiver for the MDT. The recorder activates whenever the vehicle is running code, and officers can also manually trigger the recorder from the dashboard. Newer recorders are digital models with hard drive space for 12 or more hours of video, but most recorders still use much-abused VHS cassettes. Officers also wear lapel microphones with short-range radio transmitters to capture conversations while the recorder is running.

Once on the street, a cop car receives heavy and ungentle use. The average patrol unit sees upward of 30,000 miles a year (compared with 12,000 for the average passenger car) and stays in service for three to five years

before being scrapped, sold at auction or handed down to other Midway government agencies. Patrol and traffic cops burn most of a tank of gas each duty shift and go through brake pads on a monthly basis. The MPD has a fleet fuel contract with the local franchises of a well-known national chain of gas stations (making that chain's cashiers a frequent source of street information), and officers are encouraged to wash their vehicles frequently to maintain a professional appearance. Maintenance is handled at the Facilities and Property Bureau's garage, and officers without a car either pick up a spare from the garage or pull desk or prisoner van duty.

A cruiser serves as the mobile office of the officers assigned to it. Most cops have their own preferences and rituals regarding their vehicles, such as a nightly kicking of the tires or rabid defense of their radio channel presets. As two or three MPD patrol shifts typically share the same vehicles, it's rare for officers to personalize their rides. Etiquette demands that the outgoing shift always clean the puke and blood out of the back seat so the next team doesn't have to smell it. Cops of lieutenant rank and above, as well as senior detective sergeants, can request permanently assigned cars and may leave duty gear or personal effects in them, but everyone who shares a car has to take all his personal effects out of it at the end of his shift.

Variations

Cruisers assigned to the Traffic Bureau are unmarked. The lightbar is replaced with LED strobes on the front of each side mirror, inside the grille, on the dashboard and in the rear windows. In addition, a radar gun with both front and rear antennas is mounted, and a handheld, laser speed sensor and spike strip are standard equipment.

The Traffic Bureau also uses several non-standard vehicles for unmarked highway enforcement. A handful of performance sedans, seized in drug-related arrests, have been overhauled and rigged for traffic enforcement. However, the majority of Traffic's specialty fleet are unmarked Chevrolet Camaro Interceptors (see sidebar), all of which are currently approaching the end of their service lives. As Camaros are no longer in production, Traffic is examining several alternatives for replacements. All of these vehicles have much the same equipment as Traffic cruisers save for the lack of a prisoner shield.

Units with large amounts of specialized equipment to transport receive SUVs instead of cars. The MPD uses the Ford Explorer for marked duty, such as those assigned to K-9, while the Analysis Bureau and other units without patrol responsibilities prefer larger Chevrolet Suburbans.

Detectives typically receive older cruisers that have been on patrol or traffic duty for three or more years. These vehicles have their video cameras, radar guns, prisoner shields, MDTs and gun clamps removed. Formerly marked units also lose their lightbars, and decals are repainted.

Each precinct's patrol unit has three assigned prisoner vans (the department's lawyers say "paddy wagon" is offensive to the Irish). These vehicles continually smell of unpleasant bodily functions due to the condition of their passengers. The cargo area is an aluminum box with a bench seat down each side and eyebolts sunk into the floor for securing particularly unruly subjects. A prisoner van is officially rated for eight passengers, though bar fights and other large disturbances can result in more than a dozen prisoners being crammed in at a time. A prisoner van has no windows, only a few ventilation holes, and no door handles on the inside. Van duty is the short straw of patrol assignments, as officers are reduced to picking up other cops' arrests and shuttling prisoners between the precinct's holding cells and the city jail.

What's in the Trunk?

Rather a lot. The standard inventory for an MPD cruiser's issued equipment includes the following:

- reference book of state and local criminal codes
- county and city maps
- first aid kit
- emergency blanket
- basic evidence collection kit
- narcotics field testing kit
- plastic tarp (usually used to protect rear seats from particularly disgusting prisoners)
- file box full of forms (in case of MDT network crash)
- spare batteries for every piece of electronic equipment
- highway flares
- traffic cones
- crime scene tape
- crowbar
- bolt cutters
- rain gear
- reflective vests
- two gallons of water
- plastic garbage bags
- stuffed animals (given to children as needed)

In theory, officers are supposed to check all of this equipment at the beginning of every shift. In practice, most just glance in the trunk to make sure everything looks like it's there.

In Play: Cop Cars

MPD vehicles have the following basic traits.

Police Cruiser: Durability 3, Size 14, Structure 17, Acceleration 15, Safe Speed 110 (75 mph), Maximum Speed 213 (145 mph), Handling 3, Cost •••.

Police SUV: Durability 3, Size 15, Structure 18, Acceleration 12, Safe Speed 96 (65 mph), Maximum Speed 154 (105 mph), Handling 0, Cost •••.

Police Interceptor: Durability 3, Size 12, Structure 15, Acceleration 26, Safe Speed 110 (75 mph), Maximum Speed 235 (160 mph), Handling 4, Cost •••.

A prisoner shield has Durability 3, Size 4 and Structure 7. Ballistic door panels increase the basic traits of the door (see the **World of Darkness Rulebook**, p. 142) to Durability 6, Size 3 and Structure 9. As noted above, the upgraded elec-

trical systems of police vehicles have a distinctive sound. A character can recognize this with a successful Wits + Drive or Wits + Streetwise roll.

Other Departments: Vehicle Options

The Crown Vic Police Interceptor is the dominant police cruiser in North America, comprising 85% of all police cars on the road. Departments tend to prefer large rear-wheel drive cars over anything else. Smaller, more economic vehicles don't have enough room for police equipment, a prisoner shield and four handcuffed suspects. Front-wheel drive cars are more likely to sustain disabling damage when an officer hits a curb or pothole at high speed. Finally, some manufacturers just won't certify their cars for police duty because of liability concerns. Other vehicles offered with factory police prep packages during the 2006 model year include the Chevrolet Impala (front-wheel drive but popular with large city departments for better gas mileage), Dodge Charger and Dodge Magnum (marketed primarily for K-9 and other specialized units that need to transport more gear than usual).

Rural departments use SUVs wholly or exclusively in place of cars, as do some departments in northern climates where four-wheel drive is a necessity rather than a market trend. These vehicles tend to be working SUVs such as Ford Explorers and Jeep Cherokees rather than luxury models. Police SUVs are not rated for pursuit duty, though they see their share of it anyway. Those SUVs offered with factory police packages include the Chevrolet Tahoe, Ford Explorer and Ford Expedition.

Some departments in less urbanized areas, typically those that don't assign officers to patrol as partners, issue employees their own marked cars. Cops who live within these departments' jurisdictions receive the privilege of using their assigned vehicles while off duty. This benefits the department by keeping additional marked cruisers on the streets, raising the visible police presence. However, officers who take advantage of this arrangement must respond to traffic accidents or other emergencies they witness until on-duty colleagues arrive on-scene.

Communications

MPD officers use a wide variety of communication systems. The introduction of in-car radios in the 1930s vastly increased the ability of patrol officers to learn of and respond to problems quickly, and subsequent technological advances have given the department ever-increasing options.

Radios

Radio communication has been the standard method for keeping officers in contact with the rest of the department for the last half-century, and every MPD vehicle has a radio. In addition, every patrol and traffic officer wears a personal unit on his duty belt.

Each personal radio is programmed to broadcast on a unique frequency that only that radio and a single linked vehicle radio are assigned. The vehicle radio system picks up these transmissions and relays them on the department's main communication frequencies, likewise re-broadcasting incoming transmissions back to the personal unit or units assigned to it. This enables officers to stay in contact when they leave their vehicles without relying on the short range (about a half-mile, less in downtown areas) of their personal radios. Officers can also switch their personal radios to "tactical" channels and talk directly to one another.

Vehicle radios have a much longer range (five to 10 miles). Each precinct has its own main radio frequency for its dispatchers, which is the default channel for patrol and traffic officers to monitor when they're not busy. Each precinct's detectives also have a separate set of frequencies. In addition, another set of frequencies is designated as car-to-car channels to which individual units can switch for semiprivate conversations that don't clutter the main dispatch channels. Finally, three other channels are department-wide: the assistance channel (which dispatchers use to request emergency assistance from neighboring precincts), the interagency channel (which is reserved for coordinating action with the MFD, Washington County Sheriff's Department and other emergency services) and the command channel (which is used to issue centralized orders in citywide emergencies). The department records all radio traffic on all channels except the tactical and car-to-car frequencies.

Officers consider their radios as indispensable as their guns, if not more so. A radio can be a cop's only connection to the rest of the department between incidents. On a slow, dark night, it's not uncommon to hear brief bursts of white noise as cops periodically key their transmit switches to make sure their radios are still working. Good dispatchers likewise worry if they aren't hearing their officers talking and will call for radio checks if the precinct channel is too quiet.

Every precinct has radio dead spots, areas where geography or architecture prevents consistent radio reception. Radio repeater stations on top of city-owned buildings can eliminate some, but others dead spots persist. Patrol cops know where these spots are and try not to stay in them for prolonged periods.

Mobile Data Terminals

The MPD began installing notebook computers in its vehicles in the mid-1990s. Today, every marked vehicle, as well as every unmarked patrol and traffic enforcement car, has a Mobile Data Terminal (MDT) and its associated accessories. The core of an MDT is a notebook computer connected to a dedicated radio transceiver. This network operates on different frequencies from the radios that emergency services use for voice communication. Through the network, a user can access law enforcement databases or relay communication to other users. These data queries cut down on the amount of chatter on communication frequencies and vastly increase the efficiency with which officers in the field operate.

Early MDTs provided only basic search functionality for looking up vehicle registration and performing background checks against local arrest records. As notebook computers' capabilities grew, so did those of law enforcement software. Current models provide not only text and photo data distribution but also national criminal database searches, GPS-integrated mapping and secondary car-to-car communication. MDTs aren't infallible, though. Radio dead spots also interfere with the wireless network, and central database systems are subject to frequent delays and outright crashes during times of peak usage.

Mechanics

With a successful Intelligence + Computer roll, a character can perform any of the following tasks through the MDT. Unless otherwise noted, assume that the task in question requires two to five minutes (response times are variable depending on how many data requests the network is handling at once). A user unfamiliar with the software (such as a civilian who shouldn't be using the system) suffers a –3 penalty. A trained officer suffers no penalty to this roll for lacking the Computer Skill, however.

In most cases, the following mechanics indicate a variety of "always-on" bonuses for the basic task in question, such as VIN or license plate numbers. Many of the following tasks are all but impossible without the requisite piece of information, yielding *at least* a –5 penalty, assuming the Storyteller wishes to allow the task at all.

• **Check vehicle registration:** The character "runs the plates" (or vehicle identification number) of a specific vehicle. Data returned via this request includes vehicle registration, the owner's criminal history, whether the owner has a concealed handgun permit and any crime or accident reports in which the vehicle appears. Having the license plate number or VIN offers a +2 bonus to the roll.

• **Records search:** Starting with a name, the character searches for matching individuals who maintain residence within the MPD's jurisdiction, as well as checking national databases for felony records. A partial name or alias inflicts a –2 penalty to the search, while the subject's driver's license or other identification provides a +2 bonus. Success yields the search target's current address of residence, criminal record, vehicle registrations, history of previous official contacts with the MPD and concealed handgun permit status. If the target has a criminal record or a weapons permit, the system also displays the most recent mug shot or ID photo on file.

• **Check call history:** The character checks the history of 911 calls from, and emergency responses to, a given address. Most uses of this system occur when an officer is en route to a call and wants to know if she's likely to walk into something like a domestic violence situation or a crack house. The address itself provides a +2 bonus to this roll.

• **Map route:** Given any two points within the MPD's jurisdiction, the character can create a street map showing the least-time route between them, as well as alternate routes. This function doesn't require connection to the network and takes 30 seconds. Using this map to get from Point A to Point B quickly provides a bonus equal to the number of successes on the roll to appropriate Drive rolls. Other functions that don't provide mechanical bonuses include finding alternate routes for diverting traffic around accident scenes and marking the specific coordinates of things such as street construction and undercover narcotics operations.

• **Distribute photo:** A digital camera enables the character to quickly copy a photo — for example, a parent's picture of a missing child or a driver's license dropped by a fleeing suspect — and distribute the photo across the network as needed.

• **Instant message:** The network provides car-to-car or beat-wide instant messaging capability. While this is available as an emergency backup in case voice communications go down, the primary use of this functionality is for low-priority questions ("Anyone know if a bag of whole blood is a controlled substance that would give me PC to search this car?") and personal message traffic ("Let's get a sandwich once you finish with that accident report."). Wise officers remember that the channel is logged at headquarters and keep the chatter clean. This function requires no roll to use and takes as long as any other instant messaging.

Other Subjects

Police work is far too involved to cover in any amount of detail in this chapter. The following information focuses on a collection of topics directly relevant to, or useful in, an MPD police story.

Corruption

In the real world, police corruption is a subject that generates headlines in a volume wildly out of proportion to the actual rate of occurrence. The vast majority of police officers take their oaths of office seriously. Something in the media culture savors the downfall of a hero, and any dirty cop whose exploits come to light

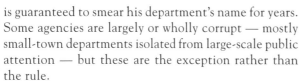

is guaranteed to smear his department's name for years. Some agencies are largely or wholly corrupt — mostly small-town departments isolated from large-scale public attention — but these are the exception rather than the rule.

Legally speaking, corruption occurs when a public official abuses his authority to gain personal benefit, to commit crimes that would not have been possible without that authority or both. In the case of police officers, corruption usually involves selective neglect or excess in their primary duties of law enforcement. Most cases of police corruption involve one or more of the following aspects.

Bribery

As government employees, most cops earn less than the majority of the citizens the cops protect. While overtime and secondary income are options, corrupt officers are willing to minimize or ignore criminal activity in exchange for money or property. Giving in to bribery can be a crime of opportunity, as in a motorist handing over a roll of cash along with his license and registration, or a regular source of cash, such as monthly payoffs from a local pimp. Bribery is a frequent predecessor to more severe forms of police corruption. Knowing this, IAB investigators look first at an officer's finances and standard of living when searching for signs of corruption.

In Play: Pay Scales

Mechanically speaking, the salary of an entry-level officer through SPO allows for no more than Resources 1. Sergeants and lieutenants can expect to maintain a lifestyle commensurate to Resources 2. Captains and majors, being the equivalent of senior managers, typically come in at Resources 3. A cop who takes on a lot of overtime, lives frugally or has a working spouse can justify a level of Resources one greater than his rank would normally allow, but anything more will have IAB peering very closely at his sources of income.

Extortion

Not content to take bribes as they're offered, corrupt officers are compelled by greed or need to actively seek supplemental income. Cops involved in extortion pursue it in much the same manner as organized criminals do (see p. 55), but cops' threats for non-payment tend to involve "official" action. Extortion may be systematic, such as demanding protection money from businesses on an officer's

beat. Extortion can also be opportunistic, such as offering to accept cash payment on the spot for "no points on your license" traffic citations.

Invasion of Privacy

Law enforcement personnel have access to a lot of information about the average citizen. A name, address, license plate or other unique identifier is sufficient for an NCIC query on the subject's criminal history. This can also facilitate a check against local databases for non-criminal encounters with the Midway justice system (such as paying someone else's bail). Official presence can also gain an officer access to business records. Easy compliance has been less frequent within the past few years due to rising concerns over privacy, particularly in the banking and telecommunications industries. However, many smaller businesses without privacy policies will still release information without a warrant in order to avoid official scrutiny. In the end, the defining line between investigation and invasion of privacy is not always the nature of the information the officer obtains but rather its relevance to a known or suspected criminal case.

Harassment

All cops know certain repeat offenders in their precincts. However, knowing someone's sold drugs before doesn't give an officer open license to shake that person down every night on the off chance that he might have crack on him at that moment. Official harassment occurs when an officer bends or breaks the rules of probable cause to repeatedly interfere with a citizen's activities without sufficient proof of wrongdoing.

Excessive Force

A certain amount of controlled aggression is necessary for street cops to be successful. Common wisdom among police officers holds that criminals, similar to other predators, can sense weakness and timidity. Officers who aren't willing to step in and wrestle with suspects won't last long on patrol duty. Those officers who exceed their authority, however, are guilty of violent crimes as any other citizen would be, typically starting with aggravated assault and ranging upward from there depending on the case.

It's worth noting that the news media has a tendency to portray any exceptional use of force as "police brutality." In truth, many use-of-force incidents are fully justified in the eyes of both the law and the department itself, though the average citizen may not feel the same way. Similar to every law enforcement agency, the MPD has a use of force policy (p. 64) that regulates the degree of force an officer is entitled to apply against a certain threat or to gain compliance in a given situation. This policy serves to protect officers (by giving them a legal basis for self-defense) and suspects (by limiting the amount of force they face if they comply with officers), and a clearly defined policy indemnifies the department against a great deal of civil liability. The vast majority of cops err on the side of restraint when interpreting these guidelines, as witnessed by the number of knife-wielding suspects the cops *don't* shoot on a daily basis. Following cinematic examples of proper use of force, however, is a quick route to a small cell.

Criminal Conspiracy

The most egregious abuses of power occur when officers use their positions to actively assist or commit criminal acts. The possibilities are endless — virtually any crime is easier with an insider's knowledge of how, where and when the local department works. Some such corruption begins with ignoble acts committed in the pursuit of arguably noble goals, such as when officers administer "street justice" to criminals whom the officers know are guilty of heinous crimes but can't arrest due to a lack of evidence. Other instances accommodate no such opportunities for self-deception. One notable case in the 1st Precinct involved a patrol squad committing burglaries on neighboring beats while the officers responsible for those areas were engaged in other incidents.

World of Darkness: Corruption in the MPD

In the World of Darkness, we're assuming that the rate of corruption is higher than it is in the real world. As well, crooked cops manage to get away with corruption more than they would in the real world, despite the stable funding of the department and the vigilance of (most of) its officers — that's the assumption we're making for the film-noir and horror genres we wish to present. Feel free to adjust this factor according to the needs of your own chronicles.

We haven't formally defined the degree of corruption that the MPD faces, however. This is intentional, as it allows Storytellers to fine-tune the MPD of their stories to fit the tone they want to set. A largely honorable MPD has an aggressive Internal Affairs Bureau, a strong culture of personal accountability and senior officers who set an irreproachable example for their subordinates. A MPD rotting from within has leaders and an IAB that are themselves corrupt or fail to discipline wayward personnel. In the World of Darkness, where most institutions suffer from some degree of decay, the first case is unpleasantly likely.

Mechanically speaking, a corrupt officer is most likely to misuse his authority in accordance with his Vice (see the **World of Darkness Rulebook**, p. 103). However, this is not always an absolute, and Storytellers should portray characters in accordance with the needs of the story as well as their own moral foibles.

Gender Issues on the Street

The MPD's almost 1,000 patrol officers who are female frequently find themselves called upon for certain duties because of their gender. Male officers may be uncomfortable (or fear sexual harassment lawsuits) when searching female prisoners. Studies have shown that in the aftermath of violent crimes that involve women or children as victims or witnesses, contact with female detectives and medical personnel is vastly less threatening than receiving the same interviews and treatment from males. In addition, some ethnic groups have strong matriarchal family structures, and women who establish rapport with the matrons who lead these communities can often obtain information that their male counterparts never would have heard.

Police Chaplains

A police chaplain is an ordained person of faith who is attached to a law enforcement agency, either as an employee or as a volunteer. His primary responsibility for the department is to assist officers, civilian employees and their families in all ways consistent with the duties of his religious office. Department chaplains typically are not cops themselves, though many come from law enforcement families and a rare few may be both ordained religious leaders and sworn officers.

The most important function that most police chaplains provide their departments is counseling. The daily grind of police work can be a crushing weight on an officer, even without the unique stresses inflicted by violent incidents or extended undercover assignments. Police officers are notorious for refusing to discuss emotional difficulties for fear of being seen as weak or unworthy by colleagues, and a chaplain's position makes him someone who both understands a cop's job and won't pass judgment on him. At times, this duty takes on certain urgency. National statistics indicate that for every one cop killed in the line of duty, three commit suicide, and five die of stress-related illnesses within five years of retirement.

In addition to seeing to the emotional and spiritual health of the departments, chaplains also visit ill or injured officers at home or in the hospital, assist negotiations in suicide or hostage standoffs, liaise with other local clergy regarding law enforcement matters and bring death notifications to fallen officers' next of kin. The chaplains' departments may also consult them on religious matters relevant to current cases or ask them to serve on disciplinary or promotion review boards.

Not all departments employ full-time chaplains. Particularly in a smaller agency, the chaplain is a volunteer with a church and congregation who provides his services to the department in addition to his normal duties. The MPD, itself a large department, employs three chaplains as full-time members of the chief's staff. The department also avails itself of the services of a handful of volunteers, who mainly provide services as needed to precinct houses near their places of worship.

World of Darkness: With Badge and Cross

On a force whose officers encounters unspeakable atrocities and inhuman horrors on a nightly basis, department chaplains are even more important. Officers troubled by things they can't put in their reports may confide in chaplains out of fear for their sanity. A career of such confidential discussions can give a chaplain a better picture of what his department faces than virtually any other member. Chaplains' academic knowledge may be vital to solving investigations of crimes involving religious or occult practices. In the gravest extreme — and in a story in which faith yields tangible results — a chaplain may be the only member of a department upon whom officers can call to put down a threat that firepower can't stop.

Blue-on-Blue

One particular hazard for an undercover or off-duty officer who deals with situations on the street is being shot by other cops who can't tell that he's a fellow officer. A handful of such incidents occur every year, usually when uniformed officers respond to a confused report and encounter a plainclothes officer struggling with a suspect or holding him at gunpoint. A common term for these situations is "blue-on-blue encounters," taken from the military terminology that describes similar cases of mistaken identity. (In military exercises, the "blue force" is the allied side and the "red force" is the opposition.)

Departments have experimented with various methods for plainclothes officers to identify themselves immediately in high-stress situations, ranging from hand signs to a specific color of shirt that changes daily. The MPD's solution is a code word that changes every day at the beginning of First Shift. Officers receive notification of the next week's worth of code words during every roll call briefing.

Reserves

To meet staffing demands during large events or wide-scale disasters, some departments use reserve police officers. The definition of a reserve officer varies depending on the department, but most view these personnel as trained and sworn officers who are not full-time department employees. Some reserve officers are paid, but most reserve programs draw on unpaid volunteers.

Training standards for reserve officers vary. At the upper extreme, reservists are required to pass the same academy curriculum as full-time officers. (Some reservists are former street cops who moved on to other professions but still feel a call to duty). Less stringent requirements still call for some measure of certification, as well as background checks and physical fitness qualifications equivalent to those for academy graduates. In almost all cases, departments require reservists to serve a minimum number of hours per month and attend monthly training.

When on duty, reserve officers must remain under the constant supervision of regular officers at all times. In practice, this means that reservists get called up when departments are shorthanded and pull a lot of grunt work, such as directing traffic at accident scenes while sworn officers write reports, working crowd control for summer festivals or providing an extra set of eyes in the passenger's seat of the cruiser during civil unrest. The degree of flexibility and authority that most departments give their reservists is directly related to the departments' training requirements.

Reserve officers are a topic of contention among cops. Depending on the observer's department policies and personal experiences, opinions on reservists range from "helpful backup" to "useless wannabes."

Police Culture

Just as any other specialized field of employment, law enforcement has its own specialized subculture. Most citizens have distorted views of police work thanks to popular entertainment or cultural issues, resulting in a gulf of misunderstanding between officers and the civilians they protect. Consequently, cops find it hard to openly socialize with ordinary citizens when off duty. It's not uncommon for an officer to find that by his fourth or fifth year in uniform, his entire circle of friends is made up of other cops.

Stress

Law enforcement is a high-stress occupation. The physical hazards are bad enough — knives, guns, tire irons, HIV, tuberculosis, auto accidents and a host of other dangers. Most statistical analyses of officer injuries and deaths in the line of duty focus on these. An even greater hazard, though, is less well documented: the emotional and psychological consequences of police work. Officers spend their shifts worrying about the physical threats while dealing with the dregs of society and experiencing stark boredom punctuated by mind-numbing terror. Cops have a firsthand view of the after-effects of homicides, suicides, drug overdoses, rapes, child abuse and the entire panoply of man's inhumanity to man.

Statistically speaking, officers are five times more likely to die of stress-related illnesses than they are to be killed in the line of duty. Despite being able to retire with a full pension after 20 years of service, many don't live much past 50.

Coping Mechanisms

Officers recognize the hazards of stress in their jobs and tend to watch out for one another. The tightest bonds form between partners, but almost every cop is willing to lend an ear or step in to resolve a situation if it looks as if another officer might be on the verge of losing it. In many situations, talking to other, more experienced cops is more comfortable than professional help, as slow, reasoned therapy is antithetical to the mode of instant assessment and action in which a street cop's brain operates.

Good street officers tend to work out regularly. Knowing that one night their survival may depend on fitness and ferocity, many cops study martial arts that emphasize ground fighting and grappling. Others maintain gym memberships or engage in physically demanding hobbies such as rock climbing or rugby when off duty.

Even the most sensitive officer eventually develops a sick sense of humor. The grislier the death scene, the more likely the responding officers are to crack jokes about it. Wise officers are careful to keep their comments out of earshot of reporters or family members. Emergency medical personnel are equally irreverent.

The department does take care of its own, too. After any officer-involved shooting or a particularly bad violent crime scene, the precinct commander arranges a critical incident debriefing as soon as possible. This is a semi-formal review of the event that a department psychologist or chaplain directs but doesn't lead. Every officer who was involved in the incident is encouraged, but not required, to attend, as is the dispatcher who handled the radio traffic and any MFD personnel who were on scene. Studies have shown that officers who do attend such debriefings are much less likely to experience residual psychological problems stemming from the event.

Herbivores and Carnivores

A behavioral dichotomy exists in law enforcement between aggressive and non-aggressive officers. Some refer to these, respectively, as carnivores and herbivores. Few cops exclusively fit into one category, but it's easy for cops to assess coworkers' positions on the scale. Some of the major points of difference include the following.

Carnivores have street eyes. When on patrol duty, they're alert and aware of their surroundings, always scanning sidewalks and alleys for trouble. By contrast, herbivores stare straight ahead and try very hard not to notice any potentially threatening situations they might have to get involved in. When a call for service goes out, a carnivore assesses how interesting the situation will be, while an herbivore considers its potential for violence.

Carnivores are assertive and confrontational. Most like to fight, or at least don't mind it, not out of masochist urges but rather out of competitive ones. By comparison, herbivores are non-aggressive and more likely to attempt to talk through a situation even when a greater degree of force is probably necessary.

Carnivores practice marksmanship on a weekly basis and take additional classes in defensive tactics. Herbivores practice marksmanship once a year, before annual qualifications, and rely on their pepper spray.

Carnivores accumulate a wide array of minor-to-moderate injuries in the line of duty. Most of these are sustained in fights or foot pursuits. Herbivores, who tend to avoid violent confrontation, rarely suffer minor injuries but are much more likely to be killed on duty. Cop killers often state that they wouldn't have had the opportunity to kill their victims if the officers had been better at controlling the encounters.

Carnivores accrue many more citizen complaints than herbivores, but also have higher clearance rates on their cases.

Herbivores are more likely to become involved in department politics at higher levels and have much higher rates of stress-related illness.

Cop Bars

Most large cities are home to at least one cop bar. Such an establishment is never part of an established chain — a cop bar is a small, locally owned business, invariably with a current or retired cop in charge. While outsiders aren't explicitly barred from entry, the place isn't easy to find or well advertised, and those who do wander in receive a general vibe of not being welcome. Cop bars spring up because officers want a place to unwind where they can speak freely, and because those who go to public establishments always run the risk of encountering someone they've previously arrested.

A cop bar looks much like any other small bar at first glance. It's rare to see a uniform in one unless an on-duty officer needs to talk to a colleague there, as department policies universally forbid cops from drinking while on duty. Décor tends toward department memorabilia: old badges, academy class photos, patches from other agencies and a memorial wall for officers killed in the line of duty.

The 13th Precinct's cop bar is Bailey's, with which the precinct house shares an alley.

Anonymity

Police officers who've lost their sense of newness in the Job tend not to advertise their occupation when off-duty. Because of the unpredictable reactions of citizens upon learning what an officer does, the cop humor T-shirts stay in the closet and the police organization stickers come off their vehicles. If asked, a common response is "I work for the city" or "I'm in sanitation."

Officers also have safety concerns, particularly if they have families, and don't want criminals identifying them when they're not working. Because, as civil employees, officers' names are a matter of public record, married officers sometimes register telephones, houses and personal vehicles in their spouses' names. Cops in some jurisdictions can also list their departments' addresses on their driver's licenses, checks and other official documents. For reasons of officer safety, MPD policy also forbids assigning an officer to the same precinct in which he lives.

New Character Options

Character creation guidelines for officers in various assignments are scattered throughout this chapter. The following new options may also prove useful for players wanting to create MPD characters.

Physical Merits

Fighting Style: Combat Marksmanship (• to •••••)

This Merit has been reprinted from **World of Darkness: Armory**, both for the Merit's utility and because several characters in the following chapter possess it.

Prerequisites: Strength ••, Dexterity ••, Composure ••• and Firearms ••

Effect: Your character is not only proficient with firearms, but has trained extensively to maintain her accuracy during the stress of combat. She most likely has experience in law enforcement or the military, though she may simply be a self-defense advocate or a dedicated hobbyist with uncommon self-possession.

Dots purchased in this Merit allow access to special combat maneuvers. Each maneuver is a prerequisite for the next. So, your character can't have Tactical Reload until she has Shoot First. The maneuvers and their effects are described below, most of which are based on the Firearms Skill.

Shoot First (•): Your character's trained reflexes give her a split-second edge in a gunfight. Whenever she begins a combat situation with a firearm already in her hand, she gains a bonus to her Initiative roll equal to her Firearms Skill. If she also has the Quick Draw Merit for firearms (see the **World of Darkness Rulebook**, p. 113) and draws a firearm during the first turn of combat, this bonus is added retroactively, starting at the beginning of the second turn of combat.

Tactical Reload (••): Your character's muscle memory enables her to reload without conscious thought. Once per turn, she may reload a firearm that feeds from a detachable magazine or use a speedloader to reload a revolver, as a reflexive action.

Double Tap (•••): When using a lever-action, pump-action or semi-automatic firearm, your character may make short burst attacks as if her gun were capable of autofire.

Bayonet Range (••••): Your character can maintain accuracy and control even when facing an opponent at arm's length. The target's Defense does not apply to firearm attacks your character makes within close-combat range (see p. 155, the **World of Darkness Rulebook**).

Rapid Fire (•••••): Your character's concentration is such that she can unleash a hail of bullets. In a single action, she may make one extra Firearms attack for each point by which her Composure exceeds 2. Each extra attack is made at a cumulative –1 modifier. Thus, she can perform a total of two attacks at Composure 3 (the second of which is at –1), three attacks at Composure 4 (the third of which is at –2) and four at Composure 5 (the fourth of which is at –3). She must declare the targets of all attacks before rolling the first one. Each attack not directed against her initial target suffers an additional –1 penalty. All attacks made with this maneuver must be single shots. **Drawback:** Your character cannot use her Defense against any attack in the same turn in which she intends to use this maneuver. If she uses Defense against attacks that occur earlier in the Initiative roster, before she can perform this maneuver, she cannot use Rapid Fire this turn. In addition, your character may not use this maneuver with bolt-action or break-action firearms.

Fighting Style: Police Tactics (• to •••)

Prerequisites: Strength ••, Dexterity ••, Stamina ••, Brawl •• and Weaponry •

Effect: Your character has picked up some of the mixed bag of subdue and compliance tricks that cops learn in the academy and on the street. If he doesn't have law enforcement experience himself, he's most likely learned these maneuvers from someone who has.

Dots purchased in this Merit allow access to special combat maneuvers. Each maneuver is a prerequisite for the next. So, your character can't have Weapon Retention until he has Compliance Hold. The maneuvers and their effects are listed below.

Compliance Hold (•): When trying to overpower an opponent you have grappled (see the **World of Darkness Rulebook**, pp. 157–159), you gain a +2 bonus to your Strength + Brawl roll if you attempt to immobilize or disarm him. You must choose your maneuver before making your roll, rather than after it, to gain this bonus.

Weapon Retention (••): An opponent who has grappled you must score successes equal to your Weaponry score on his Strength + Brawl roll to choose a "disarm" or "turn a drawn weapon" maneuver against you.

Speed Cuff (•••): If you have a pair of handcuffs or equivalent restraints drawn while grappling, you may choose "cuff" as an overpowering maneuver. With success, you get the cuffs on one of your opponent's wrists. With exceptional success, you cuff *both* wrists.

Social Merits

Sworn Officer (• to ••••)

Prerequisite: The character must meet the basic requirements to be an officer in the department she selects. See p. 36 for the minimum requirements for an MPD officer.

Effects: You character is a sworn law enforcement officer, with all the rights and duties thereof. She is empowered within her jurisdiction to make arrests, use department equipment and resources, view confidential information, request assistance from other agencies and use force during the course of her duties. She may legally carry a concealed deadly weapon anywhere in the United States not prohibited by federal law, even when off duty. When in another agency's jurisdiction, she also can expect professional courtesy (see p. 60), subject to local customs and policies.

This Merit differs from Status (see the World of Darkness Rulebook, p. 116) in that Status represents a character's standing within an organization, while Sworn Officer indicates that the character actually is a duly empowered law enforcement officer. The civilian director of the Midway Forensic Science Center may be an MPD employee with Status (MPD) ••••, but he's still a civilian, not a sworn officer.

The number of dots purchased in this Merit determines the extent of the jurisdiction of the agency for which your character works. One dot indicates a small to mid-sized town or a rural county. Two dots indicate a major city (such as Midway) or a densely populated county. Three dots indicate a statewide agency. Four dots indicate a federal agency with national jurisdiction.

Note: For a police-centered story in which most or all of the characters are officers, the Storyteller is strongly encouraged to provide this Merit free. In such a case, being a cop is an intrinsic part of the story and players should not be charged points for playing characters that fit the game's concept. However, an individual player who wants to play a cop character in a non-police-focused chronicle must still purchase this Merit.

STATE'S
EXHIBIT

Chapter Three: Roll Call

I'm not against the police; I'm just afraid of them.

-Alfred Hitchcock

This chapter depicts the various personalities who inhabit the 13th Precinct. Each has his own interesting story, habits, tales to tell and cases he's currently investigating.

About half of these characters have connections to the supernatural. That's intentional on our end, and you'll note that those individuals touched by the supernatural don't necessarily know how close they've come to it. One of the hallmarks of the World of Darkness is that the strangeness of the environment leaves no one outside its cast shadow. Whether or not those individuals realize that they've had a brush with the mystical depends on the individuals' awareness or disposition.

Unless otherwise specified, each police character (not the ambulance crew, etc.) carries the standard complement of police-issue gear while he's on shift. That includes the weapons, armor and other accouterments described on p. 69.

As well, Storytellers will have a little room to modify characters to best suit their own chronicles. For example, some characters have overlapping Allies or Contacts, or such "outside" individuals have been left without details. Switch these about, fill in the blanks or otherwise adapt them so as to keep players on their toes and the characters in question fully and broadly connected to their beat.

The Officers and Detectives

Det. Pauline Reed, Senior Field Investigator

Quote: *"Well, I'm not one to complain, and I'm sure the captain is doing the best he can . . . all things considered."*

Background: Pauline has the greatest seniority of anyone in the 13th Precinct other than the captain and Sid Routman (who harbors no political ambitions). She also strongly believes that she should be the next captain and is in fact incensed that the current captain was promoted over her. She is convinced that this is either because she is black or because she is a woman. To the extent that discrimination plays any part in Pauline being passed over, it is because of the mistaken belief in some quarters that she is a lesbian. In fact, Pauline is heterosexual but has a near-phobia of sexual relations due to her being date-raped by a fellow police academy cadet named Stephen Carter more than 20 years ago. Pauline never reported the incident because Carter was related to the then police chief, and she was afraid that by bringing charges against him she might hurt her career ambitions. Carter was shot and killed six years later, and a 17-year-old Latino suspected of gang connections was arrested and convicted of the shooting. If Pauline ever felt any guilt over murdering her rapist and sending an innocent boy to the electric chair for her crimes, she has never shown it. The real reason that Pauline was passed over for the captain's bars was simple patronage — the current captain was a fraternity brother of one of the mayor's major campaign backers.

Description: Pauline is an attractive but somewhat aloof black woman in her mid-40s. She prefers pantsuits to dresses but still maintains her femininity. She is in excellent shape and jogs regularly. She maintains professional and cordial relations with her fellow officers but gets along with the women somewhat better than the men. She goes to great lengths to cover up her personal dislike for the captain of the 13th Precinct.

Storytelling Hints: Pauline is a capable and efficient police officer with 20 years' experience in the Robbery Division. As such, she can be an excellent mentor to detectives and even patrol officers who aspire to detective rank. She bonds more easily with women than with men, and a male officer who seeks to gain her trust should keep the relationship on a strictly professional basis, as she will instantly grow cold to any male coworker who makes romantic overtures.

Attributes: Intelligence 3, Wits 3, Resolve 3, Strength 2, Dexterity 2, Stamina 2, Presence 2, Manipulation 3, Composure 2

Skills: Academics (Forensics) 3, Brawl 2, Computer 2, Drive 2, Empathy (Detecting Lies) 3, Firearms 3, Intimidation 2, Investigation 2 (Crime Scenes) 2, Medicine 1, Politics 2, Stealth 1, Streetwise 2, Subterfuge 3, Weaponry 1

Merits: Contacts (Fences, Organized Crime) 2, Fighting Style: Police Tactics 1, Status (City Police) 3, Sworn Officer 2

Willpower: 5

Morality: 6 (Suspicion, mild)

Virtue: Justice

Vice: Envy

Initiative: 4

Defense: 2

Speed: 9

Health: 7

Neil Hurst, Rookie Patrol Officer

Quote: *"Don't fucking tell me to calm down!"*

Background: Officer Hurst is a third-generation MPD officer. Neil dedicated himself to becoming a police officer in the memory of his own father, Ted Hurst, who was killed in the line of duty just months after Neil was born. To fulfill this dream, Neil has worked to overcome the stigma of being the only child of a single mother and a lifetime of anger management issues stemming from growing up without a father. Less than a year ago, Neil graduated from the MPD training academy, and although he was nowhere near the top of his class, his performance was respectable. Recently, however, the stress of his job has been wearing at his ability to cope with his anger, and Neil's fiancée has broken off their engagement out of concerns over his potentially violent mood swings. Neil is caught between concern over his constant mood swings and his fear that seeking psychiatric help may end his police career. In fact, things are much

worse than Neil could ever imagine.

The truth is that Ted Hurst was not Neil's father. Rather, Neil is the product of an affair between Neil's mother and a longtime friend named Eric Holland, who also happens to be a werewolf of the Iron Master tribe. Ted discovered that his wife was carrying another man's child and attempted to murder Holland. Instead, the werewolf killed Ted in self-defense, altered the crime scene to make it look like a gangland slaying and left Midway till the heat was off. Unfortunately for Neil, the Uratha blood runs true, and Neil's increasingly uncontrollable anger is the result of an immanent First Change that may well occur in front of fellow officers while he is on call. The local Iron Riders are aware of this situation but are uncertain of what to do, since no one with as high a profile as a MPD officer has ever undergone the First Change. Some Uratha even argue that it would be best to simply kill him before he Changes rather than risk a catastrophic breach of the Veil.

Neil is currently partnered with Alex Quintero.

Description: Neil clearly shows the Black Irish ancestry of both his mother and his true father, with black hair and thick bushy eyebrows. His eyes have a smoldering intensity that draw women like moths to a flame, at least until his moodiness and barely sublimated anger frighten them away. When not in uniform, Neil favors comfortable jeans, tennis shoes and T-shirts or jerseys carrying the logo of one sports team or another. Neil is in superb physical condition. He works out almost every day, and he avidly studied kung fu until a few weeks ago when he accidentally broke three of his instructor's ribs in a sparring mishap. Since then, Neil has been too embarrassed to return to his training.

Storytelling Hints: Neil is the epitome of the expression "still waters run deep." Even when he is totally calm, the young man gives the impression of someone barely holding his temper in check. He is very easily provoked into anger, and only the calming influence of his partner, Alex Quintero, has prevented a few incidents that might have gotten Neil brought up on police brutality charges, or worse. Recently, his moodiness has also been increased by his insomnia, the result of recurring nightmares about going on an inchoate rampage and tearing apart drug dealers, pimps and gang members with razor-sharp claws and teeth. Neil knows something is happening to him and would be grateful to anyone who could help him — unless that "help" cost him his job on the force. Neil's role as a police officer is so integral to his self-identity that he would certainly face difficulty over the obvious impossibility of serving on the force while adapting to life as a werewolf.

Attributes: Intelligence 2, Wits 3, Resolve 2, Strength 3, Dexterity 3, Stamina 2, Presence 3, Manipulation 2, Composure 2

Skills: Academics 2, Athletics 4, Brawl (Kung Fu) 4, Computer 1, Drive (High Speed Chases) 2, Firearms 3, Intimidation 2, Investigation 1, Medicine 1, Socialize 2, Stealth 2, Streetwise 2, Weaponry 2

Merits: Fighting Style: Combat Marksmanship 2 (see

World of Darkness: Armory), Fighting Style: Kung Fu 4, Fighting Style: Police Tactics 3, Sworn Officer 2
Willpower: 4
Morality: 7 (After his First Change, Neil's Morality rating will convert to a Primal Urge rating. See **Werewolf: The Forsaken**.)
Virtue: Justice
Vice: Wrath
Initiative: 5
Defense: 3
Speed: 11
Health: 7

Sgt. Mal Lesperance

Quote: *"You say the officer put his hand where, now? And this was while he was holding his flashlight? How's that possible?"*

Background: Police work is exceedingly difficult. Officers face threats to their well-being as part of the job, and their actions come under intense scrutiny. Complaints by citizens are taken seriously, particularly in light of scandals such as the Los Angeles Police Department's Rampart program and the Amadou Diallo shooting in New York City. When an officer's actions and integrity come into question, he often turns to his local union representative for assistance. Officers of the 13th Precinct have a determined advocate in the person of Sergeant Malcolm Lesperance.

Mal's father was a prosecutor for an East Coast District Attorney's office. The older Lesperance was a dogged lawyer who viewed his work as a conflict between good and evil and a personal battle with every defense attorney he faced. His legal skills served him well, and he developed a reputation as a fearsome adversary. He studied other cases diligently, seeking out every advantage he could use to punish the guilty and humiliate his opposite number. Defense attorneys regularly accepted Lesperance's plea-bargain offers.

Mal set out to follow his father's path. He spent only a year in law school, however, before dropping out and joining the police force. He saw and studied cases in which police procedure was called into question, resulting in the perpetrator going free, the officer being penalized or both. Let his father prosecute the guilty, Mal decided. Police officers deserved legal protection as well, and the younger Lesperance began studying the tactics of criminal defense attorneys.

Police work agreed with Mal, and his father's reputation opened doors for him. He developed his own reputation as a real cop's cop, avoided any hint of scandal or corruption and got involved with the police officers' union. He leapt at any chance to further solidify his standing with his fellow officers, and was elected to the position of union representative before he turned 30. His first test as an advocate came when a citizen filed an excessive force complaint against Mal's own partner. Mal investigated the complainant and

Neil Hurst, Pauline Reed, Sid Routman, & Mal Lesperance

discovered that the man had made at least two complaints of a similar nature against other officers every year. More than half of the accused officers had received some kind of punishment. Mal examined the complainant's medical records, finding no trace of the kind of injury the man reported. When his partner was exonerated, Mal contacted a colleague of his father and filed a slander suit against the complainant. The suit was resolved out of court, and the accused officers' records were cleared. Mal's popularity skyrocketed.

Similar to his father, Mal studies legal precedent and current cases. He spends many off-duty hours in courtrooms, learning how defense attorneys use seemingly insignificant missteps and violations of procedure to further their cases. He applies these tactics to his defense of officers under investigation, casting doubt on the veracity and reliability of accusers. Where his father used the results of police investigations to punish the guilty, Mal ensured that officers were able to do their jobs without fear of petty retribution and constant second-guessing. The two Lesperances exchange information about their cases, and both men are proud of each other.

For all of his advocacy work, Mal is notoriously unforgiving of officers who grossly abuse their authority, such as Wade Whitfield and Stew Green. Mal holds his fellow policemen to high standards, and cops who decide that they are above the law can find themselves left high and dry. He looks at law enforcement as much more of a calling than a mere career, and wants only the best men and women the city has to offer serving as its protectors. The force's reputation for corruption sickens him; he sees MPD's bad officers in the worst possible light.

Mal is unmarried, with a couple of steady girlfriends. He prefers the company of fellow officers, and is starting to look toward continuing the family line. He is incredibly popular among the police department's rank and file. Officers rely on his knowledge of procedure and legal precedent.

Sometimes called the "angels' advocate," Mal attends service at Garcia Road Episcopal, and was one of the officers who encouraged Father Calhoun to become a police chaplain. Mal and Calhoun regularly consult with one another, and each man sends troubled officers to visit the other.

Description: Mal is tall and imposing, and can generate an aura of genuine menace as easily as turning on a light. He has a pronounced widow's peak, and his remaining dark brown hair is kept tightly trimmed. His face is deeply lined from the stresses of more than two decades of service to Midway's citizens and the officers who protect them.

Storytelling Hints: Mal is dedicated to protecting the officers he represents from investigation and severe punishment. He is an aggressive and sometimes vicious opponent, using tricks more suited to a high-priced defense attorney. Mal's never satisfied with his own achievements, and when an officer he represents is reprimanded by the department, Mal sinks into a deep funk. He takes every complaint and investigation personally. No matter what he does, though,

someone out there does it a little bit better. Mal measures everything he does against the achievements of someone else, and he feels that he comes up short.

Attributes: Intelligence 3, Wits 2, Resolve 3, Strength 3, Dexterity 3, Stamina 2, Presence 2, Manipulation 3, Composure 3

Skills: Athletics 2, Brawl 2, Drive 2, Expression 2, Firearms 2, Intimidation 3, Investigation 3, Persuasion 3, Politics 3, Streetwise 2, Weaponry 2

Merits: Allies 2, Disarm, Fighting Style: Boxing 2, Strong Back, Status (MPD) 3

Willpower: 7

Morality: 6

Virtue: Fortitude

Vice: Envy

Health: 7

Initiative: 5

Defense: 2

Speed: 7

Lt. Sid Routman,
Senior Homicide Detective

Quote: *"Excuse me, sir, I'm sorry to intrude, but I just had a few more questions."*

Background: Sid Routman is the longest-serving officer in the 13th Precinct and is the ranking Homicide detective there. At age 63, he is almost eligible for retirement, but is unsure if he will quit when his time is up. Sid is something of an oddity among the Homicide detectives. Most officers feel some degree of tension between work and family, but not Sid, who is a devoted husband to his wife of 37 years and a loving father to three grown daughters. His fellow officers marvel at how Sid can handle the grotesqueries of more than 20 years in the Homicide Division without being worn down by the type of cases that send lesser officers to counseling or other jobs. Instead, Sid just keeps on coming in, day after day, dispassionately collecting evidence at murder scenes, gently consoling the families of murder victims and interrogating suspects with such effortless charm that his friends compare him to "Columbo." His success rate with murder cases is the highest of any Homicide detective in the department.

What Sid's fellow officers and even Sid's own wife don't suspect is that the key to his success lies in his own unique form of insanity. Sid snapped in 1984, when his first assignment as a Homicide detective turned out to be a young woman killed by a vampire during a failed feeding attempt. The vampire attempted to silence Sid, who killed the bloodsucker in self-defense and then watched in horror as the creature disintegrated into dust. Sid's next conscious thoughts were, *This won't do. How can you arrest a murderer when he doesn't have a body?* So, Sid picked a homeless vagrant at random and framed him for the young girl's murder. And Sid's been doing it ever since.

Sid's madness takes the form of an extreme sociopathic detachment. He doesn't consider anyone around him to be real, including himself. Rather, Sid views everyone he encounters — victims, suspects, fellow officers and even his family members — as fictional constructs, with him playing a part very loosely based on an amalgam of television cop shows. Consequently, Sid never seems to have any emotional difficulties stemming from his job because he views neither the victims nor their families nor even their murderers as people. When confronted by a mutilated corpse, he is no more horrified than he would be when seeing one in a horror movie. When consoling survivors, he is gentle and compassionate, because according to the script that runs in his mind, police officers are supposed to be gentle and compassionate in such situations. And his success rate stems from his insistent belief that a good cop always gets his man. Thus, whenever he is stumped in a murder case, he carefully assesses which potential suspect (which might include other homeless people) would be the easiest to prove guilty and meticulously frames that person for the crime. Then, Sid goes home to his wife, ready to assume the role of loving husband and doting father, oblivious to the innocent life he has just destroyed.

In addition to making him a well-respected detective, Sid's insanity also makes him a boon to the Masquerade, albeit one even the local vampires don't know about. The detective is so deeply in denial about the vampire he encountered so many years ago that he conceals any evidence of occult activity he encounters in his work, even to the point of deleting the statements of witnesses to supernatural attacks — or maybe killing them. Anyone who tries to show Sid evidence of the existence of vampires will likely have no idea of what a dangerous enemy she's made.

Description: Sid is a 63-year-old, non-practicing Jewish man with black-and-gray hair and a slightly receding hairline. He's just under six feet tall and fairly healthy, though age and good cooking are finally starting to catch up to him. He almost invariably wears one of his several identical brown suits except to funerals, when he wears a blue suit. While at the office, he often ditches his suit coat for a cardigan, as he often complains of how cold the detective's offices are in winter.

Storytelling Hints: No one who knows Sid has the faintest clue of his true nature. To observers, he comes off as a genial, fatherly mentor to younger officers or a sloppy visionary to suspects. Indeed, many suspects conclude that Sid is a fool, right up until they answer some innocuous question with a detail that gives them away. Sid is a preternaturally good liar, especially on the witness stand, and no jury has ever doubted his presentation of evidence against a defendant. To most of his coworkers, Sid's chief character flaw is his insistence on showing off pictures of his new grandchildren to everyone he meets. Beneath this almost comically placid exterior, however, lies a calculating, ruthless mind. As a sort of intellectual

exercise, Sid frequently comes up with contingency plans for how he could frame or kill almost everyone he meets and get away with it. If he thought someone was close to penetrating his secrets, he would not hesitate to put such plans into effect.

Attributes: Intelligence 4, Wits 3, Resolve 3, Strength 2, Dexterity 2, Stamina 2, Presence 2, Manipulation 4, Composure 3

Skills: Academics (Forensics) 3, Athletics 1, Brawl 1, Computer 2, Drive 1, Empathy 3, Expression 2, Firearms 3, Intimidation 1, Investigation (Crime Scenes) 4, Larceny 4, Medicine 2, Persuasion 3, Politics 3, Science (Falsifying Evidence) 3, Socialize 2, Stealth 3, Streetwise 3, Subterfuge (False Testimony) 4, Weaponry 2

Merits: Encyclopedic Knowledge 4, Fame 2, Fighting Style: Police Tactics 1, Status (Police) 3, Sworn Officer 2

Willpower: 6

Morality: 3

Derangements: Hysteria, severe (triggered by exposure to supernatural); Sociopathic Detachment with Homicidal Tendencies, severe — triggered when Sid cannot solve a case. (See above.)

Virtue: Charity

Vice: Pride

Initiative: 5

Defense: 2

Speed: 9

Health: 7

Sgt. Gena Buehler,
Undercover Narcotics Detective

Quote: *"Well, looking like an addict is part of my job, after all."*

Background: Gena Buehler has been on the MPD force for 11 years, the last eight in Narcotics. During that time, she has been a highly respected officer at the center of a number of high-profile drug busts that have made the MPD Narcotics Division one of the most successful Narcotics units in the nation. And somehow, she has done so despite her own addiction to crystal meth.

Gena became addicted seven years ago, when she was forced to take the drug in order to avoid blowing her cover in a dangerous sting operation. She was able to conceal her illicit use from her fellow officers, but not her husband, Greg Buehler, who divorced her four years ago. Greg has sole custody of their two-year-old child, Amanda, which was his condition for not revealing her addiction during the divorce proceedings. Since then, Gena's drug use has increased significantly, and the only thing that has prevented her exposure has been the nature of her newest addiction: a methamphetamine derivative known on the street as "crimson."

The MPD Narcotics Division has become increasingly alarmed at the proliferation of this new designer drug, which chemically appears identical to normal crystal meth, but also

has several unique properties. Crimson, as its name implies, appears to be bright red instead of the normal rock-salt appearance of meth. More importantly, crimson is just as addictive and leads to much longer highs. However, despite the fact that the demand for crimson is very high, its street price seems to be kept quite low, suggesting that the process for making crimson is much more efficient than conventional meth. The final effect is unknown to the Narcotics Division — crimson is metabolized by the body more quickly than normal crystal meth, making crimson extremely difficult to detect on standard drug tests. Because of this, not one of the mandatory drug tests to which Gena has submitted during the last year has detected her use and addiction. Gena's suppliers have kept her in generous supply of crimson in exchange for advance warning of Narcotics Division operations designed to bust the supply ring. Gena lives in mortal fear of the day her betrayal of her fellow officers will lead to one of their deaths. Her greatest fear is that, when that day comes, she'll be so in the thrall of crimson that she won't even care.

Description: Gena was once very attractive and still can be if the situation calls for it. But her beauty is fading, worn away by years of stress and obscured by the hunted expression common to undercover officers. A natural blonde, Gena stands about five foot seven. She is in good shape but no longer exercises regularly. While undercover, she tends to dress vaguely "slutty," but when in the office, she favors dress pants and crisp pants, and she keeps her hair pulled back in a ponytail.

Storytelling Hints: Normally, Gena exudes professionalism when around other cops. She is mildly dismissive of patrol officers, and indeed any fellow officers who do not perform undercover work, as she feels only fellow narcs truly understand the stresses of her life. If confronted with the truth of her addiction, her reaction may be suicidal despair or genuine relief that she no longer needs to keep up the pretense of normality — and possibly both emotions at the same time.

Attributes: Intelligence 3, Wits 2, Resolve 2, Strength 2, Dexterity 3, Stamina 2, Presence 3, Manipulation 2, Composure 2

Skills: Academics 2, Athletics 1, Brawl 2, Computer 2, Drive 2, Empathy 2, Expression 1, Firearms (Handguns) 3, Intimidation 1, Investigation 2, Larceny 2, Medicine 1, Persuasion 2, Politics 1, Socialize 1, Stealth 2, Streetwise (Drug Culture) 4, Subterfuge (Concealing Addiction) 3, Weaponry 2

Merits: Contacts (Drug Dealers, Junkies, Party Promoters) 3, Fighting Style: Police Tactics 2, Sworn Officer 2

Willpower: 4

Morality: 6

Virtue: Justice

Vice: Gluttony

Initiative: 5

Defense: 2

Speed: 10

Health: 7

What Is Crimson?

Mechanically, the effects of each dose of crimson are a +1 bonus on all Strength- and Stamina-related rolls and a –1 penalty on all Composure-related rolls, due to the extreme euphoria the drug induces. The effects of a typical dose will last for about four hours. After each dose, the user must roll Resolve + Composure to avoid becoming addicted to the drug. Each subsequent dosage confers a cumulative –1 penalty in addition to the –1 penalty caused by the reduction in Composure. Addicts must have a fix at least once every 24 hours, and for every 24-hour period that passes, the user suffers a cumulative –1 penalty (maximum penalty of –5) on all Social rolls to resist taking the drug if it is offered. If the user's Vice is Gluttony, the penalty increases to –2.

In order to beat the addiction, the addict must avoid every possible opportunity to be supplied with the drug during the withdrawal period. During this time, the addict must accumulate 30 successes on an extended Resolve + Composure roll, with each roll representing one day off the drug. Even after the withdrawal period, the addiction is never permanently beaten, as the user remains permanently susceptible to the drug's effects. If offered the drug, the user must roll Resolve + Composure to resist the invitation (with no penalty), and if the user ever takes the drug again, he is automatically addicted to it once more.

We leave the true nature of the street drug crimson to the Storyteller's discretion, as its origin may change depending on the needs of the chronicle. Some possible origins include the following.

Vampires: Crimson consists of normal crystal meth that has been cut with specially treated Vitae taken from a vampire. Most likely, the process for creating crimson is the result of Ordo Dracul blood magic or perhaps through the strange powers of a bloodline, such as the Nepenthe Discipline of the Anvari (see **Bloodlines: The Hidden**).

Mages: There are a great many reasons why certain mages might want to create a magically enhanced street drug: a Mastigos who Awakened when overcoming his own addiction who seeks to enlighten others, a plot of the Seers of the Throne to come up with a way to pacify the population, a diabolical plan devised by one of the Left-Handed Legacies such as the Scelesti to win souls for their dark masters or even just a wealth-generating scheme by a particularly amoral Silver Ladder cabal.

Werewolves: Few werewolves would have the means or the desire to trigger an addiction epidemic for a street drug, but many of their adversaries might. For example, a spirit of addiction or suffering that had crossed over to the physical world might use Numina to mystically alter normal crystal meth in order to expand the spirit's influence.

Alejandra "Alex" Quintero, Patrol Officer

Quote: *"On behalf of the Midway Police Department, I am honored to speak before the Midway Latin American Unity Conference."*

Background: Alex Quintero's family moved to Midway from Cuba in 1949, but that doesn't stop people from calling her a "wetback" behind her back, and sometimes even to her face. Alex graduated at the top of her class from the MPD Academy, and since then she has been a capable and conscientious police officer, which is, of course, why her promotions have been slow in coming. It's not due to racism, as a number of people in City Hall would love to advance the career of a bright, photogenic Latina for purely political reasons, but only if they were certain she would play ball when it came to improving the MPD's shaky public image. Unfortunately, a few people in City Hall still remember that the Citadel Heights scandal that brought down almost the entire city government in the late 1980s exploded after a Hispanic female officer (the first to reach detective grade) leaked evidence of rampant police brutality to the *Midway Tribune*. Even today, almost 20 years later, there are still elements in the city government who are gun-shy about advancing officers who are both female and ethnic minorities unless such officers are certain to put the needs of the department above their ethic or gender loyalties.

And in truth, none of the politics really matters to Alex. Although she has some aspirations of being a detective someday, she genuinely enjoys patrol work and takes great pride in her status as a role model for the Latino community. In addition to numerous commendations, she has also received several public service awards from local Latin American civic organizations. Regrettably, this attention has also caused some friction between Alex and some of her coworkers, particularly a small group of white and African American officers who are united in their bigotry toward Latinos. Aside from racial issues, Alex has also had to deal with a certain amount of resentment over her ongoing romantic relationship with Brad Alford, a local public defender who is particularly skilled at getting evidence suppressed due to police misconduct. Their relationship has led to some of Alex's fellow officers accusing her of "sleeping with the enemy," and has resulted in Alex being paired with the other officer no one wanted to ride with: the possibly unstable Neil Hurst. After some trepidation, Alex has grown quite fond of Neil, though she still has serious concerns about his fitness for police work.

Description: Alex is an attractive female officer with Hispanic features: olive skin, deep brown eyes and black hair, usually pulled back in a ponytail. Her uniform is invariably spotless. When Alex lets her hair down, so to speak, she becomes a stunning beauty. Alex works out regularly and also competes every year in the Midway 10K Run. She also studies martial arts and has asked Neil Hurst to spar with her, though he refuses to do so out of fear of injuring his partner.

Storytelling Hints: Alex is very nearly the perfect officer. She's highly intelligent, well motivated and honest to a fault. Naturally, she may never see a promotion past sergeant for the rest of her career. Alex has only one major character flaw: her somewhat excessive pride in her ethnic heritage. Even then, however, her pride does not lead her to holding any prejudices toward people of different ethnicities. Rather, it's just mildly grating to her more openly prejudiced coworkers. Alex also has one potential stumbling block. While she has strong feelings for her boyfriend, Brad Alford, she has reservations about actually marrying him. More importantly, Alex's fondness for Neil Hurst is on the verge of becoming something more, despite all of her instincts screaming that an affair with her possibly unstable partner can only end in tears.

Attributes: Intelligence 3, Wits 3, Resolve 2, Strength 2, Dexterity 2, Stamina 3, Presence 3, Manipulation 2, Composure 3

Skills: Academics 1, Athletics (Running) 3, Brawl (Kung Fu) 3, Computer 2, Drive 3, Empathy 2, Expression 2, Firearms 3, Intimidation 1, Investigation 2, Medicine 1, Persuasion 1, Politics (Public Relations) 2, Science 2, Socialize 1, Stealth 1, Streetwise 2, Subterfuge 2, Weaponry 1

Merits: Fame 1, Fighting Style: Kung Fu 1, Fighting Style: Police Tactics 3, Fleet of Foot 3, Sworn Officer 2

Willpower: 5

Morality: 7

Virtue: Faith

Vice: Pride

Initiative: 5

Defense: 2

Speed: 12

Health: 8

Sgt. Arthur Delgado, Night Shift Desk Sergeant

Quote: *"Evening everybody. There's donuts in the break room. Sorry, but they were out of jellies."*

Background: Art Delgado has served 28 years with the MPD and is still going strong. Art was never a particularly ambitious cop, but he has always been well liked by his coworkers and at least competent at his job. Nine years

Wade Whitfield, Arthur Delgado, Alejandra Quintero, & Gena Buehler

ago, he was diagnosed with a persistent heart murmur that effectively ended his career as a patrol officer, but he had enough friends in high places — younger cops who had been mentored by Art on their way up the political ladder — that he was put on partial disability and allowed to continue on the force. Art's pension would not have vested until after 20 years on the force, and anyway, Art loved being a cop so much (even a low-ranking cop with little authority) that his friends were eager to find him a job as a desk sergeant that would let him continue wearing the uniform even as the job kept him off the streets. The Third Shift position was the perfect fit, as Art is a self-proclaimed night owl and the shift is often so light that Art can bring a book to read. Art used to joke that he would make it to retirement or die trying. He was partly right.

Six months ago, Art Delgado passed away peacefully in his sleep. Then, that night, when it was time for his shift to begin, he got up, got dressed and came in to work as if nothing were wrong. Exactly how and why Art became one of the walking dead is unknown, and not even Art himself noticed the change at first. It wasn't until six months after Art's "death" that his repeated inability to check his own blood pressure after exercising lead to the realization that he had no pulse. After a brief panic, Art quickly realized the benefits of his condition. Whatever force animates Art's body has made it more healthy than ever before, other than the fact that his heart no longer functions. In truth, Art no

longer needs to eat, drink or even breathe. His body can still process food and liquids normally, but if he were deprived of sustenance, he would not even notice. Art is also free of all the aches and pains that had plagued him in his later years, and he is much stronger and faster than a man of his age should be, though he carefully conceals these benefits from those around him. He heals injuries at an astonishing speed and seems almost immune to pain.

Art is single and has never been married, except to the force. Since discovering his condition, he has contemplated trying to find some way to get back out into the field, since he might now be a much more effective police officer than he was even in his younger days. Such ideas cannot overcome his sense of caution, however. Art has avoided doctors and anyone else who might discover his true nature, and he is actually quite frightened of being discovered. His head is often filled with wild conspiracy theories about sinister corporations or government agencies that might dissect him for the secret of immortality if he were discovered. Sometimes, his mind wanders back to the comic books he read in his youth and wonders if he should become some sort of masked vigilante superhero, but then he shakes his head at such an obviously absurd idea and returns to the safety of his dispatch job, as he tries to remain inconspicuous while he decides what to do next.

Description: Art is 61-year-old white male who is clearly too out of shape for field police work. He has gray hair and glasses and is portly, bordering on obese. Despite his age and apparent health problems, his coworkers describe him as "pretty spry." In fact, he conceals great physical strength and agility behind the demeanor of an over-the-hill cop counting the days to retirement.

Storytelling Hints: Art is friendly to almost all of his coworkers, and it takes almost overt rudeness on another person's part for him to get on Art's bad side. He is fairly efficient at his job, but he's also the guy who can be counted upon to bring in a 12-pack of donuts or to remember your birthday with a card. Art is a lapsed Catholic and completely dismisses the possibility of a religious or supernatural origin for his newfound abilities. Despite this general geniality, it is possible that Art might become more forceful or even violent if someone confronted him with evidence of his inexplicable nature, particularly if the confrontation were threatening. Beyond that, he will take any nonviolent steps to avoid blowing his own cover, as he is deathly afraid of all of his friends in the precinct thinking him some kind of freak.

The Strange Case of Arthur Delgado

In addition to incredible vitality, Art heals at a vastly accelerated rate and is almost unkillable. He heals one bashing health point every turn, one lethal health point every minute and one aggravated health point every hour. This healing continues *even after Art is dead*, and if he is killed, he will spring back to life immediately once all of his accumulated damage is healed. Although Art doesn't know it, he can be killed in one of four ways. Decapitation will kill him permanently, as will removal of his heart or his genitals. Finally, if he takes sufficient aggravated damage that would normally be fatal and his body is left in a situation in which his body will take continual damage (such as dumped into an incinerator), he will die permanently if he is prevented from reanimating for a full 24 hours.

Attributes: Intelligence 2, Wits 3, Resolve 2, Strength 6, Dexterity 4, Stamina 6, Presence 2, Manipulation 2, Composure 3

Skills: Academics 2, Athletics (Jumping) 4, Brawl (Boxing) 3, Computer 1, Drive 2, Empathy 2, Firearms 3, Intimidation 1, Investigation 2, Medicine 1, Persuasion 2, Politics 1, Science 1, Socialize 2, Stealth 3, Streetwise 2, Subterfuge (Discretion) 3, Weaponry 2

Merits: Allies (Police Administration) 2, Fighting Style: Boxing 1, Fighting Style: Police Tactics 1, Status (Precinct) 2, Sworn Officer 2

Willpower: 5
Morality: 7
Virtue: Justice
Vice: Envy
Initiative: 7
Defense: 3
Speed: 20 (species factor 10)
Armor: 3 (natural toughness)
Health: 11

Sgt. Wade Whitfield, White Supremacist Patrol Officer

Quote: *"What the hell makes you think I care whether you're guilty or not, asshole?"*

Background: Wade Whitfield is a 12-year veteran of the MPD and the ACLU's worst nightmare. After his second disciplinary review, Wade has finally learned to keep his mouth shut about his racist, bigoted and homophobic views, at least around people who don't share them. Among his pack of friends at the 13th, Wade won't hesitate to blame the "problems" in the precinct (whatever they might be) on PC liberals who force the MPD to give police spots to blacks, Mexicans (which includes all officers of Hispanic descent) and even gays. Wade openly despises Richard Bucknell, but has been told bluntly by his superiors to refrain from antagonizing Midway's most prominent gay police officer. Instead, Wade amuses himself by terrorizing the city's gay prostitutes, arresting them on specious charges, and then beating them for "resisting arrest" in what can only be described as legalized gay-bashing. Thus far, all of Wade's victims have been too afraid of him to bring charges.

Wade is related by blood to George O'Dell, a legendary racist and Klan member who served as Washington County Sheriff during the 1920s and whose Mob-connected family still runs much of the county as a corrupt fiefdom. Wade was eight years old when he went to his first Klan rally, and the roots of his hatred run deep. Despite his intensely violent nature, however, Wade is a fairly honest cop. He works in the MPD rather than the Sheriff's Department solely because he wants nothing to do with the O'Dell family's criminal activities, and he has turned down several offers from family members to fatten his wallet with bribes or to work as a partner in various illegal activities. However, he has not reported any of these criminal acts to his superiors due to the strength of his family connections.

In terms of personality, Wade is an unabashed redneck whose entire worldview comes from listening to talk radio jocks who make Rush Limbaugh look moderate. Consequently, much of his speech is peppered with conservative buzzwords such as "West Coast elites" and "gay agenda." Wade listens to no music other than country and western and despises rap. He is currently in the middle of his second

marriage, though it may soon go the way of his first. His first wife, Tina, unable to tolerate his abusive personality, simply ran off one night while Wade was at work and got a quickie divorce in Nevada. He and his current wife, Molly, have been married for four tumultuous years — Wade slapped Molly exactly once, six months into their marriage. She responded by kicking him in the balls and threatening to castrate him if he ever raised a hand to her again. Currently, Molly is eight months pregnant with their first child, a boy, and she is considering asking for a divorce after the birth rather than expose their son to Wade's personality. The prospect of fatherhood has had an intense effect on Wade, and if Molly threatens to take his boy away, he might actually try to change his ways — or he might explode in a brutal rage.

For the last six months, Wade has been partnered with Stewart Green, an African American officer who has been accused of having racist attitudes toward whites. Most of the officers in the 13th believed that this pairing was a disaster waiting to happen. A few of the more cynical officers thought it was brilliant, since one of the two widely despised officers was almost certain to quit the force rather than ride with the other, and in fact, they did almost come to blows on several occasions. To everyone's surprise, however, Wade and Stew have reached an understanding and are generally capable of working together in a professional manner. And while they still privately maintain contempt for each other, they have found common ground in their mutual homophobic hatred of Richard Bucknell.

Description: Wade is 39 years old, with red hair that he wears full in front to conceal a receding hairline. He has a wide face that could be quite open and friendly if he were capable of those demeanors. Most often, though, his smiles look more like sneers. Wade is in fairly good shape but does not work out regularly. When out of uniform, Wade favors blue jeans and T-shirts, usually featuring either patriotic slogans or depicting NASCAR stars.

Storytelling Hints: Wade is emphatically not a creature of subtlety. He is an unabashed racist bully who enjoys intimidating coworkers and private citizens. Like most bullies, he is cowardly at heart, and he won't do anything that might jeopardize his position. Instead, he sticks to tormenting rookie cops with elaborate mind games and hazing rituals and taking out his more violent frustrations on people who won't fight back, such as prostitutes and the homeless. He is easily provoked to anger, particularly by challenges to his manhood, and both Richard Bucknell and Alex Quintero are good at getting under his skin.

Attributes: Intelligence 2, Wits 2, Resolve 2, Strength 3, Dexterity 2, Stamina 3, Presence 2, Manipulation 3, Composure 2

Skills: Academics 1, Athletics 2, Animal Ken 1, Brawl (Cheap Shots) 3, Computer 2, Drive 3, Firearms 3, Intimidation (Bullying) 3, Investigation 2, Larceny 2, Medicine 1, Persuasion 3, Politics 1, Science 1, Socialize (Carousing) 2, Stealth 2, Streetwise 3, Subterfuge 3, Weaponry 2

Merits: Contacts (Sheriff's Department, Bar Owners) 2, Fighting Style: Combat Marksmanship 2, Fighting Style: Police Tactics 2, Sworn Officer 2

Willpower: 4

Morality: 6

Virtue: Justice

Vice: Envy

Initiative: 4

Defense: 2

Speed: 10

Health: 8

Officer Stewart "Stew" Green, Black Supremacist Patrol Officer

Quote: *"Well, of course. As a white man, you would think that, wouldn't you?"*

Background: If Wade Whitfield is the ACLU's worst nightmare, then Stew Green is the Klan's — an African American street cop with the build of a professional wrestler and the political views of a Black Panther. Stew decided to go into police work at the age of 17, after his brother was killed during the race riots that resulted from the 1980s Citadel Heights scandal. After completing a criminal justice degree and two years in the Marine Reserves during Desert Storm, Stew had no problems making it through the MPD Academy at the top of his class. Well, there was one minor problem — when he "accidentally" broke the arm of a white instructor with a nightstick during a "training mishap."

After the academy, Stew quickly found employment with the MPD, and he was highly regarded as a rookie officer, despite the grumblings of some of his fellow officers who thought he was an arrogant showboat. Things came to a head when a fellow officer made the mistake of referring to the Midway African American community as "you people" in a conversation with Stew, and accusations of racism and reverse-racism quickly degenerated into a fistfight. Stew almost lost his job, but the intervention of a prominent employment discrimination attorney (combined with a mayoral administration terrified of another racial controversy) not only saved Stew's job but won him a promotion. Emboldened by the experience, Stew went on to help found the MPD Black Officers' Council, a support organization for African American police officers who claimed to have been victims of racial discrimination and bias.

The BOC's stated purpose was laudable, but the organization's practical effect was to rip the MPD apart. Stray remarks were blown wildly out of proportion as the BOC sought to find discrimination everywhere in the department. Meanwhile, the legitimate grievances of other officers who suffered real discrimination because they were women, gay, Hispanic or Asian were ignored as the BOC monopolized the city's attention. To make matters worse, the BOC's agenda often conflicted with that of the Police Union, and many African American officers who had been good union members for decades found themselves caught

Sammy Atkinson, Stewart Green, & Richard Bucknell

in the middle. Eventually, the BOC imploded in 2002, when several of its key members were caught in a bribery sting and fired. The BOC dissolved, and while the MPD established a standing Committee on Departmental Race Relations, the police chief deliberately excluded everyone who had been involved in the BOC, including Stew, although he was not implicated in any way with the bribery scandal. Embittered, Stew became convinced that he was being scapegoated by the white power structure within the MPD, aided and abetted by the cops who belonged to other minority groups who were "jealous" of the BOC's success. This attitude was reinforced when Richard Bucknell, in a newspaper interview given shortly after he was outed, rejected the possibility of forming an organization for gay officers because of "the destructive impact of the BOC." As a result, Stew's long-standing bigoted views about whites began to extend to women, Hispanics and especially to homosexuals on the force.

After the BOC's collapse, Stew was reassigned to the 13th, where he went through a number of partners who were unable to work effectively with the bitter and racially inflammatory officer. Eventually, he was paired with Wade Whitfield, a borderline white supremacist, and the two nearly came to blows within hours of the assignment. Much to everyone else's surprise, however, the two officers came to an understanding, mainly due to their mutual realization that the higher-ups wanted them to get into a fight so that

both could be dismissed from the force. Since then, they have reached an uneasy truce and even found common ground: both Stew and Wade despise Richard Bucknell and, to a lesser extent, Alex Quintero.

Description: Stew is a 36-year-old African American who stands six foot eight and weighs nearly 300 pounds, almost all muscle. He keeps his head shaved at all times and prefers wearing the archetypal cop mirror shades. He has a tiny scar on his left cheek, a memento of Desert Storm. Stew's uniform is always finely ironed, and he polishes his uniform boots every night with the attention that only an ex-Marine can give them. When out of uniform, he favors comfortable clothes with a slight ethnic feel to them. For years, he insisted on wearing a Malcolm X cap when off duty to annoy the white officers. A few months back, someone who works at the 13th stole it from his locker as a prank, to his barely concealed consternation.

Storytelling Hints: The parallels between Stew Green and Wade Whitfield are almost disturbing. Both are profoundly racist, though directed toward different ethnic groups. Both are bullies, though Stew is much more subtle than Wade, opting to loom over and stare down his adversaries rather than actually threatening them. Stew is not afraid of controversy, but he has become almost paranoid in recent years, convinced that the police administration is just looking for a pretext to fire him. Given his intensely divisive personality, he's not really wrong. If Stew gave the

matter any thought, he would be surprised at the success of his relationship with Wade — the two men obviously hate each other but still seem to work well together. Largely, this is because they share many of the same bigotries. So long as Wade sticks to abusing white or Hispanic rookies and leaves the African American ones alone, Stew will not interfere and will even help out, advising Wade on some new, sick prank to pull or how to "get" somebody without crossing the line and risking an official reprimand. The main difference between the two is in degrees of subtlety — where Wade would simply write "faggot" on a fellow cop's locker, the more cerebral Stew would deliver a cutting remark that could be laughed off while making Stew's contempt obvious to the target.

Attributes: Intelligence 3, Wits 3, Resolve 2, Strength 4, Dexterity 3, Stamina 3, Presence 3, Manipulation 3, Composure 2

Skills: Academics 2, Athletics 3, Brawl 3, Computer 2, Drive (Defensive Driving) 3, Empathy 1, Expression (Cutting Remarks) 2, Firearms 3, Intimidation (Looming Over Suspects) 3, Investigation 2, Larceny 2, Medicine 1, Persuasion 2, Politics 3, Science 1, Socialize 2, Stealth 1, Streetwise 3, Subterfuge 2, Weaponry 2

Merits: Fighting Style: Combat Marksmanship 3, Fighting Style: Police Tactics 3, Stunt Driver 3, Sworn Officer 2

Willpower: 4

Morality: 6

Virtue: Hope

Vice: Envy

Initiative: 5

Defense: 3

Speed: 12

Health: 8

Sgt. Richard Bucknell, Night Shift Evidence Lockup Officer

Quote: *"Right. Now if you'll just sign for this evidence here. And here. And initial here. And here."*

Background: Richard Bucknell is a 12-year veteran of the MPD, and he spent most of that time deeply in the closet about his sexuality. Four years ago, he was made the senior officer in charge of maintaining the 13th Precinct Evidence Room. Shortly thereafter, Richard was approached by men in the employ of a local drug kingpin who threatened to expose him as a homosexual if certain forensic evidence didn't disappear from the Evidence Room. Without a moment's hesitation, Richard promptly informed both Internal Affairs and the Narcotics Division of the attempted extortion and also of his homosexuality, and he subsequently participated in a sting operation that helped bring down both his would-be blackmailers and their entire drug network. Richard received a special commendation for his role in the sting, but, as a result of the publicity, he was not only outed to his fellow officers, but before the entire city as the department's most prominent gay officer.

Reaction from fellow officers was mixed. While most were generally supportive, especially in the administration and among the detectives, the homophobia of some of the patrol officers remains pronounced. Stew Green and Wade Whitfield in particular have repeatedly made Richard the target of immature jokes and pranks, such as leaving women's underwear in his locker. Although some of his friends have urged him to report such juvenile behavior, Richard refuses, thinking that it will only make Wade and Stew martyrs to political correctness. That hasn't stopped him from discreet retaliation, however, and Whitfield never did figure out who planted a dead squirrel in his car's air-conditioning unit.

It helps that Richard fulfills few of the stereotypes of homosexuality. He is neat, but by no means "flaming," and he's quite conservative in his political views — not only is he a Log Cabin Republican, he's in the NRA as well. Richard is also an avid hunter and bowler, and he has established an unlikely friendship with Sammy Atkinson, who is on the 13th Precinct bowling team with Richard and with whom Richard regularly goes duck hunting. Most recently, Richard has been dating Ron Quintero, a cousin of Alex Quintero, who fixed the two up. Richard enjoys Ron's company, but has little in common with the 22-year-old party boy. In fact, Richard is on the verge of having a crush on his staunchly heterosexual friend Sammy, but refuses to do or say anything that might threaten their friendship.

Description: Richard is 37 years old and very good-looking, with blond hair and piercing blue eyes. His uniform is always immaculate. When off duty, he favors semi-casual attire, with chinos and nicely pressed shirts. In conversation, Richard is highly literate and professional, but quite conservative in his views on every topic other than sexuality. Even there, Richard is dismissive of what he considers the sex-obsessed lifestyle of most gays, and he longs for a steady monogamous relationship, complete with a civil union (as opposed to a same-sex marriage, which Richard opposes).

Attributes: Intelligence 3, Wits 2, Resolve 2, Strength 2, Dexterity 3, Stamina 2, Presence 3, Manipulation 2, Composure 3

Skills: Academics 2, Athletics (Bowling) 3, Animal Ken 2, Brawl 2, Computer 2, Drive 3, Empathy 2, Expression (Public Speaking) 3, Firearms 2, Intimidation 1, Investigation 2, Medicine 1, Persuasion 2, Politics 2, Socialize 2, Stealth 2, Streetwise 1, Subterfuge 2, Survival (Hunting) 3, Weaponry 1

Merits: Fame 1, Fighting Style: Police Tactics 2, Status (Precinct) 1, Striking Looks 2, Sworn Officer 2

Willpower: 5

Morality: 7

Virtue: Fortitude

Vice: Lust

Initiative: 6

Defense: 2

Speed: 10

Health: 7

Sgt. Sammy Atkinson, K-9 Officer

Quote: *"Yeah, I do tend to like dogs more than people. You have to work at it to make a dog want to leave you. People don't need a reason."*

Background: Sammy has served in the MPD for nine years. He is divorced, and his wife Beth has custody of his two children, Sam Jr. (age 6) and Lisa (age 3). Sammy still dreams of getting back together with Beth and rebuilding his family, but those dreams are about to be dashed. Beth will soon break the news to Sammy that she is remarrying and moving out of state, taking the kids with her.

Since the divorce, Sammy has become a bit of a loner, and he doesn't know what he'd do without Kita, the German Shepherd assigned to him in the K-9 unit. Sammy had been a "dog person" all his life, but sadly got rid of his last dog eight years ago because Beth was allergic to pet dander. Although Sam had worked with K-9 dogs before, he was still surprised and pleased at how intelligent and affectionate Kita is. He would be even more surprised if he knew that Kita is actually smarter than her owner. He might also be frightened to learn the depths of his animal companion's feelings for him, and how Kita is contemplating taking some sort of action against Beth if she continues to bring Sammy such pain. To Kita's mind, Sammy is her beloved alpha, and no rival bitch will come between them.

Description: Sammy is 41 years old, having served for several years with the National Guard and with the Washington County Sheriff's Department before moving to the MPD. He is a bit overweight and somewhat out of shape, but not so much as to fail to meet MPD standards. Sammy has a wide face with an infectious grin, and his sandy brown hair is only just starting to gray. Sammy's police uniform is slightly small for his expanding frame, and he insists that the uniform "shrank in the wash." When out of uniform, Sammy favors blue jeans, work boots and comfortable flannel shirts. He almost invariably wears some kind of cap, whether an MPD K-9 Unit cap or any one of a dozen or so baseball caps.

Storytelling Hints: Sammy is reasonably intelligent but not well educated, and he can best be described as a "good ol' boy." He doesn't have a genuinely racist bone in his body, but he is utterly obtuse when it comes to cultural differences with people of different ethnic backgrounds, so he occasionally says things that African American and Hispanic officers find offensive. He is always quick, however, to sincerely apologize when he realizes that he has offended someone with an ignorant remark. Sammy is mildly homophobic, but he has genuinely worked to overcome this attitude. He now considers Richard Bucknell a friend (to their mutual astonishment). They are both on the 13th Precinct's official bowling team, and they regularly go duck hunting together.

Attributes: Intelligence 2, Wits 3, Resolve 2, Strength 2, Dexterity 2, Stamina 3, Presence 2, Manipulation 1, Composure 3

Skills: Academics 1, Athletics 2, Animal Ken (K-9 Tactics) 3, Brawl 3, Computer 1, Drive 2, Empathy 2, Firearms (Shotguns) 3, Intimidation 1, Investigation 1, Larceny 1, Medicine 2, Persuasion 2, Science 1, Socialize 2, Stealth 1, Streetwise 1, Subterfuge 1, Survival (Hunting) 3, Weaponry 2

Merits: Brawling Dodge 1, Fighting Style: Police Tactics 2, Sworn Officer 2, Toxin Resistance 2

Willpower: 5
Morality: 7
Virtue: Fortitude
Vice: Sloth
Initiative: 5
Defense: 2
Speed: 9
Health: 8

Kita, the Huntsman's Companion

Obviously, Kita is more than she appears to be. Shortly after finishing K-9 training, the four-year-old German Shepherd was claimed by a dog-spirit called the Huntsman's Companion that had recently crossed the Gauntlet and sought to conceal itself from Uratha and other predators. The Companion is unusually smart for an animal-spirit, as its nature — the perfect hunting dog — requires it to have intelligence so as to better serve its "alpha." The bond between the companion and Kita has raised Kita's intellect to that of a human, though the *duguthim* (the dog/spirit hybrid) carefully conceals the extent of the changes from the humans around her.

Although Kita is kept in a pen behind Sammy's house, it is quite easy for her to escape every night and go on discreet patrols of the surrounding environs. During the last six months, she has killed two "intruders" in the neighborhood, as well as one 12-year-old boy who was walking his pet Labrador, and hidden their bodies. She has also stalked and killed a half-dozen minor spirits in her territory and battened herself on their Essence, though she is careful only to devour spirits whose natures are complementary to her own so as to avoid adopting magath characteristics. The local Uratha packs are aware that some spirits have been slain by unknown assailants, but the packs have attributed this to normal internecine conflict between rival spirits and have not yet noticed any sort of pattern. For her part, the *duguthim's* preternatural senses allow it to detect and avoid any Uratha who approach too closely, and the

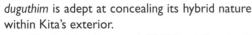

duguthim is adept at concealing its hybrid nature within Kita's exterior.

Mental: Intelligence 1 (4), Wits 4, Resolve 3

Physical: Strength 4 (6), Dexterity 3 (4), Stamina 3 (4)

Social: Presence 4, Manipulation 1 (4), Composure 2 (4)

Mental Skills: (from spirit) Occult 3, Persuasion 2, Subterfuge 2

Physical Skills: Athletics (Running) 4, Brawl 3, Stealth 1, Survival (Tracking) 3

Social Skills: Animal Ken 4, Empathy 3, Intimidation 4

Willpower: 5 (7)

Health: 7 (8)

Initiative: 5 (8)

Defense: 4 (4)

Speed: 13 (16)

Synthesis: 3

Essence: 7

Ban: The Companion cannot disobey a direct order from the person she considers her alpha (currently Sammy Atkinson).

The traits in parentheses represent Kita's traits since the merging with the Companion and are normally the traits used unless the Companion leaves or is exorcized. The *duguthim*'s Synthesis trait is a Supernatural Attribute possessed by Spirit-Claimed beings. Kita's Synthesis trait is added to her Resistance Attribute on all resisted rolls against supernatural powers. The *duguthim* also has the following supernatural powers:

• **Dark Sight:** Kita can see in complete darkness.

• **Sharp Senses:** Kita's senses are preternaturally acute, even for a dog. She can hear a whispered conversation in the next house and see up to a mile away if there are no obstructions. She can track anything not obscured by supernatural effects without a roll, and she can detect the presence of spirits or Uratha within a quarter mile with a reflexive Wits + Composure roll.

Janessa Burch, Vice Squad Sergeant

Quote: *"Fifty bucks for a blowjob? No problem. Only, instead of doing it in an alley, let's go someplace more intimate . . . like jail. You're under arrest, pal."*

Background: Janessa Burch is a 10-year veteran of the MPD and has spent the last five assigned to the 13th Precinct as an undercover Vice detective. Janessa is extremely good at her job, but she is beginning to find the work demeaning — as the best looking African American woman in the precinct, she spends a disproportionate amount of her time standing on street corners wearing what she refers to as "slut-wear," and usually freezing half to death while she does it. Her job constantly exposes her to lewd propositions from a wide variety of men, whose sexual desires she alternately finds either disturbing or hilarious. Despite her frustration with Vice, she has excellent working relations with her coworkers and indeed with most of the officers of the 13th. A few years ago, she was briefly involved in a romantic relationship with Stew Green, but eventually, she became frustrated with his constant racial paranoia and broke up with him. She is very good friends with Alex Quintero, Sid Routman and Richard Bucknell, but she finds Pauline Reed to be off-putting.

Janessa herself has a healthy sex life. She is single, but enjoys dating and is the closest thing to a social butterfly the precinct has. She was raised by a single mother in a rough neighborhood, but Janessa managed to evade most of the pitfalls of that living environment. When many of her childhood friends were becoming single mothers themselves, she was studying to get into a good college and out of the ghetto. She went to Midway University on a basketball scholarship and finished with a pre-law degree. Unable to get into law school, Janessa applied for the police force on a lark, and was hired. The academy was more difficult, but Janessa remained an excellent and intelligent student as well as a gifted athlete, and she graduated near the top of her class. After a period of relatively quick advancement, however, she ended up on the Vice squad and has been stuck there ever since, getting sent out every other week or so dressed like a streetwalker. She is already signed up to take the Law School Admissions Test again next fall, just in case she can't get a promotion or a transfer to another division. She also has what she thinks might be another way to get out of Vice — breaking a case that no one else knows exists.

During the past year, Janessa has become acquainted with most of the regular prostitutes who work the streets of Midway. She's also heard a few of their stories, some of which hint at a team of serial killers who prey on streetwalkers, junkies and homeless people in the city. Actually, the stories aren't really about "serial killers" but "vampires." At first, she scoffed at such stories as mere urban legends. Since then, a few of her regular contacts have been found dead due to what looks strangely like advanced pernicious anemia. She's seen the medical reports that show no signs of foul play, but years of experience on the force have made her more than a little cynical about the quality of the medical examiner's work, particularly in the case of low-profile victims such as Janessa's dead contacts.

Janessa now has a theory that she keeps strictly to herself. She suspects that there is a serial killer active in Midway, or possibly a small group of serial killers, who either has a severe delusion or else belongs to some sort of "vampire cult." These "vampire killers" have been killing street people for years, capturing victims and drawing off their blood with surgical equipment or even drinking it. Janessa thinks that if she can break this case, the notoriety of capturing serial killers who think they are vampires will be her ticket to the big leagues. In fact, even if there's nothing to her theory, it might make a good idea for a novel. And so, Janessa Burch continues to keep her eye on the streets, looking for any hints of "vampire activity" without any idea of how dangerous her quarry really is.

Description: Janessa is an extremely attractive, 33-year-old African American female with long, black hair and regal features. When undercover, she is dressed as a typical street hooker, with a shirt that shows off abundant cleavage and borderline obscene shorts. When not undercover, she is considered a plainclothes officer, and she usually dresses professionally but very stylishly and fashionably (or at least as fashionably as she can on a cop's salary). Her off-duty attire is usually the same as her plainclothes attire. Janessa is about five foot seven. She is in superb physical shape, and she has been studying kickboxing for the last eight years.

Storytelling Hints: Janessa is professional but easygoing. Around men, and especially available men, she is often flirtatious but not easy. She is eager to either advance her career or find a better one, but she will not do so in a way that compromises her morals, though those morals are a bit more fluid than, say, Alex Quintero's. That is, Janessa would at least consider sleeping with a superior to advance her career, but she would never participate in any illegal activity in exchange for a promotion, or even embark on an affair with a married superior. In the field, Janessa is very cool under pressure. If she actually does encounter a vampire in the field and the creature gives Janessa a chance to adapt to the existence of the undead, the vampire may be in as much danger from Janessa as she is from the vampire. In fact, a greater danger for Janessa is that, if she does discover the existence of vampires, the person she is most likely to tell would be Sid Routman. How he would react is up to the Storyteller, but Sid would most likely react poorly to having vampires intrude into his nice, orderly life once again.

Attributes: Intelligence 3, Wits 3, Resolve 2, Strength 2, Dexterity 2, Stamina 2, Presence 3, Manipulation 3, Composure 2

Skills: Academics 2, Athletics 2, Brawl (Fighting Dirty) 3, Computer 2, Drive 2, Empathy 2, Expression 1, Firearms 3, Intimidation 1, Investigation (Street Crimes) 2, Larceny 3, Medicine 2, Persuasion 2, Politics 2, Science 1, Socialize 2, Stealth 2, Streetwise (Hooker Culture), Subterfuge 2, Weaponry 1

Merits: Contacts (Street) 2, Brawling Dodge 1, Fighting Style: Police Tactics 3, Sworn Officer 2

Willpower: 4
Morality: 7
Virtue: Charity
Vice: Greed
Initiative: 4
Defense: 2
Speed: 9
Health: 7

Father Paul Nelson Calhoun, Episcopal Chaplain

Quote: *"There's a difference between doing the right thing and doing what you want to be the right thing."*

Background: Father Paul Calhoun was ordained into the Episcopal priesthood in his mid-20s, completing a goal he'd had since boyhood. Fascinated by the church's role in history and the continued importance the church holds in the modern world, Paul took to his duties with great enthusiasm and kindness. His marriage to a young woman from his parish caused a minor scandal among the more conservative members, but his devout service to the church won over most detractors.

Paul loves the church and his parishioners. He feels God's power in the rituals of worship and praise, and believes that the true strength of the rituals lies not in the actions, but in the congregation's faith in the rituals, the words, their priests and one another. The thought of abusing his status in the church appalls him, and although he is secure in his faith and beliefs, he grows uncomfortable with the idea of pressing his views on anyone clearly uninterested.

Three police officers are members of Garcia Road Episcopal Church, where Paul serves as assistant pastor. Discussions with the officers about their work led Paul to pursue a chaplaincy with the Midway Police Department. His superiors within the church granted his request, and while Paul is still carried on the roll at Garcia Road, he spends more of his working hours with the city's police and emergency workers. Paul works daily with the best and worst that his city has to offer, hearing formal and informal confessions, comforting family and friends, providing guidance in questions of law versus morality and doing his best to keep intact the souls of those he comes in contact with. At the same time, he seeks answers to his own questions about God, humankind and the church and his place in the world.

In the eight years he has spent as precinct chaplain, Father Paul has heard countless stories from both sides of the law and been called to almost as many crime scenes as the average police officer. Father Paul's faith and training assure him of the existence of things outside the pale. The unexpected evidence provided by his senses has cemented this certainty.

A rookie officer responding to his first fatal car accident provided Paul with his first brush with the supernatural. The young officer, Chris Gosser, was overwhelmed by the violence of the accident, and came to the chaplain wracked with a certainty that a victim would have lived if Chris had been able to "do something more." Throughout the conversation, Paul saw and heard a young girl nearby who wanted to comfort the officer as well. Paul at first dismissed the officer's lack of reaction at the girl's presence as shock, and conveyed her messages to him. After a couple of days, the officer spoke to Paul again, and when Paul described

Father Paul Nelson Calhoun, Alana Bailey, Lance Schachter, and Janessa Burch

the girl, Officer Gosser paled — the description matched the accident victim down to her clothes.

As time passed, Paul had more encounters. He has seen a handful of ghosts while counseling officers and citizens at crime and accident scenes. He passed himself on the street not so long ago. A number of previously violent or threatening suspects have either recoiled in terror from his presence, or collapsed before him, with no more explanation than the priest "had their number." He has yet to speak to his superiors in the church about it, but Paul performed an impromptu exorcism on a man arrested for attacking a bar full of football fans, and has no doubt that the presence he felt leave the man's body was demonic.

The ghosts trouble Paul the most. He's beginning to recognize one or two, and one appeared during a church service Paul conducted. His faith warns against consorting with familiar spirits; Paul's unsure if that prohibition would apply in cases in which the spirits just seem to show up from time to time, but where his eternal soul is concerned, Paul is growing unwilling to take chances. He's started reviewing the church's rituals of exorcism and defense against supernatural forces, and is preparing to try and send one of the spirits away once and for all.

Description: Paul is slightly above average in height and thick bodied, and has brown hair trimmed close to his scalp. When not in his chaplain's garb, Paul prefers slacks, comfortable shoes and dress shirts, often with the emblem

of his seminary or the local university embroidered somewhere. He keeps a Palm PDA with several translations of the Bible and eBook versions of spiritual and counseling texts close to hand.

Storytelling Hints: Father Paul believes strongly in the power of Christian faith and the sanctity of human life. He is certain that his place in life is to serve others and to spread his faith through example. Paul is friendly and compassionate, with a ready smile. He'll listen intently to anyone's story, and offer hope and reassurance.

Paul's numerous brushes with the supernatural have led him to deeper studies of and meditation on what lies outside normal human experiences. The Bible contains many accounts of the paranormal, and Paul believes that his encounters are simply latter-day incarnations of these ancient events.

Paul has no doubts at all about the existence of a greater world than the eye can see. God is with him every moment of his life, and has chosen him to spread the Good Word, comfort the afflicted and save lost souls. On the other hand, Paul's rising prominence in the church and his status with the police department has gone to his head. He can be stubborn, and is occasionally aggressive toward those he sees as challenging his faith.

Attributes: Intelligence 4, Wits 3, Resolve 4, Strength 2, Dexterity 2, Stamina 3, Presence 3, Manipulation 2, Composure 4

Skills: Academics (Religion) 3, Athletics 1, Drive 1, Empathy 3, Expression 2, Investigation 2, Occult 2, Persuasion 2, Politics 2, Socialize 2

Merits: Allies (Police 2, Episcopal Church 3), Inspiring, Status (MPD) 2

Willpower: 8

Morality: 8

Virtue: Faith

Vice: Pride

Health: 9

Initiative: 7

Defense: 3

Speed: 10

Officer Lance Schachter,
Ex-Aviation Squadron Lieutenant

Quote: *"Midway Airport, this is MPD Air Support 228. Are you showing any air traffic over Murakami Industrial Park?"*

"Ah, negative, MPD 228. Do you have something?"

"Yeah, it looks like . . . aw, hell. Like . . . well, like a discolored area in the sky, maybe 100 yards across."

"MPD 228, discolored sky?"

"Affirmative, Midway Airport. Kind of a shimmering greenish circle. What the — "

[Quick bursts of static, followed by the sound of a helicopter engine throttling up rapidly.]

"Midway Airport, MPD Air Support, get somebody out to Murakami now! Something just hit my damn helicopter!"

"MPD 228, say again. You have collided with another aircraft?"

"Not an aircraft. Oh, shit, here it comes again!"

[Unintelligible words from MPD 228. The helicopter's engine noise rises and falls. MPD 228 announces an emergency landing and requests assistance. A loud thump is heard, then repeats, then the MPD signal ends.]

— Transcript from an incident report, police helicopter crash, August 15, 2001.

Background: From childhood, Lance looked to the sky and dreamed of being among the clouds. His after-school jobs paid for flying lessons, and a Coast Guard recruiter offered Lance the opportunity to fly helicopters. He signed up, eager to rescue stranded mariners and interdict drug smugglers. He completed flight training, received his commission and began flying Blackhawk helicopters from the deck of a high-speed cutter in the Gulf of Mexico.

Lance's promising Coast Guard career came to a halt when his parents were diagnosed with a form of early-onset senile dementia. Lance reluctantly applied for a hardship discharge and returned to Midway to care for his parents. The call of the sky was still as strong as ever, and Lance's particular skills earned him a spot on the police air support unit. The work was close enough to what he had done in the Coast Guard, and being close to home made things easier.

After the deaths of his parents, Lance decided to stay on with the MPD. The force was glad to have him. He was promoted to lieutenant and assumed a share of air support's administrative tasks. Lance kept himself on flight rotation as much as possible.

On a clear summer afternoon, Lance and his observer, a veteran officer named Art Punnett, were returning to MPD's flightline after providing assistance to a high-speed pursuit on the city's freeways. Art caught sight of something unusual near a newly opened industrial park, and Lance turned the Jetranger helicopter toward the park. Six minutes later, the helicopter was on the ground, Punnett was dead and Lance had broken both of his legs. Lance insisted that a creature similar to a prehistoric pterodactyl had flown at the helicopter, striking it twice and damaging the helicopter's engine. No trace of this creature was found at the crash site, and the crash was severe enough that the helicopter could not be repaired.

The destruction of a very expensive helicopter, death of a longtime officer and an explanation described as "delusional and irrational" in the final report cost Lance his flight certification. He was reduced in rank and assigned to traffic patrol, with mandatory monthly psychiatric evaluations. Throughout the investigation, Lance insisted that the creature was real, coming dangerously close to a psychiatric discharge. His union representative convinced him to tone down his claims and try to work his way back into MPD's better graces.

Lance has adapted to his grounding as well as he can. After reassignment, he doesn't speak of the incident unless another officer brings it up, and he has started to wonder what really happened that afternoon. A few officers have spoken to Lance in private about similar events. Lance has looked for reports from other pilots involving encounters with large flying creatures, especially the "thunderbird" in Alaska and the American Southwest.

In addition to his assigned gear, Lance keeps a digital camera in the front seat of his cruiser. His partner accepts this quirk, as it seems to give Lance some inner peace. Lance hopes that another air support officer will encounter a creature as Lance did (hopefully without a fatal crash), and he will be vindicated. For now, he watches the sky, much as he did when a child. Only now, instead of cataloging as many aircraft as he can, Lance keeps his eyes open for a large, leathery-winged apparition. Photographs would go a long way toward vindication, and a downed creature would help even more.

Description: Lance could have stepped out of a recruiting poster. Tightly curled blond hair frames a handsome, boyish face with deep blue eyes and a disarming smile. His patrolman's uniform sports a worn set of aviator's wings over the nametag.

Storytelling Hints: Although a dedicated officer, Lance distrusts the MPD's highest ranks and positively loathes the Internal Affairs Division. He treats his assignment to a patrol car as an exile, and would do anything to get back into a pilot's seat.

The right must prevail: Lance is committed to protecting the innocent, even at great personal cost. He relies on the spirit of the law than the letter. Lance wants to clear his name and get back into the air. He looks for chances to prove that what he saw was real, and puts his career and those of some of his fellow officers at risk.

Attributes: Intelligence 3, Wits 4, Resolve 2, Strength 3, Dexterity 4, Stamina 3, Presence 3, Manipulation 2, Composure 3

Skills: Athletics 1, Brawl 1, Drive (Helicopter) 4, Firearms 2, Intimidation 2, Investigation 2, Occult 1, Persuasion 2, Politics 1, Streetwise 1

Merits: Language (Spanish) 2, Direction Sense, Stunt Driver, Status (MPD) 1, Striking Looks 2

Willpower: 6

Morality: 7

Virtue: Justice

Vice: Pride

Health: 8

Initiative: 7

Defense: 2

Speed: 12

Sgt. Fernando Raia

Quote: *"Evening, ladies. What's the issue here?"*

Background: Fernando Raia is a second-generation MPD officer. His father was one of the force's first Hispanic cops and instilled a powerful sense of duty in his children (Fernando's older sister was an ER nurse and his younger brother works in the city's extensive civil service system). A son by Fernando's first marriage is completing his rookie year on the force, showing the same promise as the previous Raia men. Fernando is approaching MPD's mandatory retirement age, and is planning to establish either a private detective agency or a security consultancy before hanging up the badge and gun for good. He knows he still has plenty of years left, and the thought of a couple of decades tending a garden or fishing fills him with dread.

Raia has served as a uniformed officer for almost his entire career. He took and passed the detective's examination, but returned to uniformed duty after finding plainclothes work ultimately unsatisfying. His record with MPD is considered exemplary — he has a reputation as a solid and incorruptible officer, with citations and letters of commendation from the city government, civic organizations, and private citizens. His ethnic background provided Fernando with opportunities to establish friendly relations and strong ties throughout the city's minority communities, and Officer Fernando is a regular visitor to elementary schools and community centers.

Fernando has put in time in every precinct in the MPD, usually changing bureaus and even divisions with every transfer. He has an extremely wide base of experience as a result of these transfers and has friends in every squad room in the city. Old friends trade information with Fernando on a daily basis, and younger officers are often directed to him

for advice and suggestions on conducting investigations. As his retirement date approached, Fernando requested transfer to the 13th precinct, planning to end a long and respected career in the city's most hard-edged assignment. His posting to the third watch was an added request, gladly granted by the precinct captain.

A young marriage ended in divorce when Raia's wandering eye led to an affair. His ex-wife, Noemi, has since remarried and long since forgiven her former husband; the two are now good friends. His second wife died in a car accident, and the stepson maintains a distant relationship with Raia.

Working the graveyard shift keeps Fernando intimately connected with the police force, working instead of simply marking time. He enjoys working with younger officers, passing on his knowledge to a new generation of police. He's heard plenty of stories about unearthly goings-on, and answered a few suspicious calls himself. He doesn't believe the incidents are anything more than the result of stress or drugs. A lapsed Catholic, Fernando often talks with Father Calhoun about the existence and nature of good and evil, and in spite of his own opinions, refuses to completely discount the accounts of other officers.

Raia is popular among the force's minority officers, especially Alex Quintero. He is a source of constant encouragement and advice, with enough regard among the department's leadership that careers have been made or broken as a result of his recommendations or condemnations. He considers himself a public servant in every sense of the word, committed to the common good above all else.

In his professional life, Fernando tries to be as colorblind as possible. Racism and bigotry have no place in his police force, even though this view has brought him into occasional conflict with other officers. His father's experiences in the early days of enforced integration left a bad taste in Fernando's mouth. He's seen the best and worst out of people, and concluded that skin color is just about the worst possible predictor of behavior. In his decades on the force, he's pursued, investigated, arrested, and assisted people of every stripe, and has been cursed and praised in equal measure.

Description: Sergeant Raia is a solidly built Hispanic man in his late 50s with close-cut, graying hair and a neatly trimmed mustache. His uniform is spotless, every crease razor-sharp, shoes polished to a reflective shine that you could comb your hair in. He keeps his posture ramrod straight, even in civilian gear. Off duty, Fernando goes for jeans and buttoned-down shirts. A crucifix tattoo covers his left bicep, and both of his hands are covered with tiny scars.

Storytelling Hints: Raia has a reputation as a cop's cop, and does his best to live up to it. He knows exactly where the line between acceptable and suspect behavior lies, and will not step over it. If you're a good cop — or a good citizen — Raia is the best friend you can have. He always has advice of some kind, the result of better than three decades of police service. Sergeant Raia is even-tempered and follows a strong personal moral code. He tries to maintain a professional demeanor at all times, relying on his authority as a police officer and his personal force of will to achieve his goals while on the job.

It must be said, however, that Fernando has a real eye — and weakness — for the ladies. He has one ex-wife, one wife killed in a traffic accident and a string of ex-girlfriends, and still flirts with just about anything that comes down the pike. His job provides ample opportunity to indulge, and sometimes his drives are too much to handle.

Attributes: Intelligence 2, Wits 3, Resolve 3, Strength 3, Dexterity 2, Stamina 3, Presence 4, Manipulation 2, Composure 3

Skills: Athletics 2, Brawl 3, Drive 2, Firearms 2, Intimidation 3, Investigation 4, Medicine 1, Persuasion 1, Politics 2, Socialize 1, Streetwise 2, Weaponry 2

Merits: Allies (Police 2), Contacts 1, Danger Sense, Language (Spanish 2), Disarm, Status (MPD) 3

Willpower: 9

Morality: 8

Virtue: Temperance

Vice: Lust

Health: 8

Initiative: 5

Defense: 2

Speed: 10

Ambulance 130

Harriett Stockwell's crew and ambulance are veterans all around. Well trained and well equipped, they provide a vital service on the city's streets, supporting MPD officers and assisting distressed citizens. The EMTs answer nearly as many calls as the police officers the EMTs work with, and the requests for assistance range from life-threatening to downright absurd.

Harriett Stockwell

Background: Harriett started putting Band-Aids and casts made of wet paper towels on her dolls before kindergarten. Every Halloween, she was a nurse. She earned her Girl Scout First Aid award at age nine. After high school, Harriett served a six-year hitch in the Army as a combat medic. When she mustered out, she came home to Midway, passed her EMT certification tests with flying colors and put on another uniform: Midway Fire Department Rescue Squad.

Harriett's time in the military took her to the Middle East in the years following the first Gulf War. She spent two years ministering to the injuries of British and American soldiers enforcing the no-fly zones and manning garrisons established after the war. She saw combat twice, and acquitted herself well under fire, taking command of a squad of infantrymen at one point. Her superiors commended her ability to maintain order while patching up wounded soldiers, and offered her a string of incentives to stay in uniform when her enlistment ended.

Harriett found herself part of a three-person ambulance crew on an experimental program. A civil service study showed that more than 80% of overnight ambulance calls required police presence or investigation. The MPD initiated a program whereby each police precinct would be assigned an ambulance crew. Harriett and Ambulance 130 drew the 13th.

Because of her military service and higher grades of certification, Harriett is the EMS team's lead officer. She runs a tight ship, and Ambulance 130's response times and lives-saved numbers are setting records in the Midway Fire Department. The crew jokes that their success is because of the ambulance itself.

In violation of MFD policy, Harriett carries a semiautomatic pistol on the ambulance. She takes her commitment to lifesaving very seriously, but has seen some very dicey situations and places greater priority on her own life and those of her crew than on that of a gangbanger defending his turf or of a spouse whose temper led to the ambulance call in the first place. Harriett's crew knows about the weapon, as do many of the police officers that Ambulance 130 works with. So far, she hasn't had to go for the gun when on a call.

Harriett is a physical fitness enthusiast, following the Army's fitness regimen even in her civilian life. She runs several hours every week, and is working her way up to marathons. She maintains friendships with coworkers away from the job, but refuses to date anyone from either the police or fire departments. Harriett is an avid basketball fan, wrangling assignments to games whenever she can.

Description: Just past her 30th birthday, Harriett is in terrific physical condition. She keeps her long, black hair tied back or tucked under a cap while on the job. Her dark blue BDUs are covered with patches displaying her lifesaving qualifications, as well as the insignia of the MFD and the infantry unit she served with while in the Army. Away from work, she prefers a softer, dressy style.

Storytelling Hints: Harriett is a professional, and her job is the most important thing in her life. When she and her crew are at an incident site, she gives orders and expects them to be followed to the letter. In more relaxed situations, she's talkative and friendly, and flirts with everyone. Harriett is dedicated to easing suffering and saving lives. Her job involves placing herself in harm's way for the good of others, and she embraces it wholeheartedly.

She's also one of the best EMTs in the city, and she knows it. On duty, Harriett can be domineering and a little bitchy, with an attitude bordering on "my way or the highway."

Attributes: Intelligence 3, Wits 3, Resolve 3, Strength 2, Dexterity 2, Stamina 3, Presence 2, Manipulation 3, Composure 4

Skills: Athletics 2, Drive 2, Empathy 1, Firearms 1, Medicine 3, Persuasion 1, Science 2

Merits: Fleet of Foot 2, Status (MFD) 2
Willpower: 7
Morality: 7
Virtue: Charity
Vice: Pride
Health: 8
Initiative: 6
Defense: 2
Speed: 11

Marshall Purdum

Background: All-City football team. Starting quarterback for the Midway University Horsemen. Heisman Trophy candidate. Marshall looked forward to a career in the National Football League, until an unlucky hit in the Rose Bowl broke his right leg and tore his anterior cruciate ligament.

With his football dreams destroyed, Marshall finished his physical therapy and took a hard look at his life. He craved action. The nearly completed degree in business management promised a career behind a desk and on the phone. Driving home from a late-night visit to an old teammate, Marshall came upon a traffic accident. He stopped his car to help, and kept a young man awake and alive until paramedics arrived. He watched the EMTs work, and found his new calling.

The Midway Fire Department jumped at the chance to bring Marshall on board. He was still well known throughout the city, and a local football hero turned ambulance crewman would make for great public relations. Marshall readily agreed to be a spokesman for MFD's charities and public service programs. His smiling face graced posters and television commercials for months.

Marshall eventually asked to be assigned to an EMT squad. He agreed to continue making occasional promotional appearances for the department, and moved into his career in emergency medical services. He adapted to the demands of lifesaving very quickly, working hard to prove himself as a competent paramedic. His teammates recognized Marshall from his time on the football field, but Harriett Stockwell cut the new EMT no extraordinary slack. Marshall was — and still is — grateful for Harriett's demanding leadership.

Ambulance 130's reputation for excellence continued with Marshall's assignment. He enjoys the odd hours and incredibly demanding work. The police officers at the 13th Precinct like having a minor celebrity in their midst, and Marshall enjoys the continued fame. He has requested some cross-training with firefighters; among his closest friends, he confides that he plans to seek promotion into MFD's highest levels and become the city's fire chief before his 50th birthday. His friends have little doubt that he'll make it.

Fernando Raia, Emmet Pritchard, Harriet Stockwell, Tyron Sevy, & Marshall Purdum

Marshall is married to Tameka Carrel, a patrol officer in the 5th Precinct. Their work shifts allow for limited time together, and their rare shared days off are spent in each other's company, phones turned off and the outside world shut out.

Marshall's fame among the city's football fans has produced an unexpected bonus in his new line of work. Injury victims sometimes recognize the former star athlete, and his presence puts them more at ease.

Description: Blond, muscular and handsome, Marshall could pass for Lance Schachter's brother. Marshall is fit and maintains a dedicated workout regimen. He wears a flexible brace on his right leg.

Storytelling Hints: Marshall loves being a paramedic, and answers every call as if it were a championship game. He's easygoing, and has a gift for making injury victims feel relaxed. He is a rabid college football fan, managing several teams in fantasy leagues.

Marshall isn't one for giving up. When his football career was ended by a freak hit, he moved on to a new path instead of sinking into despair and self-pity. Marshall relies on his ideals as a source of inspiration and drive. Marshall remembers the days when he was a nationally famous athlete fondly, and the occasional adoration from an old fan goes to his head.

Attributes: Intelligence 2, Wits 3, Resolve 3, Strength 4, Dexterity 3, Stamina 4, Presence 3, Manipulation 2, Composure 2

Skills: Academics 1, Athletics 2, Drive 1, Medicine 3, Persuasion 2, Science 1, Socialize 1

Merits: Danger Sense, Fame 2, Quick Healer, Status (MFD) 1

Willpower: 5

Morality: 7

Virtue: Fortitude

Vice: Pride

Health: 9

Initiative: 5

Defense: 3

Speed: 12

Tyrone Sevy

Background: Tyrone built and raced cars from the time he was 15. He developed a reputation as a skilled mechanic and driver, and some of the city's most notorious racers took their cars to Tyrone for repair and modification. He dreamed of becoming a professional race driver, but no one was looking for a black driver during the 1960s. Tyrone put his dreams on a shelf and joined the Army.

Uncle Sam gave Tyrone a job maintaining tanks, armored personnel carriers and other heavy vehicles. He served in Vietnam, came home and used the GI Bill to pay for two years at a city technical college. Afterward, Tyrone found a job with the city's Emergency Services Division. His driving skills and technical aptitude served him well, and a

professional driving career came his way — only in highly modified vans instead of hot-rodded muscle cars.

Having grown up in a segregated society, Tyrone began to take part in social change movements after his time in the military. He studied the history of race relations, read anything he could on Midway's equality programs and became a leader in his community. He came into contact with Fernando Raia long before assignment to the 13th Precinct, and the two men developed a deep friendship.

Tyrone's assignment to Ambulance 130 and the precinct sits well with him. He appreciates the ambulance crew's professionalism and the interaction with most of the police officers. He tries to maintain a positive outlook in the face of racism and prejudice, but sometimes lets himself show up those whose opinions he considers less than enlightened.

Happily married and the loving father of three children, Tyrone never stopped tinkering with cars and engines. He keeps an eye on Midway's street racing scene, and manages to use a love for and in-depth knowledge of cars to forward his personal agenda of racial peace. It's a long road, and Tyrone has no illusions about seeing his goals achieved during his lifetime, but he is committed to fighting the good fight as long as he can.

Description: Well into his 50s, Tyrone is an elegant and handsome man. His hair and mustache are both neatly trimmed and graying, and the lines in his face lend character, rather than show signs of advanced age. He has a booming laugh that comes on unexpectedly and quickly infects those around him.

Storytelling Hints: Tyrone is looking forward to a comfortable retirement in a few years. He is close to his children and grandchildren, and plans to spoil the younger generation silly. Tyrone also wants to stay involved with social issues for a few years. Tyrone's social activism is a result of his desire to eliminate racial division and strife. He works hard to provide a better world for future generations.

Behind the wheel, Tyrone is calm and unflappable. He keeps his cool, no matter what. During downtime, he'll trade sports stories with Marshall and Army yarns with Harriett.

Tyrone has to work at keeping his fiery temper in control. He knows that violence will only set his dreams back, but sometimes it seems like the best and more effective answer.

Attributes: Intelligence 3, Wits 4, Resolve 3, Strength 2, Dexterity 3, Stamina 2, Presence 3, Manipulation 4, Composure 4

Skills: Athletics 1, Drive 3, Empathy 3, Expression 3, Medicine 3, Persuasion 2, Politics 2, Streetwise 2

Merits: Allies 2, Contacts 2, Fast Reflexes 2, Fresh Start, Stunt Driver, Status (MFD) 1

Willpower: 7

Morality: 8

Virtue: Hope

Vice: Wrath

Health: 7
Initiative: 9
Defense: 3
Speed: 10

The Ambulance

Midway Fire Department Ambulance 130 is a 1997 Ford Econoline 450 chassis with an Ultramedic III ambulance body, painted in the white-on-blue EMS scheme. The ambulance has a handful of nicks and scratches from years of service, but the big turbocharged diesel engine is in excellent condition and the rescue equipment on board is state of the art.

Number 130 has transported countless patients, accident victims, unlucky bystanders and self-destructing citizens. Officers and paramedics have hidden behind its huge flanks when a perpetrator has decided go out in a frenzy of violence and a hail of bullets. A few children have been born inside the ambulance, and more than a few lives have ended on board.

Kelly van Sant was born in Ambulance 130, halfway between her parents' house and Four Winds Regional Medical Center. Five years later, a traffic accident badly injured the little girl, and she died on the way to the same hospital in the same ambulance. Kelly's spirit attached itself to the machine that had seen her enter and leave the physical world.

Ambulance 130's invisible fourth crewmember helps out whenever she can. The EMTs find necessary equipment falling quickly to hand, and patients seem to cling a little closer to life inside the vehicle's body.

The ambulance's supernatural assistance comes with a side effect unknown to its crew — or the spirit. Because of the vehicle's proximity to scenes of death and suffering, as well as the spiritual energy contained inside, the barriers between the physical and spiritual worlds are weakened around Ambulance 130. Sensitive individuals notice something not quite right, and particularly painful or traumatic death can weaken the barriers sufficiently to allow easy crossing between the worlds.

Medicine dice pools inside the ambulance or within a few yards of it receive an additional +1 bonus. If a death is sufficiently powerful, in the Storyteller's judgment, the death may briefly increase the manifestation modifier for ghosts and spirits by +1 or +2 in dire circumstances. See p. 210 of the **World of Darkness Rulebook** for information on manifestation and manifestation modifiers.

Civilian Staff

Emmet Pritchard, Civilian Personnel

Background: Emmet is not a police officer or even an employee of the city. Instead, he works as a custodian and head janitor for the 13th Precinct by virtue of a contract between the city and G&V Janitorial Services. However, G&V does more than provide 24-hour janitorial service — the company is also a front organization for Midway's Guardians of the Veil (see **Mage: The Awakening**). G&V maintains contracts to provide janitorial services for all city offices and for a number of private businesses in Midway. For the most part, G&V's employees are exactly what they appear to be: honest, hardworking employees who receive just under eight dollars an hour to clean toilets and empty wastepaper baskets. Occasionally, however, the Guardians will have a special need to know what's going on with one of their clients, such as when an investigation originating out of the 13th Precinct is edging too close to mage activity.

When that happens, the janitor gets a little something extra in his weekly paycheck — a dozen or so business cards, each bearing the name of a location in the precinct where the card is to be hidden. Each business card is sympathetically linked to a Guardian temporarily assigned to monitor the activities of certain police officers, and the cards are secreted on each officer's desk, in the offices of their commanding officers and even in the nearest bathrooms. Most G&V employees have no idea why they are required to plant these cards, and even if one did question the activity, it wouldn't matter, as all employees are placed under a mental compulsion to not worry about the significance of the cards. Even if the employees weren't, the extra $1,000 cash in untraceable bills each janitor receives along with the cards would eliminate most concerns. Emmet is an exception to the rule, as he is a Sleepwalker and thus knows about the existence of mages. His late wife was an Obrimos Guardian, and he suggested using janitors to plant magical listening devices many years ago. His son, also an Obrimos Guardian, currently runs both the business side of G&V and its surveillance activities.

Description: Emmet, similar to most janitors, is almost invisible to many of the precinct's personnel who simply don't notice custodial staff members unless they draw attention to themselves. Anyone who actually paid attention to Emmet would see a tall, almost regal African American with piercing eyes that betray a lively intelligence. He is somewhat thin, but his janitor's uniform conceals wiry muscles that are stronger than one might expect. Emmet is genial and good-natured to those who pay any attention to him, despite the fact that he is essentially a deep-cover spy in potentially enemy territory. While on the job, he invariably wears a brown shirt with the G&V logo, blue jeans and comfortable shoes. Off duty, Emmet dresses casually, and is something of a homebody — other than his duties for the Guardians, Emmet considers his adventuring days behind him.

Storytelling Hints: If Emmet does his job correctly, most characters will never even notice his presence or even remember his name unless someone has spilled something Emmet will need to clean up. While on the job, Emmet is genial and polite to all police personnel, almost to the point of being obsequious. Pauline Reed slightly disapproves of his attitude, presumably because it rankles her to see a black man in a janitorial position fulfilling so many stereotypes held by white police officers. Mages who encounter Emmet will get an entirely different view of him, as he will possess an encyclopedic knowledge of police procedure and internal police politics, as well as a wealth of information about Midway's supernatural community built up over decades working as a mortal agent for the Guardians of the Veil. Indeed, while some mages are dismissive of the importance of Sleepwalkers, the leaders of the Midway Guardians consider Emmet more valuable to their work than most of the mages who report to them.

Attributes: Intelligence 3, Wits 3, Resolve 3, Strength 2, Dexterity 2, Stamina 2, Presence 2, Manipulation 3, Composure 3

Skills: Academics 2, Brawl 1, Computer 2, Drive 1, Empathy 3, Expression (Acting) 3, Firearms 1, Intimidation 2, Investigation 3, Larceny (Sleight of Hand) 3, Occult (Guardians of the Veil) 4, Persuasion 3, Politics (Mage Politics) 3, Science 1, Socialize 2, Stealth 2, Streetwise 3, Subterfuge 4, Weaponry 1

Merits: Allies (Local Mages) 3, Resources 3, Status (Midway Guardians of the Veil) 3

Willpower: 6

Morality: 7

Virtue: Fortitude

Vice: Pride

Initiative: 5

Defense: 2

Speed: 9

Health: 7

Eve Kanagy, Assistant District Attorney

Background: As a little girl, Eve Kanagy was picked on for anything and everything. Glasses. Braces. Too tall. Too skinny. Cooties. She had few friends and fewer joys. She made a promise that someday she would punish anyone who hurt someone weaker or less powerful. She would turn her private pain into justice for everyone.

Eve started her career in the district attorney's office with a stunning conviction on largely circumstantial evidence. Her vicious questioning of an accused rapist caused the perpetrator to break down on the witness stand and scream his confession at the jury. Eve's face and name were on the *Midway Tribune*'s front page the next morning, every TV station in time was calling for interviews and the city's chief prosecutor announced that she was the office's new star.

Rapid and unexpected success went to Eve's head. She met with a humiliating courtroom defeat when a judge prevented crucial evidence from being presented. Eve had other evidence almost as strong against the accused, but had built her entire case around the forbidden piece. Unwilling to accept responsibility for blowing the case, Eve tried to shift the blame to the investigating officers, using the defense's accusation of sloppy police work.

Eve stormed into the precinct house and proceeded to viciously dress down the officers who provided the case's evidence, permitted and rejected. The officers' protests fell on deaf ears. Eve knew she had been set up to fail by cops who were jealous of her higher position in law enforcement. She promised the officers that they would lose their badges and never work in law enforcement again before tearing out of the station and back to her office downtown.

Word of Eve's tirade spread quickly throughout the police force. Officers soon learned that Eve was a volatile ally, driven as much by ego as by a love for justice. She demanded flawless police procedure in her cases. Omission of even the tiniest facts was evidence of incompetence and corruption within the police force. A handful of officers have refused to work with Eve, even under threat of suspension or termination.

Eve actually is a gifted prosecutor, able to turn a suspect's most insignificant statements into near-confessions. She is adept at punching holes in a defense attorney's position, but hasn't gotten past her reputation as a cop-hater. The DA's office rarely assigns her as a lead prosecutor in a case, instead turning her abilities toward supporting more experienced or level-headed attorneys.

Description: Eve is sharp-featured. She dresses in fashionable suits that compliment her figure. She is prone to quick movements, and in the courtroom is almost predatory in manners.

Storytelling Hints: Eve is convinced that she can do no wrong. She remembers any slight against her and files it away for future revenge. She demands perfection from everyone around her. Eve is blind to her own laziness. She believes her status in the DA's office places her above the need to do any research into the evidence presented to her. She subconsciously ignores other DAs doing that very thing.

Eve lives to see the guilty receive their mandated punishment. Those who break society's laws deserve society's codified revenge, and those who have been wronged deserve to see their victimizers suffer for the crime. For all of her professed hard work and sacrifice, though, Eve wants all of the material necessary for a conviction to be handed to her before any case goes to trial. She feels that any kind of legwork is beneath her and should be handled by the police.

Attributes: Intelligence 4, Wits 4, Resolve 4, Strength 2, Dexterity 3, Stamina 3, Presence 3, Manipulation 3, Composure 4

Skills: Academics 4, Athletics 1, Empathy 2, Expression 1, Intimidation 3, Investigation 3, Persuasion 2, Politics 3

Merits: Allies 2, Status (Legal System) 2

Willpower: 8

Morality: 7

Virtue: Justice

Vice: Sloth

Health: 8

Initiative: 7

Defense: 3

Speed: 10

Katy Garriga, Public Defender

Background: The basis for the American legal system is that a defendant is innocent until proven guilty beyond a doubt, and no one can be denied legal representation. In a society in which a significant number of the accused cannot afford legal defense, the system has a responsibility to provide for the accused. Toiling away in relative obscurity, countless numbers of public defenders across the nation provide impoverished defendants with legal representation.

Katy Garriga's parents were classic '60s radicals. Children of privilege, they spoke out against social ills, attended rallies and did their best to establish a better nation. The Garrigas instilled a love of social activism in their only daughter, and were overjoyed when she announced a desire to attend law school and defend the less fortunate.

Katy's law school career was undistinguished. She graduated in the middle of the pack and took a position in civil service instead of the powerful law firms she had dreamed of. Katy decided to make the best of her situation and establish a reputation as a passionate and skilled defender, and when a private firm came along, she would jump at that chance.

Her plans did not survive contact with reality. Instead of the city's downtrodden, working poor and unfortunates, Katy's clients turned out to be petty criminals — low-level drug pushers, prostitutes and others at the low end of the social strata. Her caseload overwhelmed her, and her goal of providing the best defense possible changed to a hope of shielding defendants from the worst predations of the city's prosecutors. Societal and bureaucratic pressure to reduce massive backlogs of criminal cases led to dozens of backroom deals and dozens of plea bargains during the course of a week at work.

The District Attorney's office developed a working relationship with Katy. Deals were struck in countless marginal cases, allowing the prosecutors to pad their conviction rates while Katy became known for getting minimal sentences for her clients.

Katy spends a couple of hours every week at the precinct house, interviewing officers and prisoners. She is committed to protecting a defendant's civil rights, and her passion has earned her the respect of many of the precinct's officers — this public defender is more popular here than her counterpart in the District Attorney's office. She consults Father Calhoun when a perpetrator seems genuinely repentant.

Because of the stresses involved in the job and its demands on her time, Katy has no significant other in her life. She has a couple of "friends with benefits," and refuses to let anything get more serious than that. She goes home to a small but comfortable apartment and an attention-starved cat most nights.

Although she is unaware of it, one of the city's largest organized crime rings has its eye on Katy. She has helped a few of the ring's low-level members out of trouble, and the ringleaders see some real potential in the young public defender. If the offer is made at the right time, Katy will probably jump at the chance for greater rewards for her efforts.

Description: Katy dresses well and takes great pains to put forth a professional appearance. She is neither attractive nor unattractive — she's "normal" in an unremarkable sort of way. Because of long hours and stress, she usually has dark circles under both eyes.

Storytelling Hints: Katy still has a great passion for social justice and equal rights for everyone. She works hard, with 70-hour weeks fairly common. She's usually tired, but maintains a good cheer as much as she can. Katy talks off the record with the precinct's cops to get a better feel for her clients. She grabs quick naps at her desk a couple of times every day. Katy is a deliberate and careful thinker. She gives her clients a good defense, and when she knows she's beat, she gets the best deal the prosecution will offer.

Big-time defense attorneys can make a lot of money and become famous on the coattails of their clients. Katy wants these things, and she's giving real thought to how best to get there.

Attributes: Intelligence 4, Wits 4, Resolve 4, Strength 2, Dexterity 3, Stamina 3, Presence 3, Manipulation 3, Composure 4

Skills: Academics 4, Athletics 1, Computer 1, Empathy 1, Expression 2, Intimidation 2, Investigation 2, Persuasion 2, Politics 2

Merits: Allies 2, Mentor 2, Status (Legal System) 1, Status (Organized Crime) 1

Willpower: 8

Morality: 7

Virtue: Prudence

Vice: Envy

Health: 8

Initiative: 7

Defense: 3

Speed: 10

Erik Blattner, Crime-Desk Journalist

Background: Where there is crime, there is a crime story. Ask any television programming executive or book or newspaper publisher — crime stories sell.

Erik Blattner's stories sell a lot of books and newspapers.

The online and print versions of the *Midway Tribune* have close to a half-million readers every day. The newspaper considers itself an advocate for the city's citizens, and sometimes taking on unpopular positions in its editorials. The news staff has a reputation for being aggressive and determined. The *Trib* is well regarded in the national journalism community, with a half-dozen Pulitzer Prizes or nominations (Mace Calhoun' among them; see the Prologue) and scores of lesser awards to the newspapers' credit.

Newspapers and the law enforcement community often have an antagonistic relationship. Cops are wary of the Fourth Estate's influence on public opinion, the media want pieces of information that cops may be reluctant to release and both sides jealously guard their sources of information.

As the senior reporter on the *Tribune's* crime beat, Blattner covers the city's less-pleasant stories. He started out logging police reports and court records, working his way into a reporter's position. His clear writing style endeared him to harried copy editors, and his attention to details caught the eye of managing editors and the newspaper's publisher. Blattner demonstrated to the cops he interacted with that he wasn't going to use the power of the media against them, and they could trust him with sensitive information. He took the time to learn how cops do their jobs and develop a positive relationship with them. The police found an advocate of their own.

Blattner starts his day with a pot of the strongest coffee he can get his hands on. He checks his voice and electronic mail and thumbs through the reports left on his desk by the night shift's news assistants. He makes his morning calls and prepares a quickly abandoned schedule for the day. Pending stories get an update, new stories get assigned to other crime reporters or claimed by Blattner and another day on the crime beat gets underway.

Blattner's job requires him to maintain contacts on both sides of the law. He keeps his sources secret and scrupulously distinct from one another, and will regularly end a phone call with a police officer only to immediately dial up one of the city's crime figures to confirm the officer's story. Blattner's moral code has convinced him to provide evidence for police investigations on a few occasions, when the crime was particularly vile. He has used available resources to create temporary false identities for his criminal contacts when their information leads to police action against powerful criminals.

The newspaper isn't Blattner's only source of income. He writes non-fiction and crime novels under a false name, using his news stories as inspiration. A mass-market paperback or hardcover book comes out every 18 months or so, and the occasional exceptionally lurid story appears in exploitative publications under yet another pseudonym. Blattner keeps this second career hidden from his editors at the *Tribune*, and only discusses this writing with his closest friends. He plans to approach Sergeant Raia soon with a proposal to write the officer's biography once he retires.

Reason and objectivity are hallmarks of Blattner's news writing, and he keeps any hint of the paranormal out of his books. During long nights on the job, he has seen things he can't explain, and only half-jokes when he tells people that sometimes his "stories just write themselves." Occasionally, voicemails or emails have no clear origin; Blattner has learned to pay special attention to these, as they lead to good stories for at least one side of his career. Some of the cops he speaks with have similar stories, and Blattner sometimes starts planning a book on urban law enforcement mythology.

Erik Blattner, Eve Kanagy, Katy Garriga, and Jamie Biron

CIVILIAN STAFF

A young woman's suicide a couple of years ago left Blattner more rattled than he is willing to admit. Blattner had covered a story involving the woman's family, and the resulting scandal caused her fiancé to end their relationship. Since then, Blattner has had occasional nightmares in which the woman appears, blaming him for her death. Blattner has seen a psychologist about these nightmares, and is taking prescription sleep medication.

Blattner is married, with a toddler daughter. Alexandra Blattner knows about her husband's nightmares, but accepts the therapist's explanation that the woman is a manifestation of Blattner's stress. Alexandra is more proud of his books than his day job, and has sworn to never tell his coworkers about the books.

Description: Handsome and outgoing, Erik could have had a successful career as a television news talking head. He dresses conservatively, with a nod toward film noir detective styling. His shoulder bag shows the effects of years of hard use, and is always stocked with notepads and pens.

His Toyota Matrix is very nearly a mobile office. A laptop computer and police-band radio scanner are almost always onboard, and the front seat is home to city maps and a phone directory.

Storytelling Hints: Erik is respectful to just about everyone, willing to keep personal distaste under wraps so as to maintain working relationships. He's a dogged investigator, and demands excellent work from his subordinates. Erik believes that he can make the world a better place. He takes on the city's criminal elements, hoping to inspire others to do the same. Privately, he can be incredibly judgmental, and will carry a grudge for months. Probably more so than many of the city's cops, Erik hates crime. He can't wear a badge and a gun or prosecute perpetrators, but he uses the power of public opinion to persecute the city's wrongdoers.

Attributes: Intelligence 4, Wits 3, Resolve 3, Strength 2, Dexterity 2, Stamina 2, Presence 3, Manipulation 4, Composure 3

Skills: Academics 2, Athletics 1, Computer 1, Drive 2, Empathy 2, Expression 3, Investigation 3, Persuasion 2, Politics 2, Socialize 2, Stealth 2, Streetwise 2, Subterfuge 1

Merits: Encyclopedic Knowledge, Allies (Police) 1, Allies (Media) 2, Contacts (Media, City Hall, Police, Organized Crime) 4, Fame 2, Mentor 2, Status (Tribune) 2

Willpower: 7

Morality: 8

Virtue: Hope

Vice: Wrath

Health: 7

Initiative: 5

Defense: 2

Speed: 9

Alana Bailey

Background: The cop bar is a great tradition among large departments. Somewhere in the city is a place for officers to spend off-duty hours with comrades, away from families, criminals and official oversight. For the officers of the 13th Precinct, that place is Bailey's.

Alana is the fifth generation of her family to own and operate the bar, and the first woman. She grew up around the city's officers, learning about their work and the incredible pressures involved. When her father retired and offered her the bar, Alana leapt at the opportunity.

Running a bar focused on the needs of the city's cops takes some doing. Alana regularly puts in 16-hour days at her business, and the bar's small staff is expected to be willing to do the same. The bar is successful, though, and provides Alana and her family a comfortable living. Her husband, a banker, is tolerated within the bar, and takes a lot of ribbing about his wife (she kept her maiden name after the marriage).

Alana has operated the bar for more than 15 years, and hears and sees more than most people would believe. She has worked hard to maintain the trust of the city's law enforcement community and would never risk damaging that status. She knows that many of her regular customers would gladly turn a blind eye to minor infractions. To protect herself and her customers, Alana keeps her business and personal life distantly separate. She refuses any favors from the cops, keeps the bar spotless and its business records just as clean and doesn't have so much as an unpaid parking ticket on her police record. Sergeant Raia tells her that if the city had more citizens like her, he'd be out of a job.

The bar is a second home for MPD officers, and seems to be a permanent home for some. Patrons report seeing a long-deceased partner, hearing his voice or some other evidence of haunting at least once a month. Alana has found items moved between closing up and opening the next day, usually souvenirs from a deceased officer. Photographs straighten themselves after being returned to the walls, and subtle changes in the captured images show up on close inspection. Alana hears her late grandfather's baritone voice singing old drinking songs when she's alone in the bar late at night. Practical to the last, she promotes the idea of a haunted bar, telling her customers that there will always be a place for them at Bailey's, even after they're dead. The gallows humor serves her well, and seems to comfort some of the officers.

Description: Alana has wavy, auburn hair and light blue eyes. She dresses casually around the bar, favoring jeans and a buttoned-down shirt worn open over one of her many police-themed T-shirts.

Storytelling Hints: Alana is hardworking and dedicated to keeping Bailey's status as the city's premier cop hangout. She makes sure that the officers are taken care of and passes this ethic on to the bar's staff. She welcomes every officer by name, attends every wedding and funeral and, at the end of the day, goes home to her husband and kids and keeps the cops' secrets intact. Alana loves the money the bar provides, and enjoys having a specific clientele. As long as cops need somewhere to relax and get away from their troubles for a little while, Alana will be there to make a comfortable living from it.

Attributes: Intelligence 3, Wits 4, Resolve 3, Strength 2, Dexterity 3, Stamina 3, Presence 3, Manipulation 2, Composure 2

Skills: Athletics 1, Brawl 1, Drive 1, Empathy 3, Occult 1, Persuasion 2, Politics 1, Socialize 4, Streetwise 2

Merits: Contacts (Police) 1, Status (MPD) 2

Willpower: 5

Morality: 7

Virtue: Charity

Vice: Greed

Health: 8

Initiative: 5

Defense: 3

Speed: 10

Bailey's

Since opening during the first years of the 20th century, Bailey's has catered to Midway's finest. John H. Bailey established the bar on the advice of his brother, the only Bailey to actually serve in the MPD.

Originally located in a storefront building near Midway's old city hall, the bar moved to its location next to the precinct house after World War II. Inside, the lights are low, the music is usually soft and unobtrusive and pictures of cops in every situation cover the walls. There are a couple of TVs tuned to sports and news channels.

Outsiders find themselves politely but firmly excluded from the bar's camaraderie, and anyone stirring up trouble gets a single terse warning before being bodily removed from the premises. God help any uninitiated thug who decides to knock this place over for a few quick bucks.

Alana closes the bar on Thanksgiving and Christmas, and any time a police officer is killed in the line of duty. After the funeral, she opens up for the night, and somber remembrances become boisterous wakes.

Jamie Biron, Citizens' Patrol Watchdog

Background: The police can't be everywhere, and criminals of every stripe rely on this simple fact. Community policing and neighborhood watch programs attempt to make communities more aware of dangers within their borders.

Computer engineer Jamie Biron worked hard all though school, and puts forth a herculean effort in his career. He enjoys the comforts that his labors provide — a nice house, expensive car and an enviable lifestyle. He wants to protect what's his, and has found a large number of his neighbors are willing to put forth extra effort to do the same.

Jamie established a community patrol program under the guidance of MPD officers. He and his neighbors keep a close watch on their community, and their efforts have helped cut the crime rate in the area by some 70%. His project is held up as a model of citizen involvement in opposing crime.

With his neighbors, Jamie organized a schedule of patrols and observation throughout his subdivision. At least two citizens are on call at any time to assist a neighbor in need or provide a late-night escort. Because of the neighborhood watch's familiarity with the area, and their knowledge of what they can handle on their own and what requires police action, the MPD is quick to respond to calls from the area. Officers know that a call from Jamie's neighborhood is highly unlikely to be a false alarm or a nuisance call.

Description: Jamie dresses well. He isn't conspicuous about his wealth, but isn't especially concerned about keeping it hidden, either. He's aged well, looking about a decade younger than his 56 years.

Storytelling Hints: Jamie doesn't play class games based on income or occupation. As long as someone is a productive member of society, or at least, not a threat to anyone else, Jamie treats that person with respect. He has no tolerance for criminal activity, and would happily lock up the guilty and throw away the key.

Jamie is a firm believer that an ounce of prevention is worth a pound of cure. He seeks to prevent problems instead of solving them, and tries to take the long view of a situation.

Unfortunately, Jamie craves attention. He's happiest when a roomful of people is focused on him, waiting on his next word. The neighborhood watch program is a step toward celebrity.

Attributes: Intelligence 3, Wits 4, Resolve 3, Strength 2, Dexterity 3, Stamina 2, Presence 3, Manipulation 3, Composure 4

Skills: Academics 1, Computer 4, Intimidation 2, Investigation 2, Persuasion 3, Politics 2, Socialize 3, Streetwise 1, Weaponry 2

Merits: Allies 2, Common Sense, Disarm, Encyclopedic Knowledge, Resources 3, Status 2

Willpower: 7

Morality: 8

Virtue: Prudence

Vice: Lust

Health: 7

Initiative: 7

Defense: 3

Speed: 10

Chapter Four: The Blotter

Empathy was yesterday. Today, you're wasting my motherfucking time.

— Detective Lieutenant Vincent Hanna, *Heat*

This chapter is divided into two sections. The first gives a brief overview of some important issues that a Storyteller must consider when preparing a chronicle in which one or more characters is a police officer. The second section provides examples of story hooks that might attract the attention of a player's character who works as a police officer at the 13th Precinct, either because he was assigned to investigate a crime that conceals more mysterious or sinister undertones than is readily apparent or simply because he heard about some strange experience a fellow officer had while on the job.

The Thin Blue Line

When a Storyteller prepares a chronicle involving the police who patrol the World of Darkness, several factors should be considered in developing the overarching plot. The first and perhaps most important consideration is deciding what mechanism exists to prevent the exposure of supernatural criminals. As a design precept, the World of Darkness is similar to our own world, but with malignant twists. While dark supernatural forces are suffused throughout the World of Darkness, they hide themselves to all but the most astute or luckless citizens. A police officer within the confines of this setting has a greater likelihood of encountering the supernatural than most citizens and represents a much greater opportunity for exposure. After all, most any honest and intelligent cop who discovers vampires should have the training and the resources to gather evidence of the predators' activities so as to prove that such creatures exist. So why hasn't anyone done that yet?

The answer is simply that the supernatural world conceals itself with layer upon layer of conspiracy and intrigue. An individual police officer may discover evidence of supernatural crime, but will be hardpressed to prove his claims to anyone else without overwhelming evidence. Vampires typically show up blurred in photos and on videotape, causing most people to dismiss such evidence as having been doctored. Uratha are protected by the shield of Lunacy, which causes mortals to disregard even their own memories of werewolf activity. Mages who fail to exercise discretion are still protected by Disbelief and Occultation, and ultimately by their own ability to magically destroy or conceal any evidence of their activities. However, these innate defenses alone are not enough to prevent exposure of the supernatural world. But then, the supernatural world doesn't rely only on passive defenses.

Any city of any appreciable size — Midway included — may be expected to have at least some vampires, werewolves and mages. The proportions may vary from city to city, and it is possible that one group could have such an overwhelming presence that that group totally excludes the other two, but generally, all three groups will be present. While these three supernatural species have vastly divergent natures, powers and goals, they all share one single characteristic: an overwhelming need for secrecy. To that end, a character who seeks to expose the supernatural world probably faces at least three separate occult conspiracies that have spent years or even decades observing police agencies for the express purpose of preventing such exposure. And while it is unlikely that any supernatural conspiracy can be said to "control" the police force entirely, such organizations are more than capable of stopping any single investigation in its tracks or of silencing individual officers who come to close to discovering the truth.

The first step in preventing exposure of supernatural activity is simply to destroy the evidence. If a police character follows standard procedure, any evidence acquired will be carefully preserved and then stored in a guarded evidence locker (either the 13th Precinct's or Central's), which should prevent anyone from gaining access to the evidence without leaving a record of his activities. While such a system is generally able to prevent most evidence tampering, this system is woefully inadequate to deal with intruders armed with powers of invisibility, shapeshifting, mind control or a host of other abilities suited to facilitating intrusion. Thus, if the character simply turns the evidence over to a superior or to the evidence locker personnel, the Storyteller is free to simply declare that the evidence has disappeared. Depending on the supernatural antagonists the Storyteller wishes to use, characters may also find that all proof that the evidence was logged in at all is gone as well, and even any memory of the evidence might have been erased from anyone else who handled it. In this manner, characters

may discover both the existence of the supernatural and learn how pervasive its influence is, possibly gaining a healthy dose of paranoia in the process.

Characters who insist on openly speculating about the supernatural will typically draw significant negative attention to themselves, not all of which comes from supernatural creatures. A cop who insists that vampires or werewolves exist will almost certainly be required to undergo psychiatric evaluation, even if her superiors are not agents of such creatures. Officers who are more subtle in their investigations may evade censure and firing, but they still risk being tagged as "that guy," the weird officer who's seen to many sordid movies. Characters with such a reputation may find it difficult to pursue their own independent investigations of supernatural phenomena. Fellow officers may not wish to associate with apparently unstable personalities, while higher-ranking personnel may be afraid of the consequences of letting a loose cannon run wild with a badge and gun.

A wise character will choose to keep her knowledge of the supernatural world to herself, at least until she's confident that she can prove her claims beyond any shadow of a doubt, a day that may never come considering the forces allied against her. Furthermore, even if the cop conceals the nature of her inquiries from her fellow officers and superiors, concealing the inquiries from the subjects of her investigations is more difficult. Supernatural entities who learn of a police officer actively investigating super-

natural crimes may react in many different ways, but they will definitely act.

One strategy for dealing with such an investigator is to attempt to co-opt him. The supernatural conspiracies that strive to conceal the true nature of the World of Darkness have much to offer a police officer who is willing to play ball: wealth, influence and even supernatural power for the officer himself. Even an honest officer may be willing to cooperate with one of the supernatural conspiracies if it presents itself as having a benevolent purpose. For example, an Iron Rider werewolf who initiates contact with the officer may be able to persuade him that werewolves are not violent and murderous monsters but are instead "supernatural policemen" who protect humanity from the horrors of the Shadow Realm. Likewise, a mage of the Adamantine Arrow or the Guardians of the Veil might persuade the cop that the order's magic is all that stands between humankind and the corruptive influence of the Abyss. Of course, not all supernatural conspiracies can pretend to be so benign or would even be willing to try. Most of the major supernatural players have access to some kind of mind control abilities, from the blunt intimidation tactics of Uratha Dominance Gifts to the thought-shaping powers of a mage's Mind Arcana to the soul-rending addiction potential in a vampire's Vitae.

If the conspiracy cannot suborn the officer's loyalty, the conspiracy may then try simply to discredit him. Each of the conspiracies is so thoroughly insinuated into mortal society that framing someone for a crime she did not commit is alarmingly simple. Evidence is planted by invisible intruders. Witnesses are coerced to give testimony against the officer, assuming a vampire or mage doesn't simply alter the witness' memories to make him genuinely believe the officer's guilt. Puppets within the banking sector transfer funds from known gangsters to the officer to make her appear guilty of bribery. A mage's Fate spells shape the officer's destiny to make it inevitable that she will arrive at the murder scene just in time to be found alone with the body. The possibilities are endless.

Although the officer may not realize it, there is one consolation for an officer who knows the truth. Whatever the supernatural creatures do to her to prevent their own exposure, assassination is almost always the last resort. When an officer is killed, particularly one who claimed to be working on some secret case involving a mysterious conspiracy, entirely too much attention is placed on the investigation for the comfort of any of the city's supernatural denizens. One rarely knows just how many people the officer has spoken to before her demise, and nothing could be more disastrous than to inadvertently confirm the suspicions of an even larger group of investigators. Better to ignore the bee flying around your head than to swat it and summon a whole swarm in its place.

To Protect and Serve

Each vignette in this portion of the blotter has three sections. The Call describes the initial civic complaint that summoned the characters to the scene of some crime. The Twist identifies what's really going on underneath the obvious exterior and which may or may not involve a brush with the supernatural. Finally, Outcomes describes possible ways that each vignette can play out during the course of a police investigation.

The assumption underlying each of these scenarios is that a single character who works as a police officer, or possibly two who are partnered together, has been assigned either as a first responder or as an investigator to some crime scene, with the actual storyline springing out of something discovered at the scene or during the course of the investigation. While all of the players' characters may be police officers, Storytellers should keep in mind the logistical responsibilities of such a chronicle. While on the job, a police officer is expected to keep Dispatch constantly apprised of her location for reasons of officer safety. Thus, a player character's officer cannot simply stop what she's doing and join another player's character in investigating some weird phenomena without either informing Dispatch or committing a serious infraction of police procedure.

Storytellers should also keep in mind the relative freedom of police officers to investigate crimes to which they have not been assigned. Theoretically, patrol officers are free to investigate any crime of which they are aware, and investigators have considerable latitude in how they allocate their time on the job. That said, it is highly suspicious and borderline insubordinate for a patrol officer to pursue a criminal investigation on his own time, and any officer, field or investigator, who disobeys a direct order to not pursue a case can be terminated for insubordination.

In addition to the three sections described above, many of the vignettes in the blotter contain a fourth section called Role Reversals, which present story ideas for how that vignette may be played out from the other side. That is, what happens when a vampire, werewolf, mage or mortal investigator is confronted by a police antagonist? Such vignettes present scenarios in which the player characters might be forced to deal with police officers as adversaries who cannot simply be killed and disposed of.

Armed Robbery: The Girl on the Tape

The Call

Police are called to the scene of a late-night armed robbery at a local gas station. No shots were fired, and the perp, a young, black male, escaped with only about $140 in

cash. First responders will arrive on the scene just moments after the silent alarm goes off, and take initial statements from the store manager and the only other witness to the crime, a white female who identifies herself as Andrea Delaney, a 31-year-old writer who was filling up her car at the time of the robbery. Delaney claims that she was too frightened to see anything and never got a good look at the robber. With a successful contested Wits + Empathy roll (against a pool of four dice), a character will notice that Delaney seems skittish, even more so than one would expect under the circumstances, particularly when she observes the store manager turn the video surveillance tape over to the police.

The Twist

Andrea Delaney is a neonate vampire (Embraced within just the last few years) who knows little about vampiric society or physiology. Delaney thinks she won't show up on the videotape, similar to the classic horror-movie vampires who don't show up on film or in mirrors, and it's making her nervous. (The irony of the matter is that she's safe — she'll simply show up blurry and unidentifiable on the tape, but she doesn't know that.) During the robbery itself, she panicked and had neither the time nor the wits to either steal the tape before the police arrived or simply leave. Now, she realizes her mistake and knows that the investigating officers will have a name to match to the "missing" face on the tape, and she doesn't want to show up in any police reports that will make their way into the Prince's hands. The convenience store clerk also knows Delaney reasonably well. Her haven is nearby, and she stops here regularly.

This scenario can play out in many ways. If police notice that Delaney is unusually nervous and question her more forcefully (perhaps in the mistaken belief that she was an accomplice), there is a chance she might frenzy, thereby making a bad situation even worse. More likely, Delaney will give a brief statement to the police and then leave as soon as possible, hoping for the best. Afterward, the character (whether an investigator or a patrol officer) will have an opportunity to see the video and notice the strange distortion of the person he knows to be Delaney.

The character may or may not be intrigued enough to want to check up on Delaney, but he will definitely take a stronger interest in the case two days later when the videotape itself disappears from the evidence locker, along with any evidence that such a tape ever existed. A check at the address listed for Andrea Delaney will reveal an apartment completely cleaned out save for a small residue of blood on the bathroom floor.

On the other hand, if the character already has knowledge of the existence of vampires and the manner in which they appear on camera, he may realize what's making Andrea so nervous. To keep the Masquerade intact, he must figure out how to steal the videotape from the evidence locker without getting caught (easier for the investigator

than a patrol officer, but still a complication). He or his allies can also reach Andrea Delaney before whatever the Storyteller decides happens to her provided that they attempt to do so before 3 A.M. of the following night. For more information on vampire antagonists, see **Vampire: The Requiem**.

Outcomes

This story hook can introduce a mortal police officer character to the existence of vampires by showing what even a minor breach of the Masquerade looks like from "the other side," so to speak. Depending on what actions are taken by the players' characters, they may never realize that Andrea Delaney is a vampire or they may actually rescue her from an unpleasant fate and gain a valuable contact within the local supernatural community, particularly if they successfully obtain the only copy of the videotape and use it to blackmail the neonate.

Andrea Delaney, Callow Neonate

Clan: Gangrel
Covenant: Unaligned (as of yet)
Embrace: 2002
Apparent Age: Mid-20s
Attributes: Intelligence 2, Wits 2, Resolve 2, Strength 2, Dexterity 3, Stamina 3, Presence 3, Manipulation 3, Composure 2
Skills: Academics 1, Animal Ken 2, Athletics 2, Brawl 1, Computer 1, Drive 2, Empathy 2, Investigation 2, Persuasion 3, Socialize 3, Stealth 2, Streetwise 1, Weaponry 1
Merits: Barfly, Haven 2 (Location 1, Size 1), Resources 2, Striking Looks 2
Willpower: 4
Humanity: 7
Virtue: Hope
Vice: Sloth
Initiative: 5
Defense: 2
Speed: 10
Blood Potency: 1
Disciplines: Animalism 2, Resilience 1
Vitae/per Turn: 10/1

Andrea is a stunningly beautiful if somewhat vapid young party girl. Her Embrace was the result of a brash impulse by a nomadic Gangrel who should have known better and who left town immediately after the deed. In the four years since, Andrea has made a few contacts among the neonates of the Midway vampire community who have informed her of the rules of their society. She has been largely invisible to the political leadership of the city's Kindred and wants more than anything else to keep it that way.

Role Reversals

Vampire characters are often acutely aware of the effect of the blurred visage that accompanies the Embrace.

While the effects can be easily overcome just by spending a Willpower point, few characters wish to constantly spend Willpower for every scene in which they are out in public. What few characters realize is that, with the proliferation of ATMs, closed-circuit security cameras and even automatic cameras at traffic lights, people are routinely photographed without their knowledge. Of course, few American cities can compare with London, whose citizens are caught on film an average of 300 times per day. But for the Kindred, who live in constant fear of the collapse of the Masquerade, widespread photo surveillance is a frightening prospect.

The Storyteller of a vampire chronicle can use the proliferation of video technology to inject a healthy dose of paranoia into his players, or to highlight the fearsome ignorance neonates often have. For example, he can take the story hook described above, but with the characters in the place of the hapless Andrea Delaney. One or more of the characters has stepped into a convenience store to pay for gas or to get cigarettes when the store is held up. A similar outcome may play out at a nightclub that has closed-circuit television, at an ATM machine when she stops to get cash or if she is simply stopped by an officer for speeding. Most young vampires know enough about modern police procedure to realize that all squad cars now have cameras mounted on the dashboard.

Trespassing and Vagrancy: Territorial Concerns

The Call

Police are called in by Martin Adelman, a Midway real estate developer who has just purchased several condemned tenement buildings that he plans to raze and then replace with luxury condominiums. Upon a recent inspection of one of the buildings, Adelman discovered that it was occupied by a trio of squatters, two men and one woman, who became belligerent when he informed them that the building was coming down soon and that they would have to leave. Officers at the scene will find only one of the three squatters present, a filthy and irascible old man who identifies himself as "Digger." Digger will be surly but will not provoke a direct confrontation with police officers. He will, however, attempt to verify that the police were sent by Adelman and then leave the premises. As the police are leaving, a successful Wits + Composure roll will permit a character to notice two large dogs waiting in an alley across the street, staring intently at the officers. With an exceptional success on the Wits + Composure roll or a single success on a subsequent Wits + Animal Ken roll, a character may realize that the dogs are actually wolves.

According to police protocol, the character who arrived at the scene should call Adelman to follow up on the report a few days after the encounter with Digger. When she does so, a noticeably frightened Adelman will inform

the officers that he has decided to sell the property rather than develop it himself, and he sees no further reason to involve the police. If any squatters remain at the site, it's the future owner's problem. From that point, individual characters can investigate as they see fit, but officers have no official obligation to return to the scene — until a month or so later, when Adelman sells the property at a significant loss to another developer who calls to complain about the same three vagrants.

The Twist

The vagrants are actually three werewolves who have made their home in the abandoned tenement after discovering a locus inside it. Loci are physical locations at which werewolves (also known as Uratha) can more easily regain Essence, the mystical energy they use to fuel their supernatural powers. Such loci also allow werewolves to enter the Shadow Realm, the spiritual reflection of the real world. The Uratha purged the locus of the spirits of decay and despair that had been corrupting the surrounding area and then claimed the locus as their own.

Unfortunately, they did their job too well. By removing the supernatural taint inflicted by those spirits, the Uratha made the area more desirable for real estate developers such as Adelman. A quick visit to Adelman at his home terrified the developer into abandoning plans to tear down the building, but it is only a short-term solution for the three Uratha, all of whom belong to a tribe called the Hunters in Darkness, which is traditionally ill-equipped to handle issues such as property laws.

In addition to legal problems, the werewolf pack also has logistical problems in protecting their locus. The pack is very small. Only three Uratha survived their fight with the decay-spirits that previously held the territory, which makes protecting the area 24 hours a day extremely difficult. While the three have frightened Adelman off, they realize that he will simply sell the property to someone else who will eventually send more police, and the werewolves have no practical capability to legally obtain title to the property themselves. They are also compelled to handle any incursions as quietly as possible, to prevent mortal police from discovering the existence of werewolves and to prevent some other more powerful pack from learning of their locus and challenging them for it. For more information on Uratha antagonists and politics, see **Werewolf: The Forsaken**.

Outcomes

A police character who enjoys using his authority to bully and harass those he considers beneath him may get his comeuppance in this scenario, possibly by being ripped apart by a werewolf consumed by Death Rage (though this fate better suits a Storyteller character than a player's character). Assuming the werewolves are not provoked to that point, they will make every effort to deal with the police without resorting to violence or using any more overt supernatural powers. However, if an officer attempts to put any of the three under arrest, all bets are off. If a character attempts to enter the building more discreetly (such as without announcing his presence, which is against procedure), he can potentially snoop around without being caught. Digger will be the only Uratha guarding the locus at night while the other two patrol the surrounding areas, and he has an unfortunate tendency to nod off while on guard duty. A search of the building will find one room on the first floor that is used as a communal pack room. There are three nests of blankets (but no sleep-ing bags), some bottles of fresh water and lots of heavily gnawed animal bones.

In the basement, the character will find a somewhat mangy gray wolf (actually Digger) curled up in a corner sound asleep. At this point, the character must make a Dexterity + Stealth roll opposed by Digger's Perception roll (Wits + Composure; Digger gains a +4 bonus while in his wolf form). If awakened, Digger, using his Gifts and his natu-ral intimidation without changing out of his wolf form, will attempt to in-timidate the character into leaving the base-ment. If the character draws a gun, Digger will

defend himself to the best of his ability. On the other hand, if the character's Stealth roll exceeded Digger's Perception roll (unlikely but possible), the character might choose to shoot the sleeping wolf with a Killing Blow (see the **World of Darkness Rulebook**, p. 168). Doing so will cause the wolf to instantly transform into Digger's human form, now dead of a gunshot wound to the head. This may be sufficient to make the character to leave in a panic.

In the middle of the large, open basement, a circular patch on the floor has been discolored by mold. This is the locus. It is also what mages would consider a Verge: a location where the boundary between physical and spirit worlds is so thin that even a mortal can step across without any special supernatural powers. If the character steps into the discolored area, he will feel a brief sense of vertigo and then everything around him will change. The spiritual manifestation of the basement is covered in mold, slime and various crawling insects. There is no sign of Digger here, but the walls will be covered in scratches and gouges

caused by unknown but obviously large creatures. Part of the north wall has been knocked down, allowing the character to see outside or even crawl up to the surface if he desires. The spiritual reflection of the surrounding six blocks is a nightmare facade of decay and misery. Nearby tenements drip blood and pus, while zombie-like figures formed of crack cocaine shaped into human forms shamble around, searching for their next fixes.

A mortal character who crosses over into the Shadow Realm in this desolate region must make an immediate Resolve + Composure roll (at a –3 penalty for the sheer alienness of it all, unless the character is familiar with the Shadow Realm) to avoid panicking completely. On a failure, the character will be under the effects of a temporary derangement (Storyteller's choice, though derangements based on fear or delusion work best). On a dramatic failure, the character will enter a blind panic and will flee up the stairs, carefully avoiding the circle of mold that brought him here. With a success, however, the character will realize that the circle is the quickest, if not the only, way back to the physical world. Simply crossing the circle again will send the character back from where he came, and he will find a new nightmare waiting for him. Digger will be awake and in his Dalu (near human) form. In this form, he is humanoid, but nearly seven feet tall, with jagged claws, outsized fangs and shaggy fur covering his face and exposed skin.

Digger will first attempt to trigger Lunacy in the char-acter (Lunacy being a supernatural mind-altering effect induced in mortals by the sight of a werewolf in one of its unnatural forms) and then use the Voice of Command Gift to force the character to leave and never return. Lunacy is described more fully on pp. 175–176 of **Werewolf: The Forsaken** while the Voice of Command Gift is described on p. 110 of that book. For the Storyteller's ease, we simplify the combined effects of these powers as follows.

First, determine how seriously the character is affected by Lunacy by adding a +2 bonus to the character's Willpower. If the result is less than 4, add a +4 bonus to Digger's Gift roll. If the result is between 5 and 7, add a +3 bonus to the Gift roll. If the result is 8–9, add a +1 bonus, and if the total is 10 or better, add no dice. Digger has a base pool of 11 dice for the Voice of Command Gift (including three dice for spending a point of Willpower), while the character will simply roll his Resolve to resist. If Digger's roll succeeds, the character will come to his senses some time later (most likely several hours). He will most probably initially believe that everything he saw was a nightmare, at least until he finds physical evidence, for example, his urine-soaked pants lying on the floor next to his bed. Alternately, he may wake up in his car, having slept there all night or he may even awaken curled up in an alley, still shivering in fear. The character can attempt to remember what happened by spending a Willpower point and rolling Resolve + Composure. Assign this roll a penalty equal to the dice bonus that Digger received on his Gift roll due to Lunacy. One success will cause the character to have hazy memories of something horrible in the tenement basement. An exceptional success will allow clear recollection. A dramatic failure will trigger a mild derangement in the character, again probably tied to fear.

If the character killed Digger before entering the locus, the character will, of course, remember everything that happened, including the fact that Digger had two allies. What the character may not realize until later is how easily the other werewolves can track him by scent.

Digger, Aged Werewolf

Note: Werewolves have a total of five forms: Hishu (human), Dalu (nearly human wolfman), Gauru (large wolfman), Urshul (dire wolf) and Urhan (normal wolf). When the werewolf's traits change with his form, the initial trait rating listed is the rating for the human form, followed by the other four in the order listed above.
Auspice: Elodoth
Tribe: Hunters in Darkness
Attributes: Intelligence 3, Wits 3, Resolve 3, Strength 3 (4/6/5/3), Dexterity 3 (3/4/5/5), Stamina 3 (4/5/5/4), Presence 2, Manipulation 2 (1/2/0/2), Composure 4
Skills: Animal Ken 2, Athletics 2, Brawl 3, Crafts 1, Drive 1, Empathy 1, Intimidation 4, Investigation 3, Medicine 2, Occult 4, Persuasion 2, Stealth 3, Streetwise 1, Subterfuge 2, Survival 4, Weaponry 2
Merits: Encyclopedic Knowledge 4, Fetish 2, Language

(First Tongue) 1
Primal Urge: 4
Willpower: 7
Harmony: 6
Max Essence/Per Turn: 13/2
Virtue: Justice
Vice: Sloth
Health: 8 (10/12/11/8)
Initiative: 7 (7/8/9/9)
Defense: 3 (all forms)
Speed: 11 (12/15/18/16)
Renown: Cunning 2, Glory 2, Honor 3, Purity 3, Wisdom 3

Role Reversals

Few werewolves are conversant in the vagaries of property law, which can often lead to werewolf characters getting caught in situations similar to that of Digger and his pack. If a pack discovers a locus in an urban area, the packmembers may have great difficulty in readily accessing the locus unless it is either in a public place that the Uratha can visit at any time or is on private property that the Uratha is capable of purchasing. Otherwise, any attempt to access the locus requires the werewolf to trespass on another's property. While most Uratha will initially not care about trespassing on the rights of a human, a character may change her mind if the property owner calls the police to complain about squatters or vagrants (a description that might well apply to most werewolves, especially Blood Talons and Hunters in Darkness). In this manner, belligerent werewolves must either learn a bit of subtlety or else choose between abandoning their locus or threatening the Veil.

Death Report: Bum Fight

The Call

Police are called at 4 A.M. to a rundown apartment building in a slum area on a report of two deceased men who apparently fell to their deaths from the top of the 30-story building. One of the decedents is a Hispanic male approximately 60 years old and the other is a Caucasian male in his early 50s. Neither man has any identification. Both appear to be homeless vagrants who reek of booze and body odor. Both also appear to have been beaten severely before falling, suggesting homicide rather than accident or suicide. Police who investigate the roof of the apartment building will note that the door to the roof is unlocked. The apartment manager will express surprise at this, as the door is always kept locked except when maintenance is performed on the roof.

A successful Wits + Empathy roll will lead the officers to believe the manager's denial of any involvement. However, with a successful Wits + Investigation roll, police may think to interview the manager's family about his keys (or the officers may think of this without making a roll). The

manager's 16-year-old son, Michael, will appear agitated, but will attribute this to shock over the two deaths. Police will probably intuit that he knows more than he is saying (or the Storyteller may offer it to them as a result of a successful Manipulation + Empathy roll, opposed by Michael's Subterfuge pool of four dice). Police who realize that Michael knows something about the two deaths and that he also had access to the keys to the roof will have probable cause to take him in for questioning. Police station questioning should be roleplayed out, using the system for interrogation outlined on p. 81 of the **World of Darkness Rulebook**. If Michael is broken, he will tell the police everything. And then things get complicated.

The Twist

Michael's story is that he took $50 from three guys to let them have access to the roof to film two homeless men fighting so that the guys could sell "Bum Fight" videos on the Internet. The two vagrants were each given $50 to fight until one of them was unconscious, as well as some liquor to dull their pain and inhibitions and some amphetamines to give them more energy. The film crew, who apparently started this film project only recently, wanted to use the roof because it was secluded (the building was much taller than the surrounding properties) and they thought the city skyline would make a cool backdrop for the fights. The film crew and Michael were surprised and horrified when, after several minutes of brutally beating one another, one of the vagrants charged the other and their momentum carried them right over the edge of the building. The filmmakers gave Michael an extra $500 cash to forget they were ever there and quickly left.

Although none of the three amateur filmmakers directly intended to kill the two bums, the filmmakers did engineer the events that led to the bums' deaths, which could conceivably result in negligent homicide charges. On the other hand, Michael also says that the two men appeared to be perfectly willing, though they were both drunk and possibly high at the time, which may make it impossible to sustain any charges against the filmmakers. The biggest problem, however, is the filmmakers' identities: Chase Addison (grandson of the senior partner at one of the biggest law firms in town), T.J. Radcliffe (the son of investment billionaire Ted Radcliffe) and Jason Prentiss (the favorite nephew of the chief of police). All three are seniors at an exclusive Midway private school, and all three have personalities that distinctly display their privilege and entitlement — all but guaranteed to rub investigating officers the wrong way. However, while the three each epitomize the word callow, they are not stupid. None of the three will say a word outside the presence of a lawyer. All of them will deny any involvement in any "bum fights," and none is likely to break under any but the most intensive interrogation. Also, each of the three has powerful relatives who will try to pull strings to get the boys out of trouble.

Outcomes

If the characters are the type to take bribes, they can make a lot of money by helping the three rich boys out of trouble, possibly ingratiating themselves with some very influential people in the process. On the other hand, if the characters have any sort of reputation for honesty and professionalism, the boys' families will not risk adding bribery to the charges and will instead take more indirect steps such as having the officers' superiors lean on them or paying Michael to recant his testimony (since, at the moment, Michael is the only evidence tying the three filmmakers to the scene at all). In order to get any sort of conviction against any of the three boys, officers must get creative, lucky or both. While the three cannot be easily broken, other evidence does exist that might weaken their resolve.

Although no website currently exists, the domain name *www.midwaybumfights.com* is currently owned by T.J. Radcliffe under the pseudonym of "T.J. Knockout." Characters may discover this with an Intelligence + Computer roll (at a –3 penalty for obscurity and the pseudonym), but only if they think to research bum fights on the Internet.

With a successful Wits + Streetwise roll, a character may find someone at one of the city's many homeless shelters who recognizes the three filmmakers, who have spent some time scouting homeless shelters looking for likely fighters. Most likely, the character can only find someone who would make a poor witness — at best an alcoholic bum and at worst someone with deep-seated mental problems. With an exceptional success, the character may find a more respectable witness, such as a shelter volunteer or manager who remembers the three and noticed that they looked out of place. Getting such a witness to testify may require a Persuasion roll (using either a Presence or Manipulation dice pool, depending on the character's approach), particularly if one of the filmmakers' family members is a major donor to the shelter.

Additionally, Jason Prentiss, the least computer-savvy of the three, inadvertently saved a digital copy of an earlier fight. While all three of the boys have erased most of the video evidence of their activities, this one video file, already edited to include music and the *Midway Bum Fights* opening credits (which list the three boys as producers) remains on Jason's hard drive and can be easily found if the computer is ever collected on a search warrant.

Michael, Guilt-Ridden Accomplice

Background: Michael is a young kid who wants to escape the drudgery of tenement life and make something of himself. To that end, he's made a devil's bargain that he now regrets. He is terrified of being scapegoated for the homeless man's death, but if guaranteed immunity, he will agree to testify as to what he knows.

Description: Michael is a young, athletic, African American male aged 16 years. He gives the appearance of a good kid and has no gang affiliation or paraphernalia.

Storytelling Hints: You have the natural distrust of police that is common to young black males in Midway, but you feel genuinely guilty over the death of the two men. If you are certain that telling the truth will not destroy your future, you will readily do so to assuage your guilty heart.

Skills: Athletics 5, Streetwise 4, Subterfuge 4

Chase, T.J. and Jason, the Bum Fight Producers

Use the same traits for each of the three boys, except as noted.

Background: All three of the bum fight promoters come from wealthy families that have spoiled them to an unpleasant degree. None of them really needs the money that the bum fight videos would bring in — they were just bored and thought they could become famous Internet personalities and maybe parlay their success into a TV show.

Description: Chase is a young, athletic blond who favors Abercrombie & Fitch. T.J. is the nerd of the group, in that he wears glasses and is the most skilled with computers. He favors expensive pullovers and khakis, and has a shaggy mop of black hair. Jason is slightly stocky and plays lacrosse. He fancies himself a rapper and tends to wear urban, hip-hop clothes that would get him beaten to death if he wore them in the wrong part of town. He generally keeps his head shaved down almost to the skin and wears an NWA baseball cap. All three are 18 years old and attractive in a well-bred sort of way.

Storytelling Hints: Each of the three is arrogant but scared. Jason is the only one to have any real respect for police officers, and the other two may be openly contemptuous of investigators. None of the three has any particular feelings of guilt over their role in the death of the homeless men, but all are terrified of going to jail. While they will generally stick together, none of the three is bright enough to know about the Prisoner's Dilemma, and each will sell out the other two if he thinks there's any real chance of jail time.

Skills: Athletics 5, Computer 5 (T.J. only), Politics 3, Subterfuge 5

Indecent Exposure: The Streaker

The Call

While on patrol, the character observes something you don't see every day: a portly, middle-aged, naked man running down the sidewalk of a busy street during rush hour. The officer should have little difficulty catching the streaker. The character will notice that the perp is weeping uncontrollably and also blushing furiously, apparently utterly humiliated by his circumstances, and through his tears, he will ask the officers, "Will this get into the papers?" Almost any response will result in the same reaction from the streaker. While continuing to cry, he will hesitate, as if listening to some voice from behind him, and then, seemingly in despair, he will rush out into the street in front of a passing bus. A particularly athletic officer may be able to stop him from committing suicide, but doing so will require an exceptional success on a Dexterity + Athletics roll (with a dramatic failure possibly resulting in the officer being struck as well). Even if captured safely, the perp will remain non-responsive and suicidal, and will be sent to a local hospital for psychiatric observation.

The streaker will be revealed as Miles Graham, a 47-year-old, divorced stockbroker with the firm of Addison-DeWitt. His former wife, Terri, as well as his coworkers, will be shocked by what happened. Most anyone interviewed, however, will note that Graham has been acting very strangely for the past several weeks. An investigation of his condominium will reveal little, but his business records will show that he has recently made some large cash payments

to a woman named Sylvia Dashwood who manages a private club called the West Wycombe Club. A success on an Intelligence + Occult roll at a –2 penalty for obscurity will permit a character to note that West Wycombe was a village in England where Sir Francis Dashwood held meetings of the notorious Hellfire Club in the mid-18th century.

If interviewed, Sylvia Dashwood will reveal only that Graham had recently joined the West Wycombe Club, which she describes as a private club for discriminating individuals. If police come back with a warrant (which should be very difficult to obtain, as they have no real evidence connecting the club to Graham's strange actions and the club itself has powerful patrons), they will be allowed to search the grounds and will discover that beneath the club's sedate, old boy's club exterior lies an exclusive BDSM club. However, even if the character cannot obtain a warrant to search the premises, he may obtain permission to attend a private club function as a guest of Sylvia. Such an invitation will only be granted to characters who were present at Graham's apprehension (and most likely death), as those characters will have attracted some unhealthy attention.

The Twist

The West Wycombe Club is a large brownstone mansion taking up most of an entire city block in the business district of Midway. On those levels above the street, one can find all the amenities of any exclusive dining club for wealthy patrons, including a first-rate dining hall, a private gymnasium, a heated indoor swimming pool and even a banquet hall for private parties. Below the street level, however, are a number of hidden levels referred to by the members as "the Caves." The Caves contain orgy halls, Roman baths, dungeons, torture chambers and an extensive collection of bondage equipment. Unbeknownst to many of the members, the building also has a number of hidden cameras in most of the rooms so that Sylvia can tape the club members' most outrageous peccadilloes "just in case." On the lowest level lies "the Pit of Sin," a large room shaped like a Roman amphitheater where the club's elaborate initiation rituals are held.

The Pit of Sin is also a two-point locus and the lair of what purports to be the Greek god Pan. Pan is a spirit of humiliation and degradation that feeds on the club members, regaining Essence as the mortals around the spirit abandon any feelings of self-worth in pursuit of mindless pleasure (or pain, which is the same thing to many club members). Normally, Pan is content to feed on the succulent morsels of defilement that occur within the club. Occasionally, however, Pan comes across a feast. The creature's ability to draw Essence from self-degradation is related to the mortal's normal feelings of self-worth, as represented by the victim's Morality rating. When a person with a Morality rating of 6 or higher enters the Pit of Sin, Pan will pursue the person even after she leaves the club, using its Numina to torment her into deliberately engaging in acts that embarrass her. The ultimate goal for the spirit is to drive the victim

to commit suicide out of shame or public humiliation, as Miles Graham did.

If a character who has a Morality rating of 6 or better enters the Pit of Sin, he may well become a potential victim for the malicious spirit. Pan's psychic assault will begin with vivid dreams, as the spirit probes its victim's mind to find out what he finds most embarrassing. The spirit is capable of communicating with the victim telepathically and may pretend to be a demon, an angel or simply a subconscious aspect of the victim's personality, whichever the spirit thinks will work best. Once Pan has taken its victim's measure, the spirit will then attempt to manipulate the victim into doing embarrassing things. Such tricks will begin small — ordering the victim to "accidentally" leave his fly unzipped before going into an important meeting or to call his lover by the wrong name during sex. The orders will be become increasingly malicious until the victim is broken down by despair, at which point the spirit may try to manipulate the victim into a suicidal state. Significantly, however, Pan cannot directly control its victim in any way. Rather, the victim's embarrassing actions must be deliberately undertaken by him. However, the spirit can directly affect and even control those around the victim, and such secondary victims may never even realize that they are under the control of a malicious spirit. Pan has other Numina that it can use in an attempt to coerce the victim, but under no circumstances can the spirit directly harm or control anyone from whom it wishes to eventually feed (or indeed anyone with a Morality of 6+).

A character plagued by Pan has three possible ways to deal with the spirit adversary. The first, and probably easiest in the short term, is to lose Morality. Pan has little interest in driving persons of average or low Morality to their deaths as the spirit can reap significant quantities of Essence only from those with a Morality of 6+. On the other hand, while the victim no longer need fear death at the spirit's hands, he is now vulnerable to direct manipulation by a vicious and capricious spirit that may harm him in other ways. Meanwhile, significant Morality loss carries its own drawbacks, including a significant chance of madness — a character who loses Morality as a direct or indirect result of Pan's psychic depredations suffers a –2 penalty to the degeneration roll to avoid derangement due to overwhelming feelings of self-loathing.

The second way is to seek help. A priest could conceivably exorcize Pan if he could be persuaded of the seriousness of the situation (and that the officer was credible). The procedure for exorcizing an evil spirit is outlined on p. 214 of the **World of Darkness Rulebook**. If a priest is not available, someone else with an occult background could attempt an exorcism. Alternately, if the officer is aware of the existence of werewolves or mages, he might attempt to seek the help of such beings, assuming he doesn't mistakenly think that such entities are the ones harassing him.

Finally, a drastic solution is to simply destroy the West Wycombe Club. While Pan gains significant Essence from driving some victims to suicide, most of the spirit's Essence is regained from the ongoing activities at the club, which provide a steady diet of debauchery. While the club would almost certainly be rebuilt, the spirit would be at a great disadvantage in the meantime and might certainly conclude that the characters responsible were too dangerous and unpredictable to continue harassing, particularly if the individual's attack on the club attracted the attention of other supernatural beings that might provide competition for the club's small locus. Note that burning down a building is an act that will probably see the (justified) end of a law enforcement officer's career. This suggestion is included in case characters of a more radical stripe are involved, or if you're telling a "cop gone bad" type of story.

Pan,
Malicious Spirit of Self-Degradation

Rank: 3
Attributes: Power 6, Finesse 5, Resistance 5
Willpower: 11
Essence: 20 (max 20)
Initiative: 11
Defense: 5
Speed: 16
Size: 5
Corpus: 10
Influences: Humiliation 3
Numina:

Drain: The spirit can leech Essence or Willpower from a material being. Roll Power + Finesse versus the subject's Stamina + Resolve (+ any Supernatural Attribute). Each net success transfers one point of the chosen trait from the subject to the spirit (or vice versa, if the intended subject achieves more successes). Pan can use this Numen only while at the spirit's locus in the Pit of Sin, but the spirit need not materialize to do so. While away from the Pit of Sin, the spirit must materialize to use this Numen against another. Pan cannot use this Numen against a target with a Morality rating of 6+.

Life Drain: In certain specific situations, Pan can regain Essence at an accelerated rate when in the presence of someone who has died. There are two conditions. First, the person must have committed suicide out of shame or humiliation. Second, the person must have a Morality rating of 6 or higher. If the two conditions are met, then Pan will regain Essence equal to the sum of the victim's Health points and Willpower. The Essence gained cannot exceed Pan's maximum Essence pool, which is 20.

Harrow: Pan can invoke powerful feelings of shame or a psychosexual need for punishment in an enemy. Spend one Essence and roll Power + Finesse (minus the victim's Composure). The target is overwhelmed by the relevant emotion for a number of turns equal to the successes achieved and for that duration will suffer a dice penalty on all actions equal

to the spirit's Rank. Pan cannot use this Numen directly on a target with a Morality rating of 6+.

Living Fetter: Pan can link itself to a living being, allowing it to remain in the physical world without losing Essence. Roll Power + Finesse, contested by the intended host's Resolve + Composure. Once linked, Pan can use its Harrow power to compel the subject to perform humiliating acts. Pan cannot use its Harrow power to directly control any host with a Morality 6 or higher, but the spirit can use its Harrow to communicate telepathically with the host (by rolling its Harrow and getting at least one success).

Materialize: Pan can become solid and visible within the physical world. Spend 3 Essence and roll Power + Finesse. The number of successes determines how many hours the spirit can remain in the material world before reverting to ephemera. After the effect ends, the spirit's options are to sacrifice an additional Essence for each extra hour of physicality, to anchor itself to someone or something or to slip immediately back through the Gauntlet.

Ban: Pan is vulnerable to those of strong moral character, even as the spirit is drawn to them. The spirit cannot use any of its Numina to directly harm or control anyone whose Morality rating is 6 or higher. At the same time, Pan's Life Drain Numina will affect only targets whose Morality rating is 6 or higher.

Sylvia Dashwood,
Queen of the Hellfire Club

Background: Sylvia was once a successful high-class hooker and dominatrix. She was also the lover of the dark god Pan, who came to her on cloven hooves in her most erotic dreams. Over the years, she went from lover to high priestess in a cult consisting solely of herself. Her dreams led her to Midway and to a dilapidated mansion that she renovated for her "gentlemen's club." Of all the "regular girls" at the West Wycombe Club, Sylvia is the one most willing to do anything for a member. As Sylvia sees it, through degradation, she has found power that those who think to dominate her can only dream of. Power, yes, and love.

Description: Sylvia is an undeniably attractive woman in her mid-30s. Hers is the body of a slightly aging fashion model, but this maturity somehow only makes her more appealing. She looks like someone who has seen everything and is still eager to see it again. Sylvia has long, jet-black hair, and, during the day, she favors severe women's business attire that still suggests a dominatrix. At the club's revels, she often wears bondage attire or nothing at all.

Storytelling Hints: You are the high priestess and lover of a lusty god. Persons of wealth and power beg for a caress from your hand or a lash from your whip. The shame that these men and women feel when they voluntarily humiliate themselves to please Pan is almost as exciting as when you do so yourself.

Skills: Empathy 8, Expression 7, Occult 6, Persuasion 7, Politics 6, Socialize 7, Subterfuge 7

Role Reversals

While the West Wycombe Club is under the sway of a powerful spirit as written, the club could just as easily be a cover for some other supernatural characters' operations. Vampires and mages often set themselves up as cult leaders, and vampires in particular might often favor the dark, hyper-sexualized environment described in the West Wycombe Club. The problem with operating cults, particularly cults that have high-profile, wealthy members, is that sometimes these members die, and occasionally under suspicious circumstances that are not even the characters' fault. Instead of being driven to suicide by spiritual possession, perhaps Miles Graham was driven to insanity or death by the stress of his addiction to vampire Vitae or as a side effect of overwhelming magical mind control. Alternately, perhaps Miles saw something he shouldn't have when a mage cult leader attempted a ritual but was stung by excessive Paradox. Even if Miles' suicide is not overly suspicious, police are still required to investigate suicides as if they were homicides. The investigation would still raise suspicions about Sylvia Dashwood, in this case perhaps a ghoul or a Sleepwalker Retainer. And if the police don't like what they see at the West Wycombe Club, how can the characters' secrets be preserved in the face of a search warrant or, worse, accusations that the club is running a prostitution ring or some similar misinterpretation of the truth?

Criminal Mischief:
The Rakshasa of Pelham Meadows

The Call

The characters are sent to investigate the complaint of Joseph Rosen, a Jewish delicatessen owner in the Pelham Meadows neighborhood of Midway. Rosen is irate over the anti-Semitic vandalism he has been seeing all over the neighborhood lately. Specifically, someone has been spray-painting swastikas on the walls of all the alleys of Pelham Meadows, including one on the back door of Joseph's deli. Joseph does not know who has been painting the insignias, but he is suspicious of a "Middle Eastern-looking" family that has recently taken over the ownership of a convenience store down the street.

In fact, the new proprietors of the Qwik-Gas Mini-Mart are not Middle Eastern, but Indian American: Manish Jindal, his wife Prati, and his elderly father, Ashwatthama. The Jindals have lived in the United States for more than 20 years, and obtained U.S. citizenship seven years ago. Ashwatthama, however, is a new immigrant and came to live with his son and daughter-in-law in this country just a few months ago. Manish will strenuously deny any anti-Semitic feelings, but a successful Wits + Empathy roll (against Manish's Manipulation + Subterfuge) will reveal that he may know more than he has revealed.

With a successful Intelligence + Occult roll (at a –3 penalty), a character may notice that the swastikas painted in the alleyways are at right angles to the ground in the manner of Hindu swastikas, as opposed to being rotated as Nazi swastikas are typically depicted. This will probably make the officer naturally suspicious of the Jindals, and if the characters ask to speak with Ashwatthama, the old man will reveal the truth.

The Twist

The vandal is 83-year-old Ashwatthama Jindal. He has been sneaking out of his home at night to paint swastikas around the neighborhood, not out of any racial impetus but out of fear. Long before the symbol was appropriated by the Nazis, the swastika was a holy symbol of the Hindu religion, and Ashwatthama believes that if a swastika is correctly drawn on the exterior of a building and the proper prayers are said, the building will be protected against the rakshasa, malicious demons sent by the Demon God Ravana to plague humankind. If confronted, Ashwatthama will confidently reveal the omens that have alerted him to the presence of rakshasa nearby: fresh milk curdling overnight, water poured into a sink flowing down the drain counterclockwise instead of clockwise, the presence of two dead robins beneath the old man's window sill and other such esoteric phenomena.

Characters will almost certainly believe that Ashwatthama Jindal is a harmless old man motivated by cultural superstitions, though characters with an extensive background in the occult may believe that there is more to his ravings than meets the eye. Most likely, however, police will give him a stern talking to about the penalties for vandalism and about how his holy symbol is commonly misinterpreted in the United States. Ashwatthama will reluctantly agree not to put up any more "wards of protection" around the neighborhood, but he will angrily tell the characters that they will be responsible for any evil perpetuated by the rakshasa. Manish, for his part, will be more than willing to pay to have the walls scrubbed clean of the swastikas, and he will apologize profusely to Joseph Rosen, who will be sympathetic when he learns that the perpetrator was a superstitious old Hindu who believed he was helping the neighborhood.

Outcomes

Once the characters have solved the mystery of who is putting up swastikas and why, the case is officially solved. However, it is up to the Storyteller to decide whether the rakshasa is real or not. If the rakshasa is real, then police may receive continual reports of increasingly malicious crimes going on in the previously placid Pelham Meadows.

On the second day after the swastikas are removed, a young boy in the neighborhood is struck by a cab while crossing the street, resulting in a broken arm and two fractured ribs. The cab driver insists that the car's brakes failed, although they work fine after the accident. On the third day, the windows of Joseph Rosen's deli are smashed from the inside during the night, with no sign as to how such damage could have occurred. On the fifth day, Manish Jindal is electrocuted and nearly killed while changing a florescent light in his convenience store. By the end of the second week, the entire neighborhood has been plagued with mysterious accidents that have left most of the inhabitants frightened and edgy. Even the police are not immune. One officer is injured when his gun somehow discharges, still in its holster, while he is writing an accident report in Pelham Meadows. Two others are surprised when, while stopped at a red light, all four of the tires on the squad car spontaneously blow out.

Eventually, the weird events of Pelham Meadows will persuade the characters that maybe old Ashwatthama knew what he was talking about after all. If they return to speak to the old man, he will be understandably embittered over the injury of his son, who remains in a hospital after his electrocution, a fate that could have been avoided if the officers had simply allowed the old man to leave the holy symbols in place. Despite his anger, the characters can persuade Ashwatthama to help them by appealing to his sense of morality (and through clever roleplay). However, the characters' options for dealing with the poorly understood rakshasa menace are limited. The easiest way is to use the holy symbols to drive the spirit off. However, characters who work for the police department should probably balk at sneaking around the neighborhood at night to paint swastikas on the doors of local businesses, and there is virtually no possibility of persuading the locals that their problems are the result of demons from Hindu mythology. If anything, the locals will be more inclined to blame the Jindals, as they are newcomers to Pelham Meadows, and if the problem is Hindu in origin, it stands to reason that the Jindals must have brought it with them.

Ashwatthama may also be able to suggest other means of getting rid of the rakshasa, none of which should be easy for a police officer to do without potentially damaging her career, if not getting sent straightaway for a psych examination:

• If a goat is anointed with saffron and lotus blossoms and then led through the neighborhood on a leash, the rakshasa will be compelled to possess the goat. Then, the goat can be ritually sacrificed, which will slay the rakshasa as well.

• One or more persons must sit out in a public place with a large jug of *tharra*, a traditional Indian liquor made from fermented sugar cane mash, which is roughly the equivalent of American moonshine. As the drinkers get increasingly intoxicated, the rakshasa is attracted by the sweet smell of the liquor and will enter the jug, which will be revealed by the jug shaking slightly. Once the rakshasa enters the jug, the drinkers can place the cork back on it and trap the rakshasa inside by inscribing a swastika on the outside of the jug. Then, the jug is buried, trapping the rakshasa beneath the ground. Unfortunately, this strategy

requires the participants to drink a substance that is nearly 90% alcohol and still remain sober enough to notice when the jug moves slightly as the rakshasa enters it. Also, if the rakshasa is not in the area when the drinking begins, the spirit may never catch the scent of the *tharra* and thus not be drawn to it. Thus, those seeking to trap the demon may have to spend several nights getting publicly drunk on Indian moonshine before they can catch their quarry.

Role Reversals

Many supernatural characters might need to place protective sigils in some public place in order to achieve some objective, or otherwise perform some public action that can draw police attention. Mages are the ones most likely to do so, but many werewolves also use glyphs to identify their territories to other Uratha, while many vampires use sigils as part of blood sorcery rituals. Maintaining such protective or descriptive markings is difficult, however, as either the city or the private owners of the defaced buildings often attempt to clean up anything they consider to be graffiti. Whenever characters are attempting to place a sigil of some type in a public place or otherwise mark their territory, police might attempt to arrest the characters for vandalism.

Reckless Driving: Hot Pursuit

The Call

While on patrol, a police character observes one or more vehicles traveling at an excessive rate of speed. The police give pursuit, potentially resulting in a high-speed chase through the city. The characters must balance the desire to catch the reckless drivers with the need to avoid endangering citizens. The scenario is designed to give characters who are on patrol a chance to roleplay the excitement of a high-speed chase, a staple of police action stories. Pursuit rules can be found on pp. 69–71 of the **World of Darkness Rulebook**.

The Twist

The Twist in this scenario can be anything at all. The reckless drivers might be flying down the streets of Midway for any reason, including some of the following (some of which are mundane while others have a more supernatural bent):

• The driver is intoxicated or high.

• The driver is already fleeing police pursuit for some other crime. The car chase may later become a footrace if the perpetrator attempts to escape on foot. Alternately, the chase may evolve into a shootout.

• There are two or more drivers who are engaged in illegal street racing. Once the perpetrators are caught, the officers who interrogate them may learn of an underground street racing network and perhaps even attempt to infiltrate it.

• The driver is rushing his very pregnant wife (who has just gone into labor) to the hospital. If the police stop the driver before he reaches the hospital, the officer may be required to help deliver a baby (involving an extended Intelligence + Medicine roll).

• The drivers are supernatural beings in a race against time to prevent or enable some dire calamity. If the police manage to catch the drivers, the officer might be subjected to mind altering powers or even be confronted by a werewolf who enters *Kuruth* due to the frustration of being hassled by a cop when she is already under intense pressure.

• The drivers are supernatural beings, one of whom is pursuing the other. At the conclusion of the chase, the police might find themselves caught in the crossfire between two warring supernatural factions who are prepared to risk exposure of their secrets in order to destroy their enemies.

• The driver is — missing! When police stop the car at a roadblock or force it off the road, the officer will discover that the car is empty and appears to have been driving itself.

Outcomes

The precise outcome should depend, obviously, on why the reckless driver was speeding. Systems for handling high-speed chases, applying dice penalties for high-speed driving or stunts and resolving crashes and collisions, as well as other factors that might come into play in a high-speed chase are detailed in the **World of Darkness Rulebook**, pp. 142–46.

Role Reversals

High-speed chases are also an issue for characters other than police officers. Both supernatural and mortal characters often find that circumstances require them to get somewhere in a hurry, with disastrous consequences if the character is late. Unfortunately, in any urban area, police on patrol have a good chance of observing characters traveling at an excessive rate of speed and acting appropriately. Indeed, even if a character is not actually speeding, he may still occasionally be confronted with a police officer who claims that the character was, perhaps out of a desire to fulfill some quota or simply because the character looks out of place in the area in which he is stopped ("DWB" or

"Driving While Black," for example).

If characters are traveling at a high rate of speed, the Storyteller should roll a single chance die during every turn in which the driver character is required to make a Drive roll. If the roll results in a dramatic failure, a random patrol car observes the speeding vehicle and gives chase. If police are already looking for the vehicle or are otherwise on alert, then a police car may give pursuit on a simple failure of the chance roll. Finally, if the Storyteller simply wants to add some extra tension to a scene, she should roll a single chance die for every journey, even if the characters are not speeding. On a dramatic failure, an officer will attempt to pull the characters over for some trumped-up or legitimately mistaken reason.

As noted above, complications for vehicle chases are outlined in the **World of Darkness Rulebook,** pp. 142–146. Additionally, the Storyteller should keep the following general principles in mind. First, when an officer either gives chase or successfully pulls over a vehicle, he will always call in with the vehicle's license plate number to determine whether the vehicle is stolen or otherwise wanted (see p. 74). Thus, even if the characters elude the officer, the police will have a record of the vehicle's description and tag number. If the vehicle is stolen, the officer will not exit his own vehicle but, using the loudspeaker, will order the occupants to exit their car. He will do the same if the drivers attempt to evade pursuit.

If the vehicle has no outstanding warrants connected to it and pulled over immediately after the officer turned on his blue lights and siren, the officer will approach the vehicle cautiously (+2 to all Wits + Composure rolls), with one hand on his weapon, just in case. He will ask the driver for her license and take the opportunity to scan the interior through the window. As noted previously, any contraband or suspicious material visible through the windows can create probable cause to detain the characters. The Storyteller should also remember the police vehicle does have a front-mounted camera that records everything that happens while the officer is talking to the driver of the vehicle. The camera will not get a clear picture of the driver and passengers unless they exit the vehicle, in which case they will be clearly shown (pending such details as the blurred visage of a vampire).

License and Registration, Please

Most adult characters are assumed to have valid identification, and anyone with a Drive score of 1 or higher is assumed to have a valid driver's license. However, this may not be the case. A vampire whose Embrace was more than a few decades ago will almost certainly have moved on to one or more fake identities. Likewise, a mage who fears the revelation of her true name (and the corresponding risk of sympathetic magic being used against her) will also try to establish a false identity. Additionally, many werewolves are forced to abandon their former lives after the First Change and will also need false identification.

Police are generally very adept at detecting fake identification. The officer's player rolls Intelligence + Investigation and must achieve more successes than the person who fashioned the ID achieved on her Wits + Larceny roll to make the ID in the first place. If the character possesses the Occultation Merit, the officer may suffer a dice penalty equal to the Merit rating when the mage is relying on a false ID. However, this effect also undermines the validity of any ID bearing the mage's true name — if the mage presents a genuinely valid driver's license, the officer still suffers a dice penalty equal to the Merit rating, but a failure on the roll will cause the officer to believe that the ID is fake and that the mage is using an assumed name. Thus, while Occultation is generally useful in protecting the mage's true name, the Merit can unfortunately lead to a mage getting arrested when an investigating officer doesn't believe the truth of the mage's identity.

Generally, most officers will be professional and courteous (if a bit brisk) when dealing with simple speeding violations. If the officer has witnessed any driving offenses that rise to the level of a felony or even a serious misdemeanor (such as any genuinely reckless driving or speeding in excess of 30 mph in a residential or urban area), he will attempt to arrest the driver. Of course, for dramatic purposes, the Storyteller might declare that the officer is an exception to the general rules of professionalism. He might be a racist cop if the driver and passengers belong to an ethnic minority. He might have a personal animus against young people or women drivers. Alternately, he might attempt to sexually proposition a female driver, suggesting that the ticket will go away if she makes it "worth his while."

Animal Cruelty: Sacrifices

The Call

Harold Toomes, a Baptist minister and a member of the local Humane Society, has filed a complaint with the police alleging that a local church, the Church of St. Lazarus, is some kind of cult that conducts animal sacrifices. The church itself is actually part of a shopping mall near the "Little Havana" section of Midway. Upon investigation, the characters will find that Toomes is partially correct, as the Church of St. Lazarus (or la Iglesia de San Lazar, to its members) is a church for worshipers of Santeria. However, the church is not really a cult, as Santeria is fully recognized as a religion by the U.S. government.

Santeria, also known as Lukumi or Regla de Ocha, is a syncretistic religion that combines Catholic beliefs with the traditional spirit-based worship of the Yoruban people of Nigeria. In many ways, Santeria is analogous to vodoun, though where vodoun was influenced by French Catholicism, Santeria was blended with that of the Spanish. When Yorubans were brought to North America as slaves to the Spanish, the Yorubans were forcibly converted to Catholicism. Over time, the Yoruban slaves conceptually combined elements of Catholicism with their own pantheon of deities called the Orishas, who were subsequently depicted through the iconography of Catholic saints. Thus, the slaves could continue their traditional beliefs under the guise of mere devotion to the saints. The Spanish, who did not realize that the slaves were actually continuing their prior rituals under a new form, began referring to the slaves' religion as Santeria, or the Way of the Saints, due to its apparent over-devotion to veneration of the saints as individuals.

Although a fairly small religion in the U.S., Santeria is practiced throughout the nation wherever a large Cuban immigrant population exists. Animal sacrifices make up a large part of traditional Santeria rituals. Such sacrifices are performed at birth, marriage and death rites, as a cure for the sick, as part of initiation ceremonies for new members and priests and during annual celebrations. Chickens are the animals most commonly sacrificed, but pigeons, doves,

ducks, guinea pigs, goats, sheep and turtles are also used. The priest performing the ritual kills the animal by cutting its carotid artery, and the sacrificed animals are cooked and eaten, except after healing and death rituals.

The Twist

Upon discovering the church's true nature, the characters are faced with a constitutional dilemma: are police permitted to arrest a citizen on charges of animal cruelty if she kills a live chicken as part of a religious sacrifice? The initial call may require the character to simply make a guess about the constitutionality of the exercise of his police power.

There is no state statute or city ordinance either forbidding or allowing religious animal sacrifices, and the state animal cruelty statute does not apply. With a successful Intelligence + Politics roll, a character will realize that the church members are not actually violating any laws by sacrificing live chickens. At that point, the character basically has two options. He can inform Rev. Toomes that the Church of St. Lazarus is doing nothing wrong or the character can attempt to shut down the church on related charges, most likely violation of city health ordinances.

Regardless of how the officer responds, Rev. Toomes will immediately begin agitating for a city ordinance banning animal sacrifice, and the City Council will pass such an ordinance within a month. Although the church will attempt to have the ordinance struck down as unconstitutional, the church's members are fairly poor and lack the resources to get good legal help. In fact, the ordinance is plainly unconstitutional, as animal sacrifices are generally protected under the First Amendment. But until a judge strikes down the ordinance, it is still good law, and Rev. Toomes will continually call for the police to raid the Church of St. Lazarus to prevent any more animals from being killed in "pagan rituals." The characters may or may not personally arrest anyone, but at least five members of the church, including its priest, Father Gabriel Echevarria, are eventually arrested for violating the ordinance, whether or not the characters conduct these arrests.

Outcomes

From a supernatural standpoint, this case is a red herring. Many players may wrongly assume that a Santeria church engaging in animal sacrifices must have some sinister connotations. In fact, the church is just that — a church, full of decent people who have the situational misfortune of belonging to a small, unpopular religion.

This scenario can be very useful for dealing with players who see the supernatural in everything, despite the fact that their characters have never actually encountered the supernatural. Much of Santeria's belief structure is admittedly disconcerting to some people, particularly those with a strongly Christian background, and both characters and players may be forced to confront their own biases and

prejudices when it becomes clear that the church is not an innately sinister organization. Indeed, the church members may soon become sympathetic figures if Rev. Toomes continues to publicly harangue them for their beliefs. If the Storyteller wishes, some of Toomes' supporters may go beyond mere complaints to vandalizing the church or physically assaulting its members. Police characters may have to put aside their own personal views to find some way to mediate this dispute, thereby calling upon the social aspects of the game rather than the physical or cerebral sides.

Also, religious intolerance is not the only factor to be considered. Instead, a character who is an animal-lover might be appalled at the idea of animal sacrifice and might seek ways to shut down the church even if its beliefs are constitutionally protected. Sammy Atkinson (see p. 95), for example, will be repulsed at the idea of animal sacrifice, even though the church does not sacrifice dogs or cats in its services. His "dog," Kita (see p. 95), will also have a strong opinion on the subject, though a more pragmatic one. While she supports the idea of sacrifices made to appease and feed spirits in principle, she may have personal issues with a local religion supporting the Orishas, which are from a spirit hierarchy different from her own. The church itself might call upon police to complain of harassment and vandalism from animal rights groups, some of whose members might regularly protest in front of the church.

All of the preceding, of course, assumes that there are no supernatural undercurrents running beneath the church, and naturally, Storytellers are free to spice things up a bit. The Church of St. Lazarus might secretly be a front for Thyrsus mages, Bone Shadow werewolves or Circle of the Crone vampires. Or the church might simply be a Santeria church in a world in which the Orishas answer prayers more readily than they do in our own. How will the characters react when Harold Toomes drops dead of a stroke in the middle of preaching a sermon against Santeria and the church's priest claims it was the judgment of the Orishas? How superstitious and paranoid will the characters get when all the officers responsible for enforcing the city ordinance and arresting the church members begin to suffer from bad luck and strange experiences, such as each of their houses becoming infested with vermin or recurring dreams of being possessed by an angry spirit?

Rev. Harold Toomes of the Freewill Baptist Church

Background: Harold Toomes has two reasons for hating the Santeria church. First, as a fundamentalist preacher, he considers Santeria to be a corruption of Christian tradition and a pagan religion leading its followers away from God. Second, Toomes is also an animal-lover and an avid supporter of the Humane Society and the ASPCA. He is opposed even to activities such as game hunting and favors the imposition of humane treatment conditions on farms and in slaughterhouses. To Toomes, the very idea of helpless animals being sacrificed in the name of a pagan religion is abhorrent.

Description: Toomes is in his early 40s. He is slightly overweight but reasonably good-looking. However, as many pastors of small churches, he is underpaid, which is reflected in fairly shabby suits and a slightly unkempt appearance.

Storytelling Hints: Depending on the individual character's background, Toomes may come off as either judgmental and sanctimonious or genuinely pious or compassionate. His depiction may also depend on which side of the debate the Storyteller falls on, as well. Toomes is not violent and believes that the law and the political process are on his side. However, he does tend to get wound up when discussing Santeria, and when he goes on a rant, he can include some inflammatory remarks capable of setting off his more volatile supporters. He will be extremely polite and solicitous of police unless a character deliberately offends him.

Skills: Expression 8, Occult 3, Politics 5, Subterfuge 6

Father Gabriel Echevarria

Background: Father Gabriel is a devoted servant of the Orishas who wants only to be able to freely and publicly practice his religion. He considers Santeria to be not only a valid religion but an essential part of his own cultural heritage, and he tends to conflate opposition to it with anti-Cuban bigotry. A second-generation Cuban American, Echevarria strives to remain civil when confronted with opposition to his religion, but he is quick to assume that any attempt to legally interfere with his religious practices is based on bigotry and ignorance. Unfortunately, he is often right.

Description: Echevarria is a Hispanic male in his late 30s. He dresses simply and economically. In addition to serving as priest for the Santeria community of Midway, he also works as a mechanic to make ends meet, and he can frequently be seen with oil stains on his clothes and under his fingernails. However, when he is conducting Santeria rituals, he is immaculately clean.

Storytelling Hints: Echevarria is slightly paranoid, especially about the police and non-Hispanics, which is understandable since so many of them really are out to get him. Most police officers may get the impression that he struggles to hold his temper, especially when his religious views are challenged or mocked.

Skills: Crafts 5, Empathy 5, Expression 6, Intimidation 6, Occult 7

Appendix: The Subtle Key

This chapter contains a ready-made crime drama for several characters. At least one of the characters should be a Midway police officer. Other characters can also be police officers or can be any other type of character approved by the Storyteller. The plot involves a police investigation into what appears to be just a ghoulish prank at a local cemetery. As the investigation proceeds, however, the prank is only the first incident in a macabre chain of events that unleashes a malevolent predator on the streets of the city.

Overview

This story consists of a prologue, five acts and an epilogue; the story can either constitute an entire short-term chronicle or take place against the backdrop of an ongoing storyline. The story is also designed so that the Storyteller has considerable latitude in deciding what degree of supernatural activity to feature during the course of the chronicle's events. In fact, if the Storyteller wishes, it is perfectly possible to strip out all the actual supernatural events from "The Subtle Key" and simply make the tale one of police pursuing a deranged occultist with no true mystical power.

The Prologue is brief with little to no conventional "action." It consists mainly of minor ongoing controversies surrounding the impending execution of Maxine Gordon, who was convicted seven years ago of murdering her husband and two children, largely due to the investigative work of Sid Routman. In truth, Maxine is innocent and was framed by Detective Routman while he was under the influence of his ongoing derangement. Maxine, who protests her innocence to the end, is executed at midnight on the first night of the story. If "The Subtle Key" is used as part of an ongoing chronicle, the Storyteller can use the Prologue during the course of several sessions through such means as having the police confront death penalty opponents who argue for Maxine's innocence, following news reports of Maxine's ultimately futile pursuit of a pardon from the governor and even seeing Sid Routman being interviewed on television news programs as he calmly explains how overwhelming the physical evidence was in proving Maxine's guilt.

Act One and **Act Two** detail the initiation of two police investigations. The first studies what appears to be a malicious prank at a local cemetery. The second is more serious, as police must investigate the theft of Maxine Gordon's body from that same cemetery. The perpetrators of these macabre deeds are a quartet of high-school misfits who fancy themselves as Satanists and occultists. The group is led by a budding 17-year-old fiend named Troy Wilkerson who has acquired a book of menacing reputation called *The Nineveh Codex*. Contained within this book is an occult ritual for creating an artifact of supernatural power called the Subtle Key. The chief ingredient for making the Subtle Key is the severed left hand of a murderess buried in unhallowed

Successful and fortunate crime is called virtue.

— Seneca, Hercules Furens

ground, which is why the kids desecrated the cemetery with a ritually slaughtered dog. But whatever the kids intended is irrelevant, as Maxine was not truly a murderess, and their use of her left hand in the Subtle Key ritual will have vastly unexpected consequences.

Act Three takes place at Troy's home, where police will eventually be led, whether by their own investigation or later by a terrifying discovery made by Troy's mother. The investigation may lead very quickly in Troy's direction, but there is little evidence directly tying him to the grave-robbing, and police will most likely be unable to search Troy's house without a warrant. Consequently, unless the investigation proceeds remarkably fast, the characters will be too late to prevent the ritual to create the Subtle Key, but they will find all the evidence they need and more in Act Four.

Act Four will lead the characters back to the home of Troy Wilkerson after the ritual of the Subtle Key was performed and too late to prevent his invocation of powers he cannot possibly control. Investigating officers will find the mutilated corpse of Maxine in the basement and an even more grotesque tableau in the ringleader's bedroom. They will also find the *Codex* and the ghost of Maxine Gordon, although they may or may not be able to perceive her.

Act Five contains the final confrontation with Troy Wilkerson, now powerful and utterly insane. Wilkerson seeks to destroy other supernatural beings, including vampires, werewolves and mages, and his newfound power allows him to do so easily. Ironically, the power that fuels Wilkerson is such that only mortals can directly confront him without risking death — Wilkerson can annihilate supernatural creatures with a gesture. While police aware of the supernatural world may not be opposed to such activity, Wilkerson is actually accumulating power in order to use the Key in order to open a portal to some other realm, and draw forth the alien power therein.

The Epilogue is actually the setup for the continuation of the chronicle, as the characters decide what to do with the information they have acquired, which ranges from new truths about the supernatural beings in their midst to more mundane insights, such as the fact that Sid Routman has brought about the wrongful conviction of at least one person.

Prologue: Waiting for the Executioner

The Prologue takes the form of several vignettes in which characters are made aware of Maxine Gordon's impending execution and the controversies surrounding it. Police officers tend to favor the death penalty, but certainly many oppose it for ethical or even pragmatic reasons. By giving the players a chance to explore their characters' views on the subject, the Storyteller can set the stage for their reactions upon learning that Maxine was actually innocent and wrongfully executed.

The Gordon Case

Jonathan Gordon and his two children, Jon Jr. (age 4) and Emily (age 2) died 14 years ago. Jonathan was suffering from the onset of a rare brain disease, which had not been diagnosed prior to his death and which was not detected in his autopsy. The disease caused him to be seized by strong paranoid delusions. On the night of the murder, Jonathan was gripped by one such delusion that convinced him his wife was a witch who sought to sacrifice their children to Satan. Maxine had left the house at 6 P.M. to go see a movie after an argument with Jonathan, and her husband took the opportunity to poison the two children and himself with an overdose of sleeping pills. Before expiring, Jonathan wrote a rambling letter accusing Maxine of being "evil." This accusation was the only real evidence implicating Maxine at all, as the bottle of sleeping pills had only Jonathan's fingerprints on it. However, the letter was sufficient to convince Sid Routman of Maxine's guilt, and he cinched the case by planting a small residue of the drug on the fingers of a pair of rubber gloves from Maxine's kitchen, thereby suggesting that she wore them when removing the drugs from the pill bottle in order to avoid leaving any fingerprints of her own. That false evidence, combined with her unsubstantiated alibi and the letter left by Jonathan (not to mention poor representation at trial) were sufficient to ensure a guilty verdict and death sentence, which survived several appeals.

Final Appeal

As the story opens, Maxine's final appeal to the U.S. Supreme Court has just been denied, and her only hope to avoid execution is a last-ditch appeal to the governor. In an ongoing chronicle, the events leading up to the execution should play out during the course of several days. Characters may be assigned to work security at a press conference in which the District Attorney and Sid Routman will answer questions about the case. Outside the District Attorney's office, a number of death penalty opponents will be staging a protest. Precinct Chaplain Paul Calhoun will argue passionately against the death penalty to any officers who will listen, while Wade Whitfield will encourage other cops to respond to online polls to encourage the governor to deny clemency.

No matter whatever happens during the Prologue, Maxine Gordon will be executed at midnight, and buried during a small private funeral the next day at Easthaven Cemetery in Midway.

Act One: Desecration

The day after Maxine Gordon's execution, police characters are called to the nearby Easthaven Cemetery to observe what is at best a malicious prank and at worst evidence of dangerously disturbed individuals. During the night, someone left the mutilated remains of a Labrador retriever hanging from a tree at the rear of the cemetery. The groundskeeper, Vic Loomis, is the one to report the discovery, but the local priest, Father Richard McCoy, is extremely disturbed, for two reasons. First, the dead dog clearly has a crude pentagram carved into its forehead, and second, Maxine Gordon, a longtime parishioner, was interred in that cemetery earlier in the day before the dog was discovered. Consequently, Maxine Gordon, a lifelong Catholic, was not buried in holy ground. Investigating officers may or may not consider this to be an important factor, but Father Richard will be quite upset over the incident, as he had counseled Maxine throughout her incarceration and was present at her funeral. He believes very strongly that she was wrongly convicted and will not be shy about telling characters so if they seem cavalier about her execution and the desecration of her grave site.

An examination of the dead dog will reveal some information, depending on how successful characters are on an Intelligence + Investigation roll: The dog was exceptionally well groomed and was most likely a household pet (one success). It was recently wearing a collar that had been cut away (three successes). Finally, the dog looks sufficiently well bred to have been a show dog and was most likely very expensive (exceptional success).

Also, investigating officers who succeed on an Intelligence + Occult roll (–2 difficulty) will be able to tell that the dog was obviously killed in a ritual manner. However, with an exceptional success, an officer will also note that much of the precision and attention to detail usually associated with occult animal sacrifices is lacking. In particular, the pentagram on the dog's forehead is very shoddy and seems almost like an afterthought. Animal control will take the dog's body away for disposal. If police check with local animal shelters, they will learn that a

purebred Labrador retriever closely resembling the dead dog was reported missing just two days earlier by a local family. The dog, Rags, was the pet of a nine-year-old child named Mickey Osborn. If the police check with Mickey's parents, the police will learn that the dog was definitely stolen out of the family's backyard — Mickey's father, Joe Osborn, discovered footprints in the mud the morning after Rags' disappearance, and the dog's collar, to which a chain was attached, was cut away and left behind.

Serious inquiries with the Osborns' neighbors will not reveal any witnesses to the abduction, but with a successful Charisma + Investigation roll, a character may find one witness, a cranky older neighbor named Bernard Dent who will remember seeing a couple of "damned punk kids" near the Osborn house the day the dog disappeared. Dent doesn't know the names of the kids, but his description will match Troy Wilkerson and Doug Guthrie (see "Dramatis Personae"). Identifying the two teenagers solely from Dent's description will require 20 successes on an extended Intelligence + Investigation roll, with each roll representing one day of police work. Multiple characters can pool their successes for this roll.

Staking Out the Cemetery

A character with knowledge of the occult who learns about the desecration of the graveyard may suspect that the act was a prelude to something more serious and may request permission for officers to stake out the area. The police will step up their patrols of the area around the cemetery, but not to an overwhelming degree.

If the characters themselves stake out the graveyard on the night after the desecration, have each character make a contested Wits + Stealth roll against a pool of 11 dice (the highest Wits + Composure of the perpetrators plus a three-dice bonus because they are expecting a heightened police presence). Characters on stakeout are also at a –2 penalty since they don't really know what they are looking for, while the perpetrators need only to observe a suspicious car. The perpetrators also gain an additional +2 bonus on the roll if the police are in a squad car.

If, despite all this, a character beats the perpetrators on the contested roll, she will notice a quartet of teenagers, two of whom resemble the description Bernard Dent gave, attempting to scale the 10-foot brick wall that surrounds the cemetery.

Characters may attempt to apprehend the teens. If any of the teens are caught, they will deny any involvement with the dog mutilation and actually say that they were here to check out where the dog was found, as they are interested in the occult. All four have worked out a fairly plausible story that they have rehearsed just in case of capture, and the ringleader, Troy Wilkerson, will take the fall for daring the group to go to "that spooky graveyard where the satanic cult worships that lady serial killer." The luridness of their tale is calculated to convince any police that they are just dumb kids who should be let off with a warning.

Depending on the circumstances, the police may be able to arrest the four on trespassing charges, but, most likely, any captured teens will be out by morning. They are all from wealthy families who have excellent attorneys, and, in any case, they are juveniles. It is possible that a character might be convinced of the teens' involvement in the desecration and attempt to interrogate them at police headquarters, but there is not enough evidence to hold them on those charges.

In any case, the Storyteller should make every effort to put investigators off the trail of the four kids, all of whom are skilled liars. However, it is not impossible for a character to break one of the four in an interrogation with some lucky rolls and possibly short circuit much of the rest of the plot. The Storyteller should proceed cautiously in such a case, balancing the desire to preserve the plot against the need to play fairly with the players. Sometimes, cops get lucky and

break crimes before they happen, and this might be such a case. However, all of this is contingent on a character getting lucky enough to spot the kids breaking in before they can spot her. The teens are in no hurry at this point, and if they spot any police presence, the teens will simply drive on and try again another night. Unless the police get lucky, the teens will eventually be able to sneak into the cemetery and achieve their true objective — stealing the corpse of Maxine Gordon from the unhallowed ground in which the body has been interred.

Act Two: Looking into an Open Grave

Police will be summoned back to the graveyard early on the morning after a shocking grave-robbing took place. At some point during the night, the grave was quickly dug up, the cheap coffin (paid for by the church, as Maxine was penniless) forced open and the body brazenly stolen away. Unlike the earlier desecration, which was performed with the utmost caution, the teens were forced to steal the body as quickly as possible. Consequently, there is more physical evidence. Muddy footprints around the grave indicate at least four perpetrators, most likely teens due to small-sized tennis shoes (one success on an Intelligence + Investigation roll). At least one clear footprint will be

of an expensive name-brand shoe, suggesting the kids are from somewhat wealthy families or otherwise have disposable income (three successes on an Intelligence + Investigation roll). Also, police will find a discarded empty cigarette pack from which the fingerprints of Sam Randolph can be lifted.

The grave-robbing of a recently executed murderess on the heels of what the local media refers to as a "Satanic ritual" becomes the talk of Midway, and the investigation will receive a much higher priority than it had the day before. Also, unless the characters actually pushed for the investigation into the animal mutilation to be taken seriously, they will be probably be chewed out by the precinct captain for slacking off on such an important assignment. The gross unfairness of such accusations (failing to solve a crime within a day or so of its commission) is simply another part of police bureaucracy. In any case, the only real lead investigators have is still the description of Bernard Dent, but because characters are now under orders to wrap the case up as quickly as possible, they can devote more time to that aspect of the investigation, and only 10 cumulative successes are required on the extended Investigation roll. (If the characters accumulated 10 or more successes previously during the investigation, have the next successful roll return the information they seek.) Once the requisite successes are achieved, the characters will find their suspects — four disaffected high school students who have immersed themselves in the occult as a way of shocking their parents.

The ringleader of the group is Troy Wilkerson, a bright, young child of divorce currently being raised in latchkey fashion by his mother, a surgeon at a local hospital. Troy has taken to dressing in black and calling himself "Crow." He considers himself a witch, although he knows little to nothing about actual occult practices, and his "religious beliefs" owe more to media depictions of counterculture in the aftermath of the Columbine shootings than to any serious study of religion or mysticism. Despite his shortcomings, Wilkerson has the support of his "coven," which consists of only his three friends: Doug "Shadow" Guthrie, Sam "Midnight" Randolph and Lisa "Rayven" Griffin. He also has a library book called *The Nineveh Codex*, which is the cause of the current developments.

Act Three: The Subtle Key

The Nineveh Codex is a 200-year-old, handwritten translation of an ancient occult text that has been banned in several countries. *The Codex* was supposed to be kept under lock and key in the Special Collections Wing of the Midway Public Library. However, to the continual consternation of the librarians there, the book somehow keeps ending up in different sections of the library, where the book is readily available to the viewing public.

Most recently, Troy discovered the worn, old manuscript incongruously stuck among a collection of Robert Heinlein novels and, instantly fascinated, stole it from the library. He spent the next several weeks poring over the book, much of which was utterly incomprehensible. However, he was able to grasp one of the strange rituals in the book that detailed how to create an occult artifact called the Subtle Key.

According to the text, the Subtle Key is a mystical item fashioned from the left hand of a murderess buried in unhallowed ground. The Key is a necessary component in other rituals designed to invoke the presence of powerful spirit beings known as the acamoth that will reward the summoner with great power. Absent from the book is a description of what happens when the hand of an innocent person is used to fashion the Key — the artifact takes on a life of its own and the one who created the artifact becomes its slave instead. (If you don't own **Mage: The Awakening** or wish to implicate beings other than the acamoth, the choice is yours as Storyteller.)

Interview with a Grave-Robber

The ritual must be performed at midnight, and the teens will attempt to do so on the first night after they successfully steal Maxine's body. Thus, if the player achieves enough successes on the first or second day of the investigation, her character can find the four teens before they can enact the ritual.

All of the teens will be at Troy's house, as Dr. Wilkerson is on a night schedule at the hospital. Police do not have probable cause to enter Troy's house or even to arrest him based solely on Bernard Dent's description. However, a character can visit the home and ask to come in.

Troy will be wary of the police but also eager to avoid drawing suspicion to his home. Accordingly, if the character achieves more successes on a Manipulation + Subterfuge roll than Troy gets on a Wits + Politics roll, Troy will allow the officer to enter for a brief interview with the three fellow occultists and Troy. Troy will do most of the talking.

Discerning any useful information from any of the four teens will require a successful contested Manipulation + Subterfuge roll, opposed by the Wits + Composure of the teen being questioned. An exceptional success on the part of the officer or a dramatic failure on the part of a teen is required to get anyone to say anything so incriminating as to justify an arrest on the spot. Accumulating any successes at all will be sufficient to justify getting a search warrant.

Additionally, with a successful Wits + Composure roll, an officer may notice a pair of muddy tennis shoes sitting on the kitchen floor, which appear to be of the same type as the shoes that left some of the footprints around Maxine's grave. That fact alone might be sufficient to obtain a warrant to search Troy's house. Troy will not give consent to a search, and his mother will not give consent by phone unless she is present, and her shift doesn't end until 7 A.M. In fact, Dr. Wilkerson will be somewhat indignant that police suspect her son of grave-robbing, and will invite the officers to come to the house at 9 A.M. the next day and search wherever they wish.

If the police get enough information to justify a search warrant and immediately seek out a magistrate to sign off on it, it is possible that they can prevent the enactment of the Subtle Key ritual. In such a case, they will easily discover Maxine's body in the basement, minus her hand, which is in Troy's room, along with *The Nineveh Codex* and a great deal of occult paraphernalia. Officers will have more than enough evidence to arrest Troy and his associates on charges of animal cruelty, malicious mischief and grave-robbing. *The Nineveh Codex* and the severed hand will be held as evidence.

This may or may not be the end of the story, depending on the wishes of the Storyteller. Once both the *Codex* and the hand are put into the evidence locker, a Storyteller who wishes to continue this scenario can declare that some other police officer who works in the Evidence Room, such as Richard Bucknell, is mentally influenced by the book itself into completing the ritual, which is quite easy once you have a suitable (or in this case, unsuitable) hand. In such a case, Act Four can, with some retooling, be adapted to the new situation, with a newly obsessed police officer taking the place of a possessed Troy Wilkerson.

It is more likely, however, that police will simply wait until 9 A.M. the next morning to perform a consent search, since the local magistrate, Judge Wyndham, will be reluctant to grant a search warrant based on the characters' evidence. An aging liberal, Judge Wyndham is overly suspicious of police authority.

Act Four: The Ceremony of Innocence

If the police do not discover Troy's involvement and fail to intervene within 24 hours of the grave-robbing, they will be summoned to his house by his hysterical mother the following morning at 7 A.M. If they had contacted Dr. Wilkerson ahead of time about a consent search, she would have told them that they could come the next day at 9 A.M., which would have the same outcome.

When Dr. Wilkerson arrives home at 7 A.M. on the day after the grave-robbing, she will discover the mutilated bodies of Doug Guthrie, Sam Randolph and Lisa Griffin, their viscera decorating the walls of Troy's bedroom as occult sigils. Maxine's body (minus one hand) is in the basement. *The Nineveh Codex* rests on Troy's bed, open to the page outlining the Subtle Key ritual. At this point, exactly how any given character reacts will most likely depend on his general awareness of the supernatural. Characters with any genuine experience with the occult will be alarmed that someone attempted this dark ritual, while those without such experience might merely assume that Troy Wilkerson is psychotic and murdered his friends in a blind rage or while under the influence of PCP or some similar drug.

At the same time, any character who discovers the body of Maxine Gordon will also have some strange experiences. Whatever time of year it is, the basement where the body is discovered will be unaccountably cold, so cold in fact that breath mists in the air, even in July. Even more disturbing is what happens when someone touches the body. The first character to do so will be shocked when Maxine opens her eyes and sits bolt upright. She will then turn to the character with a

terrified look in her eyes and say, "Don't let him open the door!" Then, the character will blink, and the corpse will be just as he found it with no sign of Maxine's sudden awakening. No one else will observe anything out of the ordinary. Maxine may also communicate with the character through such indirect means as appearing in a mirror behind his reflection, appearing in a shower whenever a character turns around or appearing in a dream. Regardless of the circumstances, such visions are terrifying but brief, as Maxine can only deliver the same cryptic message before the connection is broken.

It is possible for characters to initiate contact with Maxine to get more information if they have any ability to commune with the dead, or if you, as Storyteller, want to create circumstances by which to allow them to do so, though characters with no occult experiences may balk at such superstitious activities. Contacting Maxine might require the characters to have access either to her body or to her grave, both of which serve as anchors for the ghost. However, unlike most ghosts, Maxine is not limited to her anchors (the third of which is the severed hand). Maxine, who had made peace with her impending death despite her wrongful conviction, should not have come back as a ghost, and she did so only because of the failed ritual.

Until the Subtle Key is destroyed, Maxine cannot move on to her afterlife. If questioned about the death of her husband and children, she will calmly explain the true circumstances of their death and also Sid Routman's role in her false conviction, all of which she came to understand after she crossed over into death. She pities Routman rather than hates him, as she can see the madness that eats at him, but she warns the characters that hers is not the only life the detective has destroyed. Maxine is constantly aware of the location of the Subtle Key (since it is a part of her), but she does not fully understand what has happened or why. She knows only that the boy who mutilated her is host to something terrible that seeks to open a door that must always remain sealed.

The Codex itself also contains valuable clues. Much of it is in Latin, but if none of the characters speak the language, Father Paul Calhoun can translate the ritual. Once translated, the ritual explains that if the Subtle Key is created with the hand of someone who does not meet the other requirements, then the summoner will have no power to command the acamoth summoned, which will then hollow out his soul and possess it, creating a composite being whose name is roughly translated as "Un-Man." The Un-Man will then seek to gain more power to free its brethren from the Abyss. The Un-Man will have great strength and power, and is immune to "those touched by the hand of the strange" as well as to "any weapon forged by human or monster." However, while the Un-Man's touch is deadly to "the strange ones," it cannot easily slay those who are "untouched by the strange." If characters ask

Father Paul what all these references to "the strange" are, he will somewhat reluctantly explain that it refers to people with a supernatural nature. If pressed, he will admit to having heard tales of vampires, werewolves and other supposedly mythical beings from certain officers among the MPD. Regardless, he will be evasive if asked whether he believes that such creatures exist. All he will say is that, according to the *Codex*, the only way to slay the Un-Man and free the mortal trapped within is with the touch of a mortal being who is untouched by the supernatural and who carries "the Sign of Marduk," a runic symbol contained in the book. The Sign of Marduk must be drawn on a mortal's hand, and the mortal must then touch the Un-Man with that hand and burn out the invading force.

Act Five: Its Hour Come at Last

In this act, the characters must pursue their final confrontation with the Un-Man, a creature of alien purpose and devotion.

Despite the spirit's vast power, few can see what the Un-Man truly is. Wrapped in the skin of Troy Wilkerson (or, potentially, Sgt. Bucknell or another possessed officer from the precinct's Evidence Room), the Un-Man appears to most observers to simply be an excessively disturbed and maybe psychotic vagrant whose strength and vitality are probably the result of drugs. Only in the presence of supernatural beings such as vampires, werewolves or mages is the Un-Man's true power manifested. The Un-Man is immune to all supernatural effects, and is able to resist bullets, fire and almost any conventional damage. The Un-Man is superhumanly strong. Most important of all, with a single touch, the being can inflict tremendous suffering on creatures of supernatural origin, absorbing their mystic potential into itself.

If this scenario is introduced as part of a long-running chronicle and some characters already have contacts among the supernatural community, the Storyteller may wish to restructure Act Five so that the final confrontation involves preventing that existing contact from meeting a gory end at the hands of the Un-Man. As written, the scenario has the Un-Man attacking the Vertigo Club, a popular nightclub where a number of vampires meet to prey on mortal vessels.

If the characters have made contact with the ghost of Maxine Gordon, she can tell them exactly where the Un-Man is, as she remains spiritually connected to the Subtle Key that's still on the Un-Man's person. If not, eventually a report will come over the police band radio about a disturbance at the Vertigo Club, involving someone matching Troy Wilkerson's description going on a violent rampage.

Characters arriving at the scene will see the Un-Man apparently strangling a large clubgoer many times the Un-Man's size. With a successful Wits + Composure roll (at a –3 penalty), a character may notice that the strangling victim has protruding fangs and claws. However, all characters will notice when the vampire victim pours out excessive quantities of blood and then collapses into a pile of ash, as reddish ethereal fumes flow into the Un-Man's body. Four other ash piles can be seen around the club, which is now empty of people except for a few bouncers beaten into unconsciousness by the Un-Man.

Police may attempt to shoot the Un-Man, but he has an effective Armor rating of 5 against guns and weapons, so stopping him this way is difficult. Also, killing the host may call for a Morality roll, especially if characters know that the possession can be ended without using lethal force.

Anyone attempting to grapple with the Un-Man risks a fatal beating, as possession gives the host a +5 bonus to Strength. However, the Un-Man's weakness is that he cannot apply his enhanced Strength against anyone wearing the Sign of Marduk. Also, if the Sign is held against the host's skin for a number of turns equal to the host's Stamina + 5, the possession ends and the host returns to normal. Or rather, the host physically returns to normal — if Troy Wilkerson were the host, he would have vivid memories of tearing his friends to pieces with his bear hands, and he would quickly go into a catatonic state.

Epilogue: Denouement

Having defeated the Un-Man (one way or another), the characters can now see to it that Maxine Gordon, complete with restored hand, is laid to rest once again, and her spirit will roam no more. This will be the easiest part of the Epilogue.

If the characters were forced to kill Troy Wilkerson, they will have to explain their actions to the Police Review Board, which, naturally, will not be amenable to explanations involving otherworldly possession.

In the long term, the characters will also face a civil lawsuit from Dr. Wilkerson, though that's a matter for the future. A more immediate problem is the fact that characters now know that Sid Routman deliberately sent an innocent woman to her death, though they have no evidence other than the declaration of a ghost. Characters will have to think carefully before attacking the reputation of one of the force's most respected officers.

Most important of all, the characters may now have a much clearer understanding of the World of Darkness in which they live. Depending upon how Act Five played out, officers may receive visits from the city's vampires, mages or perhaps even werewolves who will seek to pick the officers' minds or erase their memories of the events at the Vertigo Club, or perhaps simply attempt to bribe, blackmail or intimidate the characters into remaining silent. Such outcomes depend on where the Storyteller wants to take his chronicle.

Dramatis Personae

Death Penalty Protester

Quote: *"Why do we kill people who kill people to show that killing people is wrong?"*

Background: During the Prologue, police characters may be forced to interact with death penalty protesters opposed to the impending execution of Maxine Gordon. Such protesters may come from a wide variety of backgrounds, including idealistic students, religious figures, politicians or just otherwise concerned citizens who strongly oppose the death penalty.

Description: A death penalty protester may look like almost anyone. Statistically, however, a protester is probably a white, upper-middle-class college student with a liberal background. A disproportionate number are Catholic, and priests and nuns often play an important role in organizing anti-death penalty protests.

Storytelling Hints: Depending on the situation and the needs of the Storyteller, an individual protester may fully support the role of police officers but simply focus her ire on the legal system or she may view all police as part of the same corrupt and racist hierarchy that props up the "murder industry."

Abilities

Expression (5 dice): Protesters of all stripes are skilled at getting their points across as loudly as possible.

Politics (4 dice): Most protesters are fully acquainted with all the arguments for and against their positions.

Maxine Gordon, Restless Ghost

Quote: *"This isn't what's supposed to be."*

Background: Maxine Gordon is not a typical ghost. She was resigned to her death and had even forgiven those who testified against her. She remains on this plane solely due to the actions of Troy Wilkerson. She has no Numina except that she can Manifest within the vicinity of any of her anchors — her grave, her body or her severed left hand — and some basic communication ability. At the point the characters find her, she wants only to prevent further bloodshed and to move on to her afterlife.

Description: If Maxine manifests, she will appear as a plump woman in her early 30s with frizzy red hair. She will be wearing the same clothes she was wearing when she discovered the bodies of her husband and children.

Storytelling Hints: Maxine is a contradiction. In life, she was a fairly simple woman who clung stubbornly to her faith despite a lifetime's worth of tragedy.

Attributes: Power 2, Finesse 1, Resistance 2
Willpower: 4
Morality: 7
Virtue: Faith
Vice: Sloth
Initiative: 3
Defense: 2
Speed: 13 (species factor 10)
Size: 5
Corpus: 7
Numina: Ghost Speech (3 dice), Manifestation (3 dice)

Vic Loomis

Quote: *"How long is this going to take, sir? I have two other plots to get to today."*

Background: Vic Loomis is the caretaker of the East-haven Cemetery. He will be the one to report the presence of the mutilated pet both to the police and to Father McCoy, who officiated over Maxine's funeral.

Description: Vic is in his late 40s and is muscular but somewhat gaunt. He favors flannel shirts, filthy jeans and thick work gloves. He has salt-and-pepper hair and three days' worth of facial hair. Characters may find him to be somewhat creepy, but that will mainly be a reaction to his occupation: professional gravedigger.

Storytelling Hints: Vic is fairly laconic and a little slow mentally. He tends to view almost everything in terms of whether it will require him to work extra hours. Vic may be useful as a red herring, since his blasé attitude toward the mutilated dog may seem suspicious.

Abilities

Athletics (5 dice): Years of hard work at physical labor have made Vic relatively fit.

Awareness (4 dice): Vic is reasonably attentive. He just seldom cares about anything he sees.

Intimidation (5 dice): A combination of attitude, appearance and profession have given Vic a mildly unsettling demeanor.

Father Richard McCoy

Quote: *"Great wrongs have been committed upon those who were utterly undeserving, and you want to add names to that list."*

Background: Father Richard McCoy is a Catholic priest who serves as priest for St. Bartholomew's Church in Midway. Maxine Gordon was one of Father Richard's parishioners, and he was and is convinced of her innocence. His personal involvement with this case, which includes personally leading anti-death penalty protests throughout the city and the state, has made him a well-known figure, though some of his immediate superiors in the Church think that he is guilty of grandstanding.

Description: Father Richard is a 43-year-old white male who stands about six foot three and weighs 200 pounds. He has a boyish face and red hair, though it is receding quickly. Despite his balding pate, people usually think that he is younger than he actually is. He usually is seen wearing a traditional priest's collar and shirt, but favors comfortable pants and a sweater to a cassock.

Storytelling Hints: Before his involvement with the Maxine Gordon case, Father Richard was a bit reserved and almost shy in dealing with his parishioners. He found his voice in his efforts to save Maxine Gordon, becoming a compelling speaker and organizer. He is still coming to terms with her execution, as on some level, he had almost persuaded himself that God would send a miracle to save Maxine's life. His faith was shaken by the absence of any such miracle, and he was further enraged when he discovered that Maxine was not buried in hallowed ground. He will be deeply offended if police characters act cavalierly in investigating the events at the Easthaven Cemetery.

Abilities

Empathy (6 dice): Father Richard is a deeply compassionate man. He is also generally a good judge of character and usually knows when someone is lying to him.

Persuasion (5 dice): Father Richard is a compelling speaker, and he has a flair for using his status as a priest to "guilt trip" others, even non-Catholics, into doing what he wants.

Politics (5 dice): Father Richard has developed an extensive knowledge of the political structures of Midway and the rest of the state, gained during the course of his failed attempt to win Maxine's freedom.

Joe Osborn

Quote: *"Somebody stole my son's dog, and you're in the one house in town where I know he's not."*

Background: Joe Osborn might just as easily be called "Joe Citizen." He is a typical member of middle-class Midway society with nothing unusual about him other than the fact that his family has been the victim of a crime. Joe is an accountant in Midway, and his wife has recently gone back to work after spending eight years as a stay-at-home mom.

Description: Joe is fairly good-looking but definitely not male model material. He is about 33 years old and in excellent shape thanks to a membership at the local YMCA. He has sandy blond hair, blue eyes and a friendly demeanor.

Storytelling Hints: Similar to most honest citizens, Joe is unlikely to present any sort of challenge or obstacle to an investigating officer. He will be extremely polite and deferential to the characters, and his only interest will be in helping the police find out who stole and killed his son's beloved pet. Practically the only thing that might change Joe's attitude would be if an officer told Mickey that the dog was dead in a particularly blunt or cruel manner. Anyone who makes Joe's boy cry is going to have an angry father on his hands.

Abilities

Academics (6 dice, plus a Specialty in Accounting): As a licensed CPA, Joe is skilled with mathematics.

Politics (5 dice): Joe is well read on the subject of city politics and has a few friends in the city's bureaucracy.

Socialize (5 dice): Characters will generally find Joe to be a very likeable guy unless they go out of their way to provoke a confrontation with him.

Mickey Osborn

Quote: *"Did you find Rags, sir?"*

Background: Mickey Osborn is a typical nine-year-old boy from an upper-middle-class family. He is an only child, and he is perhaps slightly spoiled and sheltered, but not obviously or obnoxiously so. Just as most young boys of his social class, he has been raised to be in awe of police officers, who are almost as cool as firefighters and guys who drive big trucks. He is extremely sensitive about the fate of his dog, Rags, and will almost certainly react hysterically if told the unvarnished truth about Rags' fate.

Description: Many people might describe Mickey as adorable. He has black hair and large eyes that flash with curiosity and intelligence. He favors shorts, T-shirts and tennis shoes unless his mother forces him into more formal attire.

Storytelling Hints: Mickey exists mainly to tug at the characters' heartstrings. Characters who present themselves as positive role models within the police community will enjoy the look of total admiration he gives them. On the other hand, a darker would-be Dirty Harry may find it stressful to deal with a child who responds to gruffness and directness with tears.

Abilities

Athletics (4 dice): Similar to most active children, Mickey is quick and agile.

Bernard Dent

Quote: *"Goddamn punk kids are always running through the yard and stomping down my hydrangeas."*

Background: Bernard Dent is a 69-year-old retiree neighbor who is actually fond of young Mickey Osborn, but Bernard is a crotchety and sardonic old man with little patience for the excitability of youth. His testimony is relevant because he saw Troy Wilkerson and Doug Guthrie near the Osborn home on the day the dog was stolen, though Bernard didn't actually see anything more suspicious than that. His hostility toward the two stems mainly from his negative views on adolescents in general and "goddamn punk kids" in particular, though he knows nothing of youth subcultures and tends to refer to every adolescent with long hair as a "hippy." Ultimately, Dent divides everyone under the age of 50 into two neat categories: those who have neat haircuts and respect their elders and everyone else.

Description: Dent is an older gentleman who keeps what little hair he has left in a military buzzcut. At his age, Dent's once-military physique has gone somewhat to paunch, despite a lifetime of self-discipline. As a retiree, he tends to dress casually, since most of his time is monopolized by frequent gardening and other home improvement projects.

Storytelling Hints: Bernard Dent is perpetually grumpy with most everyone he meets. He may show some deference to a police officer who appears to have some military background or who appeals to Dent's vanity — he tends to see himself as the only real adult on the entire block. Officers who fail to get on Dent's good side will most likely hear a barrage of complaints about how "back in the old days, the cops did their job and you could actually leave a dog fenced up in your backyard without worrying about some goddamn punk kid stealing it." Don't play him for laughs, though. He's genuinely concerned about the lack of responsibility parents are taking for their kids and what that's doing to those kids' attitudes.

Abilities

Crafts (4 dice, plus a Specialty in Gardening): Since his retirement, Dent has thrown himself into gardening and other home improvement projects with the same intensity that he brings to everything else.

Intimidation (5 dice): A retired drill sergeant, Dent derives a perverse pleasure from frightening teenagers with his wrath, and occasionally grown-ups, too.

Investigation (5 dice): As head of the local Neighborhood Watch Program, Bernard Dent makes it his business to stay in everyone else's business.

Dr. Melinda Wilkerson, Successful Surgeon

Quote: *"Surely you don't think my son's to blame."*

Background: Melinda Wilkerson is not a bad person, by any means, though players will almost certainly dislike her. Both Melinda and her former husband went to medical school together, with Melinda specializing in cardiac surgery and her husband specializing in chasing the nurses. They divorced five years ago, and Melinda has been raising and spoiling her son, Troy, ever since. By doing so, Melinda only wants to make up for her son having to grow up without a father, but now, she is in total denial over how much of a sociopath her baby boy has grown up to be.

Description: Dr. Melinda Wilkerson is 44 years old, with somewhat mousy blonde hair and too many wrinkles around her eyes, the result of years spent as a single mother in a high-stress, male-dominated field. She is quite wealthy and isn't afraid to show it. She keeps in excellent shape with a personal trainer who works with her on the hospital's physical therapy equipment.

Storytelling Hints: Dr. Wilkerson is an extremely overprotective mother who is utterly blinded to the possibility that her child has criminal tendencies. She is something of a limousine liberal and has an innate bias against police officers, whom she tends to view as thugs with badges. She will take every step she can to protect Troy from what she is certain is just a misunderstanding.

Abilities

Academics (5 dice): Dr. Wilkerson is highly literate and well read. She has several degrees and specializations.

Medicine (7 dice, plus a Specialty in Surgery): Dr. Wilkerson is a highly respected doctor and surgeon who is regularly on call as the Chief Surgeon of the Midway General Hospital.

Politics (6 dice): Dr. Wilkerson is well aware of her rights and those of her son, and she will protect them zealously. She also has a number of friends in high places.

Empathy (6 dice): Dr. Wilkerson has an excellent bedside manner and is a good judge of character. She will be naturally suspicious of any police officer characters and will be looking for any trickery calculated to get her to waive her rights.

Troy Wilkerson

Quote: *"I don't have to answer to you."*

Background: Troy is the ringleader of a quartet of would-be occultists who seek to gain mystical power from the creation of an artifact called the Subtle Key. To that end, they have gone so far as to torture and kill a helpless pet stolen from a neighbor's yard and then rob a dead woman's grave. Troy is a mallrat stereotype of a Goth who dresses in black and uses black mascara and fingernail polish solely in an attempt to provoke some sort of reaction from his mother other than bland acceptance. Far from living a life of quiet desperation, Troy lives a life of loud desperation, complete with noisy guitars and abrasive industrial music. He has fixated on the Subtle Key ritual not out of any real desire for power so much as just a way to get noticed.

Description: Troy most commonly wears black jeans, black T-shirts (featuring some especially morbid band logo), black hair, black fingernails and black mascara. He occasionally ornaments himself with a studded collar. He also

carries a switchblade he uses to intimidate any classmates who might try to bully him.

Storytelling Hints: If not stopped somehow, Troy could be a future Charles Manson. Despite his abrasive pseudo-Goth persona, Troy is a genuinely charismatic young man who has a flair for manipulation, charm and lying. If confronted by the police, he will tell whatever lies are necessary to distract them long enough to complete the Subtle Key ritual, with which he has become completely obsessed.

Attributes: Intelligence 3, Wits 2, Resolve 2, Strength 2, Dexterity 2, Stamina 2, Presence 3, Manipulation 3, Composure 3

Skills: Academics 1, Athletics 2, Brawl 1, Empathy 2, Persuasion (Charm) 3, Socialize 3, Subterfuge (Appearing Innocent) 3, Larceny 1, Occult (Satanic Lore) 3, Stealth 2, Weaponry 1

Merits: Fleet of Foot 3, Language (Latin) 1, Unseen Sense

Willpower: 5

Morality: 6

Virtue: Fortitude

Vice: Pride

Initiative: 4

Defense: 2

Speed: 12

Doug Guthrie, Sam Randolph and Lisa Griffin

Background: These three teenagers are the members of Troy's "coven." Only Troy has any real knowledge of the occult: the other three are complete poseurs. Each is devoted to Troy, however, and he has either charmed or intimidated them into joining him in his plan to enact the Subtle Key ritual. While the three kids found it darkly exciting to kill the dog and desecrate the graveyard, actually stealing the body of Maxine Gordon is perhaps a little too intense for them. All three would wash their hands of the whole thing now if they could, but each is in too deep to just walk away.

Description: Doug is the youngest of the three at age 14. He is a self-described computer nerd with oily hair, bad complexion and a collection of ill-fitting fantasy- or sci-fi-themed T-shirts. Doug is Caucasian with dirty blond hair. Sam is a thin, 16-year-old African American male who is currently somewhat confused sexually. He favors clothing calculated to make him seem more masculine, but he can rarely pull off the effect. Lisa is a short, notably overweight 16-year-old Caucasian girl with short and spiky black hair and an overabundance of Goth makeup.

Storytelling Hints: Doug is the youngest and most frightened of the three. He would be the easiest to turn against the others in an interrogation setting. (Police get +1 on Interrogation rolls against Doug). Sam has not yet come to grips with his latent homosexuality, and

Morality: 7
Virtue: Fortitude (all)
Vice: Lust (Sam), Pride (Lisa), Wrath (Doug)
Initiative: 6 (5 for Lisa)
Defense: 2 (all)
Speed: 10 (9 for Lisa)

The Un-Man

The Un-Man is any individual possessed by a powerful otherworldly spirit as a result of a botched attempt to enact the ritual of the Subtle Key. The Un-Man retains all the memories of its host, but is obsessed with hunting and slaying supernatural creatures to steal their magical energies in order to unleash others of its kind on humanity. The Un-Man has all the traits of its host (which will most likely be Troy Wilkerson) but gains a +5 bonus to Strength, Dexterity and Stamina, as well as an Armor rating of 5. All Advantages are recalculated to take the Attribute bonuses into account. Also, the Un-Man is immune to all supernatural effects, which fail automatically when used against it. Finally, the Un-Man's touch inflicts aggravated damage on all supernatural creatures, and the Un-Man gains one point of Essence per point of damage inflicted.

The Un-Man has two weaknesses. First, its touch has no particularly adverse effect against non-supernatural creatures. Second, the Un-man cannot apply any of its enhanced Strength against someone protected by the Sign of Marduk, and it takes one level of aggravated damage from every turn of direct contact with the Sign. If the Un-Man sustains contact with the Sign for a number of turns equal to the hosts (original) Stamina + 5, the inhabiting spirit will be destroyed, and the host will be returned to normal, though the host may well have been driven mad by the possession experience.

his one-sided crush on Troy combined with a natural distrust of police makes Sam the most resistant to turning (–1 on Interrogation rolls against Sam). Lisa is very passive personality-wise, and, after Troy, she is also the smartest. She will never willingly talk to police unless her father is present.

Attributes: Intelligence 2 (3 for Lisa), Wits 2, Resolve 2, Strength 2, Dexterity 3 (2 for Lisa), Stamina 2, Presence 2, Manipulation 2, Composure 3

Skills: Academics 1, Athletics 1, Brawl 1, Computer 1, Drive 1, Empathy 1, Investigation 2, Occult 1, Persuasion 1, Socialize 1, Stealth 2, Subterfuge 2

Merits: None
Willpower: 5

CITY OF MIDWAY, Midway County

To All and Singular, the Sheriffs, Constables and Coroners of said State, Greetings.

Whereas, at the _____ Term of the Superior Court of the County Aforesaid, the Grand Jurors did find a True Bill against _____

for the offense(s) of: _____

You and each of you are therefore commanded in the name of the State to apprehend the above Defendant, and in default of his giving bond and surety in the sum ordered on the first page of this warrant, to commit him or her to the common jail of this county, to be dealt with as the law directs.

Given under my hand and seal this day,

_____
JUDGE, Superior Court, Judicial Circuit

_____
District Attorney, A.J.C.

Know all men and women by these presents, that we _____ , principal, and _____ , Surety, acknowledge ourselves held and firmly Bound unto his Excellency, _____ , Governor of Midway, and his successors in the office, in the sum of _____ Dollars. The conditions of this obligation are:

Whereas, the Grand Jury, at the _____ Term of the Superior Court for Midway County, did find a True Bill against _____ for the offenses of:

Now should _____ personally be at the Midway County Superior Court, to be held in and for the Court of Midway on the _____ day of _____ , _____ , and personally attend the Court and abide his or her trial and judgement of the Court in this case from day to day and term to term, and not depart from the Court without its Leave, then this bond is VOID, else to remain in full force and effect.

And the better to secure the payment of this bond, in the event of forfeiture, we each for ourselves and families, and as the head of our respective families, renounce and waive all right and benefit of the homestead and exemptions to the people of Midway, and each of us assert and say that we have never taken or availed ourselves of any homestead or exemption under the laws of this State, or of the United States or elsewhere.

Bond taken and approved before me.
This ___ day of _____ , _____.

_____(Seal)
_____(Seal)
_____(Seal)

THE WORLD OF DARKNESS
2006 RELEASES

World of Darkness Core RuleBook

The central product for all World of Darkness games, this book presents the complete Storytelling System. All World of Darkness, Vampire, Mage and Werewolf titles require use of this rulebook.
ISBN 1-58846-476-8;
WWP55000; $19.99

Play Aids (Coming Soon):

For use with all **World of Darkness** titles and the **World of Darkness®** Rulebook.

WoD: Character Pad
(April)

WoD: Storyteller's Screen (April)

WoD Dice
(July)

The World of Darkness
2006 Releases

For use with all **World of Darkness** titles and the **World of Darkness**® Rulebook.

Coming Soon:

Second Sight
Shadows of the U.K.
Tales from the 13th Precinct

(May)

(June)

(July)

Not every entity with supernatural powers is one of a species of creatures that prowl the night. Solitary psychics, crazed sorcerers and doomsaying cultists all share the World of Darkness. This book explores their unique abilities.
ISBN: 1-58846-487-3;
 $26.99 USD   #55100

They hunted the moors and forests in the days before Caesar came, and they prowl the towns and cities even now. For millennia, supernatural creatures have walked these islands. From the Scottish Highlands to the London streets, danger waits for the unwary.
ISBNL 1-58846-334-6;
 $29.99 USD   #0202

TFor every vampire attack, werewolf rampage, sorcerous outburst, or other strange event, some at police station is going to get a call about it. Here, then, is how the law deals with the mysterious and supernatural, from investigation through prosecution.
ISBN: 1-58846-480-6;
 $26.99 USD   #55001

Universal Supplements Available Now:

www.worldofdarkness.com

Who shall
conceive the
HORRORS
of my secret toil as I
dabbled among the
unhallowed damps of
the grave or tortured
the living animal
to animate the
lifeless clay?

PROMETHEAN

The next storytelling game in the World of Darkness®

Coming to life August 2006

among criminals

DO NOT CROSS

my sleepless intriguing mind

Oh, yes, everything's fine.

misery and wretchedness